Behold
your
God

The Weight of Majesty

This workbook is the daily devotional companion to the 12-week study

Behold Your God: The Weight of Majesty

www.BeholdYourGod.org

Behold your God

The Weight of Majesty

JOHN SNYDER

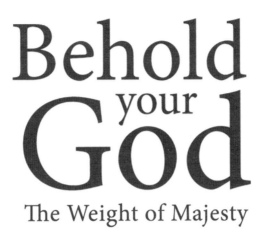

Media Gratiae
New Albany, Mississippi

Published by
Media Gratiae
PO Box 21
New Albany, MS 38652
email: info@mediagratiae.org
website: www.mediagratiae.org

Published in the United States of America 2018
First Edition

Scripture quotations taken from the New American Standard Bible® (NASB),
Copyright © 1960, 1962, 1963, 1968, 1971, 1972, 1973,
1975, 1977, 1995 by The Lockman Foundation
Used by permission. www.Lockman.org

ISBN: 978-0-9886681-8-8

Edited by Steve Crampton
Layout by Forrest Hite
Cover design by Matthew Robinson

CONTENTS

This book is warmly dedicated to

Misty

Wife and Mother
Co-laborer and Friend
Faithful Companion
Beyond Price

INTRODUCTION

When the first study in the Behold Your God series was released in 2013, we felt (as did many others) that the evangelical churches needed to face some hard questions. Many had carefully traced the symptoms of an internal decay within evangelicalism, a decay that was occurring even while outwardly there appeared to be continued successes. *Behold Your God: Rethinking God Biblically* was written with the desire to help stir God's people by pointing them back to the fountainhead—God Himself. Precious time was being wasted as Western evangelicals attempted to fix the external problems. It was our belief that the surest hope of a cure was to deal with the root issue, and that root issue appeared to be an inadequate understanding of our own God.

The response to that study, by God's grace, has been far greater than we could have imagined. During the last four years the emails, letters, and personal testimonies of those who have benefitted from the study have been gratefully received. It is always humbling to see God use our efforts as a part of something far greater than anything we could accomplish. Within these communications there has been a recurrent question: where do I go to find more resources on the character of God? Thankfully, there are many fine treatments of God's perfections. Often, however, they are either very large or very complex books. In response to this question, we have put together this second study dealing primarily with the attributes of God rather than ways the evangelical church often lives below His self-revelation. In a sense, *The Weight of Majesty* is a continuation of the theme we explored in week one of *Rethinking God Biblically*—that God Himself is the great attraction of the Christian life. By His help we hope to continue going deeper into the themes that were introduced in the first study through several forthcoming installments in the *Behold Your God* series.

HOW DOES THIS STUDY WORK?

Behold Your God: The Weight of Majesty is set up like many other studies of its type, with a few additions that we hope will prove beneficial. The study is centered upon the twelve-week workbook and is designed to be used in conjunction with the DVD series. Each week the student will work through the workbook (five days per week) in preparation for watching the DVD. *Behold Your God: The Weight of Majesty* can be used as an individual or a group study. If you are part of a group, watch the DVD at the end of the week and allow time to discuss the issues raised in the workbook and DVD lessons.

Each week's DVD is made up of three segments: the historical introduction, the sermon, and highlights taken from interviews with various contemporary religious leaders. The historical introduction is a short biographical sketch of the life of a significant servant of Christ whose life and ministry were built upon the same truths that you will be studying in this book. These were filmed on site in England, Scotland, and North America. The sketches include John Newton, John Knox, Hudson Taylor, Ann Judson, Edward Payson, and John Bunyan.

After the introduction, a sermon follows that reinforces and helps apply what you have been studying in the Bible that week. Finally, you will be able to listen to highlights from interviews with contemporary ministers whose lives and labors reflect these same truths. These ministers include Sinclair Ferguson, Conrad Mbewe, Andrew Davies, Anthony Mathenia, Geoffrey Thomas, Ian Hamilton, Jeremy Walker, Garry Williams, Jordan Thomas, Joel Beeke, and Steve Lawson. I hope you will feel, as I do, that it is a real privilege to be able to hear from these men whose gospel labors range from Ethiopia, Virginia, Tennessee, and Michigan to New Zealand, England, Wales, Scotland, and Zambia.

A WORD TO ENCOURAGE THE STUDENT

Nothing is so satisfying for the true Christian as an ever-increasing and experiential knowledge of our God. This knowledge cannot be gained safely without diligently searching the Bible. Therefore, the real purpose of this book is to guide you back into those passages which contain some of the most significant descriptions of God. Avoid the temptation to merely get through the exercises without wrestling honestly with these matters. Sit long at the feet our Heavenly Father and ask Him to tell you about Himself. We know it is too easy to check a box, fill in the blank with the correct word, and move on unaffected. Don't settle for undigested concepts or merely emotional responses to passages. Plead with God to help you adjust everything in life to fit what you are learning about Him. Bring both your mind and heart together, and bow before God in real worship as you study each day, until like Job you feel compelled to say, "I have heard of You by the hearing of the ear; but now my eye sees You!" You will not be disappointed with the Living God.

Please note that in this second study the *New American Standard Bible* has been used throughout the DVD sermons and this workbook unless otherwise noted. The exercises will be much easier if you can use this version for the study.

A WORD OF THANKS

The *Behold Your God* series is the product of the collaborative effort of many like-minded believers, especially the leadership at *Media Gratiae*. Also, I am grateful to those in Christ Church New Albany, who are attempting to live on these same truths while allowing me to continue to write. I appreciate the men who, in the midst of busy ministries, gave their time and thought to the interviews which conclude each DVD session. I am very grateful to all of those who sacrificially helped us pull together the many aspects need to produce *Behold Your God: The Weight of Majesty.*

May this study be a lifelong friend as we labor to live unto God.

JOHN SNYDER·

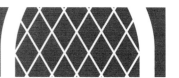

KNOWING THE GOD WHO IS INCOMPREHENSIBLE

DAY 1: KNOWING THE INCOMPREHENSIBLE GOD, PART 1

The fourth-century theologian Augustine (AD 354-430) wrote, "We are speaking of God. Is it any wonder that you do not comprehend?"[1] Stephen Charnock, in his book *The Existence and Attributes of God*, writes:

> *And whatsoever conception comes into your mind, say, This is not God; God is more than this: If I could conceive him, he [could not be] God; for God is incomprehensibly above whatsoever I can say, whatsoever I can think and conceive of him.*[2]

Referring to the impossibility of fully grasping the character of God, the twentieth-century Chicago pastor A.W. Tozer wrote: "If all this sounds strange to modern ears, it is only because we have for a full half century taken God for granted. The glory of God has not been revealed to this generation of men." These men confront us with a fundamental aspect of God's majesty—His incomprehensibility.

Incomprehensibility (the impossibility of being completely understood) may seem a strange and somewhat discouraging place to start a study of the attributes of our God. Yet these men give us a needed caution: we are entering the realm of mystery. There are facts to be studied and compared, to be grasped and lived upon. We can know our God through His self-revelation. We can, however, never fully comprehend Him.

Strangely, understanding God's incomprehensibility will keep us from two dangers:

1. The smug assumption that if we work hard enough we will fully comprehend the revealed realities of God's character.

2. The tendency to humanize God, to think of Him as one of us, only bigger.

To enlarge our thoughts of God's majesty, we must look to Scripture to see what He says about Himself. If we will humbly set our hearts and minds to examine God's self-revelation, we need not be discouraged by His incomprehensibility. In reality, incomprehensibility is one of the shining features of God's splendor, the weight of His majesty. It is a truth that separates Him from all else.

> *If we could understand God, he would not be God, for it is a part of the nature of God that he should be infinitely greater than any created mind.*
>
> — C. H. Spurgeon

INCOMPREHENSIBILITY—WHAT DOES THE BIBLE SAY ABOUT THIS PERFECTION OF GOD?

The Bible plainly teaches that God can be known; however, no created being in heaven or on earth can fully comprehend God. In fact, though much can be said that is true of Him, no word can fully represent Him, and no description can do His perfection justice. Tozer's little book, *The Knowledge of the Holy*, reminds us that God has chosen to use things with which we are familiar to teach us about His perfections. In other words, God uses familiar objects to help us grasp things that are unfamiliar to us. Even these comparisons quickly fail under the weight of His incomprehensibility. Consider Ezekiel's vision of God. Notice how he becomes progressively less precise in his comparisons as he gets closer to describing God Himself.

READ EZEKIEL 1.

Did you see it? Did you notice how the prophet becomes increasingly vague in verses 26 to 28 as he gets closer to describing God's majesty?

So, when we say that God is *like* something, we are not saying He is *exactly like* any created thing. In fact, we must remember when comparing things that there are only two categories: "that which is God," and "that which is not God"; and between these two there is an infinite gap.

One of the great English theologians of the seventeenth century wrote:

> *We may speak much of God; talk of Him, His ways, His works, His counsels, all day long; but the truth is, we know very little of Him. Our thoughts, our meditations, our expressions of Him are low, many of them unworthy of His glory and none of them reaching His perfections.*[4]

Where reason fails, with all her powers,
There faith prevails, and love adores.

— Isaac Watts

THE BIBLICAL WITNESS

The Bible uses various descriptions to convey the truth of God's incomprehensibility; below are three.

1. Wonderful

We normally use this word in a different way than the Scripture uses it. We use it to describe something that is particularly good or pleasant. When we say something tastes *wonderful*, we mean that it tastes very good. The Scripture, however, uses this word to refer to something that is beyond understanding, something that belongs to the category of mystery. It *fills* us with *wonder* because it is wonder-full. It bewilders us with its greatness.

When the LORD appeared to the parents of Samson, they asked His name. In Judges 13:18 we read His response: "Why do you ask my name, seeing it is wonderful?" In other words, the self-revealing name of God would fill them with wonder and confound them by its glory.

2.   Unsearchable/Unfathomable

Another word that portrays the incomprehensible perfection of God is *unsearchable*. In the Old Testament the Hebrew root of this word refers to something that cannot be discovered by examination, investigation, or calculation. Thus, God is not able to be searched out, discovered, examined, investigated, or calculated by any created being.

COPY the following verses, noting how they pertain to the doctrine of God's incomprehensibility.

Job 11:7-8

_____

_____

_____

Psalm 145:3

_____

_____

God's incomprehensibility is seen in the New Testament as well. In ROMANS 11:33 Paul writes:

> *Oh, the depth of the riches both of the wisdom and knowledge of God!*
> *How unsearchable are His judgments and unfathomable His ways!*

Notice that the passage contains another word regarding incomprehensibility—*unfathomable*. This is from the Greek word which means "untraceable." The apostle uses that word again when he describes the *"unfathomable* riches of Christ" that are found in the gospel (Ephesians 3:8). In Romans and Ephesians

Paul is explaining the gospel work of God, which is ultimately incapable of being fully comprehended. Note that even the apostle reaches a place where he must admit that he cannot trace the perfections of God any further!

3.   Invisible/Unapproachable

These words give us another aspect of God's incomprehensibility: He is beyond our sight or approach. In his first letter to Timothy, Paul reminds the young pastor that God is:

> . . . *the blessed and only Sovereign, the King of kings and Lord of lords, who alone possesses immortality and dwells in unapproachable light, whom no man has seen or can see. To Him be honor and eternal dominion! Amen.* (1 Timothy 6:15-16)

The perfections of God's being are beyond the sight of any creature. They create a fundamental barrier by their innate brilliance. It is always helpful to know what the saints of Scripture thought of God, and how it moved them to respond. Strangely, these unapproachably glorious realities of God's character did not discourage or dampen Paul's worship. They moved him to exalt the solitary honor of this God.

Ask yourself: when you begin to understand that your God is beyond complete understanding, do you delight to praise Him?

Day 2: KNOWING THE INCOMPREHENSIBLE GOD, PART 2

> *O Lord, enlarge our scanty thought to know the wonders Thou hast wrought;*
> *Unloose our stammering tongues to tell Thy love, immense, unsearchable.*[5]

Today we want to continue to look at the incomprehensibility of God.

FILL IN THE BLANKS using a New American Standard Bible.

1.   All of God's attributes are beyond comprehension.

THE DURATION OF GOD

> Job 36:26
> *Behold, God is exalted, and we do not know Him;* _____
> _____ *is unsearchable.*

THE LOVE OF GOD

> Ephesians 3:19
> *. . . to know the love of Christ which* _____
> _____, *that you may be filled up to all the fullness of God.*

THE ANGER OF GOD

> Psalm 90:11
> _____ *the power*
> *of Your anger and Your fury, according to the fear that is due You?*

THE PEACE OF GOD

> Philippians 4:7
> *And the peace of God, which* _____
> _____, *will guard your hearts and your minds in Christ Jesus.*

Whether it is the mystery of His eternal existence or His love, anger, and peace—the God that we are studying possesses perfections which are incapable of being accurately calculated, fully investigated, or unerringly traced.

Tell out, my soul, the greatness of the Lord!
Make known His might, the deeds His arm has done;
His mercy sure, from age to age the same;
His holy Name—the Lord, the Mighty One.

— Timothy Dudley-Smith

2. Like His character, God's actions are shown to be incomprehensible.

> Job 5:9
> *. . . [God] does great and* _____ *things,*
> _____ *without number.*

> Job 37:5
> *God thunders with His voice wondrously,*
> *Doing* _____ *things which we* _____
> _____.

3. His thoughts and decisions or judgments are beyond our comprehension.

> Isaiah 55:8-9
> *"For* _____ *are not your thoughts, nor are your ways*
> *My ways," declares the LORD. "For as the heavens are higher than the*
> *earth, so are My ways higher than your ways and* _____
> *than your thoughts."*

The decisions of God which most clearly demonstrate that He is beyond our full comprehension are those which have to do with our salvation.

Listen again to Paul in ROMANS 11:33. The context is important. He is drawing to a close a detailed treatment of the doctrines behind our salvation. What does Paul feel is a fitting conclusion to that section?

> *Oh, the depth of the riches both of the wisdom and knowledge of God! How unsearchable are His judgments and unfathomable His ways!*

It is important that we not misunderstand the reason we cannot comprehend God. The incomprehensibility of God does not flow from our sinfulness. Believers in heaven are able to see more clearly the perfections of God, yet they will never be able to fully comprehend the infinite splendor that belongs to Him. Even angels in heaven cannot fully comprehend His perfection. It is not our sinfulness that puts God beyond our present ability to "figure Him out"; it is His infinite deity, His God-ness. He alone knows Himself. As created beings, we cannot fully grasp the Uncreated Being.

To make this point a little clearer, let us consider the statements of three godly men. Each of these men knew God relationally. Each walked with God. Yet each man's life demonstrates that even the godliest cannot fully comprehend the unique majesty that belongs to God. We cannot even fully understand our own selves, much less the one who formed man from dust.

JOB

In his reply to the counsel of his friends, Job speaks of the activity of God as He rules over all aspects of creation. When he comes to the end of his description, he tells us:

> Job 26:14
> *Behold, these are the fringes of His ways; and how faint a word we hear of Him! But His mighty thunder, who can understand?*

Despite the heights Job reached in his understanding of God's supremacy, he ultimately confessed that he had only touched the fringe and heard a whisper of all that there was to experience and hear of God.

MOSES

Moses was given a vision of God's glory. In addition to this external display of glory, God gave him a verbal explanation of what he was seeing. Here was a unique privilege even for Moses. What a sight! What an explanation! Yet even here Moses was only able to see the back parts of God's majesty.

READD EXODUS 33:17-34:9 and write God's self-description.

_____

_____

_____

_____

PAUL

READD 2 CORINTHIANS 3:4-18.

Verse 18 tells us that in the New Covenant the believer is able to have a clearer understanding of God. He is the same God and it is the same faith, but Paul says the veil over our eyes is removed. Something is wonderfully better—the dawn has come and the New Covenant reveals more than the Old ever did. Yet Paul tells us that, even in the New Covenant clarity, we are only able to see God (in the person of His Son) as a man sees something in an ancient mirror, a true reflection but not a complete one.

APPLYING THIS REALITY

How is the Christian to pursue an ever clearer knowledge of a God who can never be fully known? Can this reality be applied? The glad answer is most definitely—Yes!

First, we apply the attribute of God's incomprehensibility in two ways that are connected: the way we view Him and the way we portray Him to others. We must not give in to the temptation to reduce Him to a manageable size. He is incomprehensible. That is His glory alone. We are obligated to guard this truth as we study Him and as we talk about Him to others.

Second, we must avoid abuse of this doctrine. There are many clever and deceptive abuses, and they have been around for centuries. Let's consider one abuse of the doctrine of God's incomprehensibility. We will label it _practical agnosticism._

Agnosticism is the philosophical view that God is unknown and unknowable. An agnostic is a person who refuses to believe in either the existence or nonexistence of God. For our purposes practical agnosticism may be defined as responding to God as if we were agnostics (believing God to be unknown and unknowable), though we would never think of ourselves in that way. Practical

Men may have atheistical hearts without atheistical heads. Their reasons may defend the notion of a Deity, while their hearts are empty of affection to the Deity.

— Stephen Charnock

agnosticism will make you lazy in your study of God's character and ways. You may be willing to read the Bible in order to find answers for your problems, to give advice to a friend, or even to produce a sermon, but you will give little time to the careful study of God Himself. The reasoning will sound something like this: "I can't figure out God. He is incomprehensible. What is the use of working hard at something that is doomed to fail?" You may even become impatient with ministers who spend time preaching about the character of God rather than about more "practical matters." If you are not convinced that the study of God's majesty is worth your time, you may be a practical agnostic.

Practical agnosticism may be spotted in other ways. It may lead you to focus more on experiences than objective theological truths. You say you hunger for God, but you are not interested in the study of God's person, as revealed in the Scriptures. Instead you focus upon powerful experiences in the Christian life. The result is a type of Christian mysticism; that is, a religion that prizes experiences but is not careful to make sure of two things: that those experiences are produced from a study of the scriptural truths, and that they are in fact approved of by the Scriptures. After all, it is easier to seek experiences in religion than to study the Bible.

Practical agnosticism may lead you to repeatedly return to your favorite passages, which have in the past moved you emotionally, but leave great portions of the Bible untouched. You are satisfied with a religion that provides emotionally stimulating experiences fueled by favorite phrases or thoughts regarding God. At the root, you are unconvinced that the study of God is worth your time. If these things are true of you, you are a practical agnostic.

Legalism is simply separating the law of God from the person of God.

— Sinclair Ferguson

A distinctly different way that practical agnosticism may reveal itself is by a preoccupation with Christian ethics (the moral rules of the Bible) rather than with God Himself. After all, if God cannot be comprehended fully, then surely it is wise to focus on the rules which we can understand. Rules, like experiences, are an important part of the Christian life; however, when we are eager to pass over a serious study of the perfections of God's character (the foundation of all the rules) in order to get to those passages which tell us "How to . . . ," then we may suspect that we are in danger of being practical agnostics.

Are any of these symptoms of practical agnosticism apparent in your life? Which one(s)?

_____

_____

_____

_____

THE CURE

The cure to practical agnosticism has remained the same throughout the centuries. Unlike most medications, it is pleasant as well as effective. We cure practical agnosticism by daily taking advantage of the reality that God has indeed revealed Himself to us most clearly in the person and labors of His Son, Jesus Christ! A. W. Tozer correctly wrote:

> *What is God like? If by that question we mean, "What is God like in Himself?" there is no answer. If we mean, "What has God disclosed about Himself?" then there is, I believe, an answer both full and satisfying.* [6]

The sending of Jesus changes everything! Because of Christ, there can never be a legitimate excuse for indulging any of the above symptoms of a practical agnosticism. Because of Christ, God can be apprehended by faith, though He can never be comprehended. In truth, we will never have a clearer display of God's splendor than that which we see in the person and work of His Son.

In the 17th chapter of John's Gospel, we have a prayer that Jesus offered before His closest followers. His prayer teaches us that His Father has invested Him with authority over all humanity for the purpose of bringing people to real life, eternal life.

> *. . . You gave Him authority over all flesh, that to all whom You have given Him, He may give eternal life. This is eternal life, that they may know You, the only true God, and Jesus Christ whom You have sent.* (John 17:2-3)

And now listen to John:

> *And we know that the Son of God has come, and has given us understanding so that we may know Him who is true, and we are in Him who is true, in His Son Jesus Christ. This is the true God and eternal life.* (1 John 5:20)

How do these passages define eternal life?

_____

_____

_____

We have God for ours, first, in the measure in which our minds are actively occupied with thoughts of Him. We have no merely mystical or emotional possession of God to preach. There is a real, adequate knowledge of Him in Jesus Christ.

— Alexander MacLaren

In the coming days we will be examining the perfections of God. We will do it with the understanding that we will never fully figure Him out—but we can know Him because He has come to us in His Son.

Have you personally found what God has disclosed about Himself, particularly through His Son, to be "an answer both full and satisfying"? If so, write a short prayer of thanksgiving and praise below. If not, don't despair. He delights to reveal Himself. Ask Him to do so.

_____

_____

_____

_____

_____

_____

DAY 3: THE SELF-EXISTENCE AND INDEPENDENCE OF GOD, PART 1

The greatest and best man in the world must say, "By the grace of God I am what I am"; but God says absolutely—and it is more than any creature, man or angel, can say—"I am that I am." Being self-existent, he cannot but be self-sufficient, and therefore all-sufficient.

— Matthew Henry

There is a vast variety in creation—from galaxies to blades of grass. It seems that some things in creation have nothing in common. Yet all created things and persons do share one quality: they are all dependent on someone else for their existence and maintenance. God is that someone else. He alone is the "uncaused cause" of everything. He Himself is absolutely independent of all else; therefore, He needs no one outside of Himself for His existence and maintenance. We call this the self-existence and independence of God.

As a result, certain "creature words" can never be applied to the Creator.

- If we think of someone who has an *origin* or *beginning*, we are not thinking of God.

- If we think of someone who has a *source* or *cause*, we are not thinking of God.

- If we think of someone who has a *need* or *lack*, we are not thinking of God.

Today and tomorrow you will study God's self-existence and independence by considering the biblical evidence for each as well as practical applications.

THE BIBLICAL WITNESS TO GOD'S SELF-EXISTENCE

CONSIDER the following Scriptures in relation to the self-existence of God:
PSALM 36:9, JOHN 1:3-4, JOHN 5:26, ACTS 17:25.

What truth do these passages teach us?

_____

_____

_____

God is not merely immortal; He alone possesses life and is the source of it. God owes His existence to no one. He is the source of His being. He is alone in this perfection because all other beings owe their existence to His activity. His attributes are also self-existing. All of His attributes have their source in Him and not one has been given to Him by another.

CONSIDER these examples.

Psalm 62:11-12
Once God has spoken; twice I have heard this: that power belongs to God; and lovingkindness is Yours, O Lord . . . .

Here we see that both power and lovingkindness are essentially God's. He does not receive them from another. They do not originate nor are they caused by anything or anyone outside of Himself.

Romans 11:33-35
Oh, the depth of the riches both of the wisdom and knowledge of God! How unsearchable are His judgments and unfathomable His ways! For who has known the mind of the LORD, or who became His counselor? Or who has first given to Him that it might be paid back to him again?

Using a rhetorical question, Paul reminds his readers that God possesses knowledge and did not receive it from anyone.

THE BIBLICAL WITNESS TO GOD'S INDEPENDENCE

The independence of God means that He alone is the source of His being, and of His continued existence. What He is He always will be, without the aid of any created thing. All that is not God—all created things and persons—are depending upon God for their continuance. God alone is self-sufficient. He is dependent upon no one.

COPY the following verses.

Psalm 36:6

_____

_____

Hebrews 1:3

_____

_____

_____

Colossians 1:17

_____

_____

In Psalm 104 we read of God sustaining all life on earth. After listing specific ways in which God upholds all creatures, the psalmist concludes:

> *They all wait for You to give them their food in due season. You give to them, they gather it up; You open Your hand, they are satisfied with good. You hide Your face, they are dismayed; You take away their spirit, they expire and return to their dust. You send forth Your Spirit, they are created; and You renew the face of the ground.* (Psalm 104:27-30)

While God clearly reveals Himself to be the one who upholds all things, He is not upheld by anything or anyone. Imagining this in a simple way will help us to see the absurdity of thinking that God needs anything from His creation. Imagine God holding all things, large and small, universal and microscopic, in the palm of His hand. They exist because He willed them to exist. They have continued to be because He has continued to will them to be. The exercise of His almighty determination is the sole reason they exist and endure. Now imagine one of the minuscule people that God is holding in His hand attempting to hold the being of God in his or her hand! Do you see how absurd it is to think that God needs anything from His creation?

CONSIDER carefully the following testimony from Scripture.

Psalm 50:7-15

Hear, O My people, and I will speak; O Israel, I will testify against you; I am God, your God. I do not reprove you for your sacrifices, and your burnt offerings are continually before Me. I shall take no young bull out of your house nor male goats out of your folds. For every beast of the forest is Mine, the cattle on a thousand hills. I know every bird of the mountains, and everything that moves in the field is Mine. If I were hungry I would not tell you, for the world is Mine, and all it contains. Shall I eat the flesh of bulls or drink the blood of male goats? Offer to God a sacrifice of thanksgiving and pay your vows to the Most High; call upon Me in the day of trouble; I shall rescue you, and you will honor Me.

Job 41:11

Who has given to Me that I should repay him? Whatever is under the whole heaven is Mine.

The God who possesses all things does not need the gifts of humanity, not even religious gifts. But the opposite is true: these people need God to come and rescue them.

Job 22:2-3

Can a vigorous man be of use to God, or a wise man be useful to himself? Is there any pleasure to the Almighty if you are righteous, or profit if you make your ways perfect?

Job 35:6-8

If you have sinned, what do you accomplish against Him? And if your transgressions are many, what do you do to Him? If you are righteous, what do you give to Him, or what does He receive from your hand? Your wickedness is for a man like yourself, and your righteousness is for a son of man.

Sin and obedience certainly affect humanity, but these do not give to, nor take from, the essential majesty of God.

We are too insignificant to be of any great importance in God's vast universe; He can do either with us or without us, and our presence or absence will not disarrange His plans.

— C. H. Spurgeon

We must be careful when we think of God.

- God alone cannot need.

- God alone cannot lack.

- God alone cannot be incomplete.

A seventeenth-century pastor wrote: "None ever in heaven or earth contributed the least towards the maintenance or continuance of his being; neither the creatures' goodness nor their goods do him the least good."[7] Tozer correctly affirms of God: "His interest in His creatures arises from His sovereign good pleasure, not from any need those creatures can supply nor from any completeness they can bring to Him who is complete in Himself."[8]

The biblical witness is clear: our goods, goodness, and wickedness cannot add to God nor reduce Him.

ILLUSTRATING THIS TRUTH

Imagine a place where there are breathtaking sunsets. Everyone who visits this place talks about them. They take pictures and post them on social media. The artistic observer attempts to capture the beauty of the sunset in a watercolor painting. Ask yourself: is the sunset any greater, any more spectacular because these people appreciate its beauty? Now imagine that there is a man living in this scenic place who was born blind. He has never seen the sunsets. Perhaps he tires of hearing the locals and tourists talk about them. If he decides not to believe in the splendor of the sunsets because he has never experienced them, are they in any way diminished? Are they any less beautiful, less colorful?

Even so, because He is infinitely complete and self-sustaining, God's perfections are not increased if all of humanity recognizes them, nor are they diminished if all of humanity denies them. He transcends us.

DAY 4: THE SELF-EXISTENCE AND INDEPENDENCE OF GOD, PART 2

How are we to live with the God Who is self-existing and independent?

It may seem at first glance that the doctrines of God's self-existence and independence, while true, are not particularly practical for us. However, these truths are actually essential to a right understanding of God, and a right understanding of God is essential to living out the Christian life.

SETTING THE RECORD STRAIGHT
REGARDING CREATION AND REDEMPTION

Understanding *why* God does what He does is important. Consider two of the works of God: creation and redemption (salvation). Why did He create? The answer commonly given is that God needed someone with whom to share His life. He was lonely. But if God is self-sufficient, can loneliness (or any other form of incompleteness) be His reason for creating? The truth is much more astonishing:

> *In eternity He was solitary . . . yet not lonely, complete in Himself, His infinite fullness, and lacking nothing. He did not create from a sense of His own need, but from the overflow of His fullness . . . and He did not recreate . . . fallen man from any lack in Himself. The fall of mankind did not lessen God. The rescue of a people has not added to His essential perfection. God does not need anyone or anything.*[9]

God created from an infinite fullness, not from any kind of lack. The quote above mentions the second great work of God—redemption. Have you ever really asked the question: "Why did He rescue His enemies?" The Bible teaches that God is free. This does not mean that He can be purchased without cost but rather that He is a free agent. In fact, He is the only truly free agent. He owes no one for His existence or continuance. Owing no one, He has no debts to pay, no favors to return. As the only one who is independent of all others, He is free to do all His good pleasure guided by His perfect wisdom and moral purity. This freedom is seen most clearly in His choice to save sinners.

To teach or even suggest that God made man because He was lonely or incomplete is a gross contradiction of the Scriptures. God did not create the universe because He had a need, but because He desired to make known the superabundance of His perfections, glory, and goodness.

— Paul Washer

If we correctly understand the biblical revelation of God's self-existence and independence, we can begin to understand the gospel and put to death the subtle lies of our enemy. The rescue of our souls is motivated by the purest form of grace.[10] However, there is often a subtle suspicion that God saves us because He needs us. We imagine salvation as a two-way-street, a mutually beneficial contract in which both parties benefit. Of course, we are quick to state that within this contract of salvation we receive a great deal more than God does, yet we may secretly believe that He also needs something from us.

Strangely, the root issue here is not our definition of grace. It is our inadequate understanding of God, in particular our ignorance of His self-existence and self-sufficiency. We think of God as though He were a bigger version of us. We can be selfish and quick to help those who will help us in return, so we imagine God must be the same way. But we must not attribute our selfish ways of thinking to God because He isn't like us.

EXPOSING A DUAL IDOLATRY

Idolatry comes in many forms. We are idolatrous when we attribute God-like qualities to ourselves. We are also guilty of idolatry when we do not think correctly of God and thus fail to present the true God to others. Let's consider both of these dangers.

ATTRIBUTING DIVINE PERFECTIONS TO OURSELVES

We might call this the "I AM" of human sin. There is a deeply rooted desire in all of us to be little gods. We want to live before our Maker as if we owe our existence to no one other than ourselves, as if we need nothing beyond what we can supply. We pretend that we exist by our own power and thus for our own pleasure. This thinking causes us to be indifferent toward God's rights and to be willing to justify our own self-centeredness.

FAILING TO ATTRIBUTE THESE DIVINE PERFECTIONS TO GOD IN OUR PRACTICE

It is common to see people motivated to Christian service by the idea that God needs them in His kingdom work. God is depicted as a generous-hearted king who has made too many promises and is having trouble fulfilling all His covenant obligations. What can He do? He paces heaven's floors wringing His hands. Then He stumbles upon an idea: enlist the people He is saving to help Him. Tozer expounds upon this issue:

> . . . *Thousands of young persons enter Christian service from no higher motive than to help deliver God from the embarrassing situation his love has gotten him into and his limited abilities seem unable to get him out of.*[11]

The idea that God needs us is a very intoxicating one. Think of it—the Almighty God needs you! Few things give people in modern churches a greater sense of worth than that idea—and yet it is a complete fabrication. It is a lie. If we are not careful, we will use this idolatrous view of God to help our church membership grow. "Join our church. God needs people like you on His team. There is a ministry opportunity for you here." People join thinking that they are kindly helping God. But which god are they helping?

IGNORANCE LEADS TO IDOLATRY

Acts 17:16-31 shows that the people of Athens, for all their learning, were ignorant of the fundamental truths of God. They were entangled in the lies of lesser gods, of idols. Their devotion was offered to "the unknown god." When Paul saw this deceptive portrayal of God his heart burned with zeal for God's honor.

READD ACTS 17:16-31 and answer the following questions.

1. What provoked Paul? Why did this provoke him? What was he provoked to do?

_____

_____

_____

_____

2. What did the Athenians like to spend their time doing?

_____

_____

3. What observation did Paul make about the Athenians in verse 22?

_____

_____

4. What did the Athenians need to understand about the nature of the true God?

_____

_____

5. What do you think Paul would need to say to your church to correct any wrong views of God you might have?

_____

_____

_____

THE MYSTERY OF BEING COWORKERS WITH THE ONE WHO IS SELF-SUFFICIENT!

Paradoxically, the one person who depends upon nothing and no one, who supports all things and all people continually, has called us into the glorious labor of His kingdom. Paul goes so far as to say that Christians are fellow-workers with Christ (2 Corinthians 6:1).

Two things are obvious in this partnership of labor:

First, God does not need us, but in His love and humility He has chosen to involve us in His work. This, rather than the myth that God needs us, is the true foundation for the Christian's sense of purpose.

Second, no Christian in himself is sufficient for such labor. Paul speaks to this when he says that he labors and speaks on God's behalf, but the sufficiency he has in this work is not from himself, but from God (2 Corinthians 3:5).

Why are both of these truths good news?

_____

_____

_____

CONCLUDING THOUGHTS

God has been described as the only one who is self-divine, self-luminous, self-wise, self-virtuous, and self-excellent.[12] In the coming weeks you will be studying the various aspects of God's majesty, His attributes. It is important that you see each one as self-existent. Not one of the perfections of God is caused by the activity of any angel, church, or person. His sovereignty, His immutability, His infinity, His transcendence, His faithfulness, His love, His wrath, His mercy, His justice, His patience—all find their source in Him alone.

CONSIDER the following verses and the obligation to live for the one who created us and sustains us. Fill in the missing words.

Colossians 1:16
For by Him all things were created, both in the heavens and on earth, visible and invisible, whether thrones or dominions or rulers or authorities—all things have been created _____ Him and _____ Him.

I am the Lord your God, who neither needs an assistant nor will admit a rival.

— Matthew Henry

I have received my all from God; oh that I could return my all to God! Surely God is worthy of my highest affection, and most devout adoration; he is infinitely worthy, that I should make him my last end, and live forever to him. Oh that I might never more, in any one instance, live to myself!

— David Brainerd

Romans 11:36

For _____ Him and _____ Him and to Him are all things. To Him be the glory forever.

1 Corinthians 8:6

. . . for us there is but one God, the Father, from whom are all things and _____ Him; and one Lord, Jesus Christ, by whom are all things, and _____ Him.

One of the fundamental implications of God's independence and self-existence is that "all which is not God" is dependent upon Him for existence. Each of us owes our existence to God's good pleasure. The biblical application of this is simple: we owe our all to the one who made us.

DAY 5: THE SUPREMACY OF GOD

For the LORD Most High is to be feared,
A great King over all the earth.
(Psalm 47:2)

The protestant reformer Martin Luther warned Erasmus, a notable theologian in his day, "Your thoughts concerning God are too human."[13]

Like Erasmus, we can be guilty of thinking of God in ways that are too human. But God is not like us; He is supreme. He alone is supreme. He is highest, utmost, and ultimate. He is superior, rising above all others by an immeasurable distance. How often do we slow down and really contemplate the uniqueness of God, the supremacy of the Most High? We must take the time to do so if we are to think of God in ways that are in line with reality.

Today we will study three aspects of the supremacy of our God. He is:

- Transcendent

- Incomparable

- Solitary

THE TRANSCENDENT GOD

When we speak of God as transcendent we mean that He is exalted far above the created universe, so far above that human thought cannot imagine it.[14]

The distinction between God and the rest of His creation is not merely quantitative (the same, but greater), but qualitative (God is a completely different being).

— Paul Washer

19

We often read in the Bible that God is the Most High. Let's be clear about two matters:

1. "Most High" does not refer to a physical distance. The term is not speaking of altitude, but rather of God's elevated dignity and worth.

2. The Bible does not depict God as the highest being in an ascending order of beings. God is not Most High, with the highest angel coming in a close second.

Tozer speaks to this issue:

> . . . [We] grant God eminence, even pre-eminence, but that is not enough; we must grant Him transcendence in the fullest meaning of that word. Forever, God stands apart, in light unapproachable. [15]

Reader, think of His incomprehensible greatness and majesty. Think of Him as the High and Lofty One who inhabits eternity— the heavens His throne, the earth His footstool, the light His garment, the clouds His chariot, the thunder His voice!

— John MacDuff

It is as the Most High that God revealed Himself to Abraham. Returning from a battle in which God had given his family victory, Abraham met a priest called Melchizedek. Here is what that priest said:

> *Blessed be Abram of God Most High,*
> *Possessor of heaven and earth;*
> *And blessed be God Most High,*
> *Who has delivered your enemies into your hand . . . .* (Genesis 14:19-20)

So the God of Abraham is God "Most High." His transcendence is seen in the fact that He alone possesses heaven and earth, and as sole owner of the universe He rescues Abraham and his family from their enemies.

God often reveals Himself in Scripture as the Most High from that point forward. The psalmists never tire of using this description of God.

COPY the following verses.

Psalm 9:2

_____

_____

_____

Psalm 57:2

_____

_____

In the midst of unspeakable sorrow, the prophet Jeremiah recognized that the Babylonian siege was a disciplinary action from God Most High.

Lamentations 3:38

_____

_____

The angel Gabriel told Mary that Jesus would be the Son of the Most High.

Luke 1:32

_____

_____

Later, as the apostles carried the gospel of Christ to the Gentiles, a demon-possessed slave girl in Thyatira followed Paul and Silas, crying out:

> *. . . These men are bond-servants of the Most High God, who are proclaiming to you the way of salvation.* (Acts 16:17)

We are familiar with this title, but have we ever filled our hearts and minds with the realities that it represents? Have we ever altered the course of our lives because of what it means to belong to the Most High God?

GOD'S TRANSCENDENT CHARACTER

When we say that God is transcendent, we must apply that truth to every aspect of God's character. In every attribute our God rises infinitely above all else.

CONSIDER the examples given in the passages below.

1. God transcends every limitation of time.

    Isaiah 41:4
    . . . I, the LORD, am the first, and with the last. I am He.

We think of God as too much like what we are. Put this mistake right, says God; learn to acknowledge the full majesty of your incomparable God and Savior.

—J. I. Packer

2. God transcends every limitation of space.

1 Kings 8:27
But will God indeed dwell on the earth? Behold, heaven and the highest heaven cannot contain You, how much less this house which I have built!

3. God transcends change.

Malachi 3:6
For I, the LORD, do not change . . . .

4. God transcends all comprehension and sight.

John 1:18
No one has seen God at any time; the only begotten God who is in the bosom of the Father, He has explained Him.

5. God transcends all other authority.

Psalm 115:3
But our God is in the heavens;
He does whatever He pleases.

6. God transcends the spite and resistance of His enemies.

Job 42:2
I know that You can do all things,
And that no purpose of Yours can be thwarted.

7. God transcends the "laws of nature."

Psalm 135:6
Whatever the LORD pleases, He does,
In heaven and in earth, in the seas and in all deeps.

We could write Psalm 135:6 over every miracle recorded in the Bible. Dividing the Red Sea, restraining the sun's course in Joshua's day, feeding Elijah by ravens, bringing Jesus to us by virgin birth, and raising Lazarus from the grave—all point to the same thing: God rises far above all the normal laws of nature which He has established.

There is another aspect of His transcendence that we must consider: He transcends accurate comparison!

THE INCOMPARABLE GOD

God is incomparable—He cannot satisfactorily be compared to anything in His creation.

In Scripture we find God being compared to those things which impress humanity. The outcome of every comparison is the same: God rises higher than the reach of our most exalted thoughts of Him. He is incomparable.

God, using the pen of Isaiah, poses this question to ancient Israel and modern Christians.

> *"To whom then will you liken Me,*
> *That I would be his equal?" says the Holy One.* (Isaiah 40:25)

The most splendid angel that stands in the presence of God is no more truly like God than the smallest worm that crawls upon the earth. God is incomparable!

— Paul Washer

We must give this question the consideration it deserves. The Bible tells us about many things to which God is *not* to be compared.

READ the following passages and fill in the blanks.

Exodus 15:11
Who is like You among the gods, O LORD?
Who is like You, majestic in holiness,
Awesome in praises, working wonders?

There is no comparison between God and _____.

Isaiah 40:15, 17
Behold, the nations are like a drop from a bucket,
And are regarded as a speck of dust on the scales;
Behold, He lifts up the islands like fine dust . . .
All the nations are as nothing before Him,
They are regarded by Him as less than nothing and meaningless.

There is no comparison between God and _____.

Isaiah 40:23
He it is who reduces rulers to nothing,
Who makes the judges of the earth meaningless.

There is no comparison between God and _____.

23

Daniel 4:34-35

I blessed the Most High and praised and honored Him who lives forever;
For His dominion is an everlasting dominion,
And His kingdom endures from generation to generation.
All the inhabitants of the earth are accounted as nothing . . . .

Wherever you look, nothing in creation can compare to the Most High.

THE GOD WHO IS SOLITARY

We come now to the height of God's supremacy. He is not merely Most High. He does not merely transcend all else in a manner that makes accurate comparison impossible. There is yet a higher description. He is solitary. That means no one is in His category. He is alone in His perfections—unique, unequalled, unmatched, unrivalled, unparalleled. Before anything was created, He alone was. He alone was holy; He alone was almighty; He alone was eternal; He alone was self-existing and self-sufficient; He alone was unchanging; He alone was all-wise; and He alone was sovereign.

Ask yourself: was His uniqueness diminished at all when He created all things? When He fashioned the angelic hosts to worship Him, did He inadvertently add others to His category? No. Though mankind was created in His image, humanity is obviously not in His category. Even after creation God remains solitary in His majesty.

Moses spoke the following words to the Jews prior to their entering Canaan:

> *Know therefore today, and take it to your heart, that the LORD, He is God in heaven above and on the earth below; there is no other.*
> (Deuteronomy 4:39)

"There is no other." That is a fitting proclamation for all creation.

HOW THEN ARE WE TO LIVE?

Who God is affects how every believer lives. If we believe He is supreme, the Most High who rises above all else, incomparable, unmatched in His perfection—how will that change the way we live today?

Perhaps we can start with three simple applications.

1. If God is supreme, then the Christian has been given a treasure beyond any other.

Think on this! The Most High walked with a man, a creature made of dust, in Eden. Later, the Most High sent His Son to accomplish a great rescue that would bring each Christian to know Him in a vital, experiential relationship. The Most High sent His Spirit to indwell followers of Christ, making them His living temple. The most common Christian has been set apart by these distinguishing privileges. So, Christian, set your soul's deepest and strongest longings upon God Most High!

The early church leader and theologian Augustine was an ambitious man prior to his conversion. After coming to God through Christ, this capable young man reset his focus. He wanted above all else to know the God who had saved him. He wrote: "I desire to know God and my soul. Nothing more? No, nothing at all."[16]

We have more than mere knowledge of the Most High—He has become our refuge! PSALM 91:9 speaks of this.

> *For you have made the LORD, my refuge,*
> *Even the Most High, your dwelling place.*

The Most High—the refuge and safe dwelling place for those who once hated Him! Surely, like Augustine, we want to say, "I desire to know God, nothing else."

WRITE below some things that you will need to change if you are going to know the Most High better. What will need to be removed from your life? What will need to be added to your life?

_____

_____

_____

_____

2. Sin is correctly seen when we shine these truths into the dark corners of our lives.

What is sin? How can you tell which actions are right and which are wrong? What attitudes are pleasing to God? What responses?

Perish every fond ambition,
All I've sought, and hoped, and known;
Yet how rich is my condition!
God and heaven are still mine own.

— Henry Francis Lyte

He that has light thoughts of sin had never great thoughts of God. Indeed, men's underrating of sin arises merely from their contempt of God.

—John Owen

Sin is, at its heart, taking the perfections of God and attributing them to yourself. So in this case sin is saying that you, not God, are uniquely raised above all others. Your desires, your claims, your rights, your preferences—these are all higher than those of others, even God's!

COPY ISAIAH 14:14.

_____

_____

Sin, at its root, is the desire to live as if you were the Most High, claiming all of His perfections and privileges. Consider the ways you have been living with the secret desire to claim the privileges of God.

3.   What an only one is our Jesus!

We know that Jesus of Nazareth is God and man united. This mystery is at the heart of all our hope as Christians. According to the angel, it was by the power of the Most High that this was accomplished (Luke 1:35).

How greatly our appreciation for Jesus is increased when we apply these three aspects of God's supremacy to our Lord. Jesus is transcendent, rising as the Most High above all creation in every aspect of His divine nature. Jesus is incomparable in His dignity, for He is solitary in His divine perfections.

You have an opportunity to take a long look at the supremacy of God in its three biblical categories. How will this alter your views of Christ? Don't settle for anything less than the kind of devotion that was expressed by the Scottish pastor Samuel Rutherford: "Oh what a fair One, what an only One, what an excellent, lovely . . . One, is Jesus!"[17]

O Jesus, light of all below,
Thou fount of life and fire,
Surpassing all the joys we know,
And all we can desire.

— Edward Caswall

KNOWING THE GOD WHO CANNOT CHANGE

DAY 1: THE GOD WHO DOES NOT CHANGE

To say that God is immutable is to say that He never differs from Himself.
— A.W. Tozer

Immutability—the perfection of God which ensures that He cannot be altered—is a treasure for those who have risked everything to know and follow Him. Consider how unstable every joy in the Christian life would be if our God could change. If the God who now exists is different from the God we read of in Scripture, then studying Him would be as impractical as consulting an ancient world map for a present-day road trip. God's immutability is the guarantee that all our labors to know and love Him are not wasted. If He is not precisely, in every detail, the same God who sought out Abraham in Ur, spoke with Moses from a burning bush, met with David while he kept sheep, and appeared in His glory to Isaiah—then this study is merely academic. God's majesty, to be sure, would form the most interesting study possible, but if He could change, that study would have no more bearing upon your life than the myths of the ancient idols. Hoping in a god who is changeable is no hope at all. Modern humanity desperately needs a God who cannot be modified, altered, or adapted. The extraordinarily good news is that this describes the very God to whom Jesus brings us.

We blossom and flourish as leaves on the tree,
And wither and perish, but nought changeth Thee.

— Walter Chalmers Smith

This week we will consider the immutability of God and explore how to apply it.

FINDING A WORKING DEFINITION OF IMMUTABILITY

Immutable is not a word we often use. *The Merriam Webster Dictionary* defines it as "not capable of or susceptible to change."[18]

Timothy Dwight, the grandson of eighteenth-century New England pastor Jonathan Edwards and eighth president of Yale, defined God's immutability this way:

> *He is subject to no change in his manner of being, his perfections, thoughts, desires, purposes, or determinations.*[19]

The self-existing I AM does not change. His perfection is such that He cannot diminish or grow. There is no variation in His character. In fact, He has no capacity for alteration, modification, adjustment, amendment, adaptation, or revision. Being perfect beyond measure, His inability to be revised or modified is an aspect of glory, not an evidence of some incompleteness in His character.

THE BIBLICAL WITNESS

It is well for us that, amidst all the alterations and vicissitudes of life, here is . . . One whom change cannot affect, One whose heart can never alter, One on whose brow mutability can make no furrows.

— C. H. Spurgeon

Below are passages that speak of the impossibility of change in God.

COPY the verses in the blanks below.

Malachi 3:6

_____

_____

Psalm 102:24-27

_____

_____

_____

_____

Hebrews 13:8

_____

_____

James 1:16-17

_____

_____

_____

LET'S CONSIDER A FEW OF THE IMPLICATIONS FROM THESE PASSAGES:

1.   God cannot be altered in His perfections.

Immutability comes naturally to God. It is part of who He is. It is not, therefore, maintained by any effort on God's part. We are not immutable. We change so easily that we must exert great effort to keep from changing. For example, we all change physically and go to great lengths to hide the signs of aging. We work to maintain our physical health and mental abilities. We can change in our intentions, so we have to work at keeping our promises.

Yet God is effortlessly and everlastingly unchangeable. To understand this fully you must link His immutability to His other attributes.

Consider the attribute of love. John tells us in 1 John 4:8 that "God is love." Love is one of the invariable perfections of His character. Immutability means that God's love is eternally unchangeable. He was love when He created Adam and placed him in Paradise. He was also love, unaltered, when He flooded the earth in holy wrath. He was love when He crushed His Son at the cross for His people's sins. He is love today. He will be love on the day His Son judges all creation and casts His enemies down forever.

Consider the attribute of wisdom. God was all-wise when He fashioned the plan of salvation prior to creation. He was all-wise when He created all matter to His personal specifications. He is equally wise today. His wisdom has not been altered by the passage of time nor the complexity of the human condition. His wisdom has not been rivaled by emerging technology or the rapid expansion of human learning.

There will never be a change in God—no change is necessary!

— A. W. Tozer

In an imperfect creature immutability would be a shortcoming. When we say of a person, "he will never change," we do not usually mean that as a compliment. We see our own imperfections and wish to fix them. But in the infinitely perfect Creator, the inability to change is a part of His glory. Imagine if God possessed every perfection that the Bible attributes to Him except immutability. How different our Christianity would be if God's love could be shifted, His knowledge made obsolete, His purity polluted, His word broken, or His patience depleted! Thankfully, these things can never be.

Before we move on, we need to be clear about something: when we speak of God's immutability, we are referring to His person, not His actions. Although God's perfections are unchanging, they are not invariably expressed. For example, God is always a God who possesses wrath against sin; however, God may choose to restrain His wrath at times and express it at other times. Wrath is an immutable aspect of God's person, but God expresses this wrath in a variety of ways.

2. God cannot be altered in His purpose.

The Bible clearly reveals God to be the one being who does everything according to His own purposes without depending upon others (Psalm 115:3). Of course, in an imperfect world there is continual resistance to His perfect purposes. Does that resistance cause God to alter them? Remember what Job tells us about God.

> *I know that You can do all things, and that no purpose of Yours can be thwarted.* (Job 42:2)

As we will see later this week, the salvation of sinners is built upon the immutable purposes and plans of God. In the first chapter of Ephesians, Paul tells us that our rescue flows from the "kind intention which He [God] *purposed* in Him [Christ]" and "according to His *purpose* who works all things after the counsel of His will."

We are deeply mistaken about God when we say that the cross of Christ was "Plan B," devised after the Old Covenant failed. The purposes of God are as immutable as His character—nothing can be taken from them or added to them.

3. Consider the hope that is ours when we realize that we can be altered.

Have you ever wished you were immutable? Think again! If we were locked into our present state, how hopeless we would be. Even as Christians, when we look into the mirror of Scripture, we see many areas that are yet to be brought under the rule of Christ. We long to see change and plead with God to complete His work in us. It is a hope-filled truth that we are not immutable. Christian, you can and will be altered daily by God's gracious work within you until you stand before Him complete.

Below, write a prayer of praise and thanksgiving to the one who has never known change.

_____

_____

_____

_____

_____

_____

DAY 2: GOD'S IMMUTABILITY: A REASON TO REPENT

When you drift from God and your heart grows indifferent toward Him, what motivates you to repent and return? Unbelievers in churches often think that repentance is a cheap and easy-going matter. They may find some shelter in parroting their favorite verse, 1 John 1:9, "If we confess our sins, He is faithful and just to forgive us our sins . . . ." Yet all the while they have no intention of giving up the sin they are "confessing." They daily trivialize God, sin, and repentance.

The true follower of Christ has a very different attitude regarding sin and repentance. The Christian knows that sin is a denial of the rights of the eternally enthroned God. In addition, the believer knows that sin is against divine love. Sin is no longer considered a small matter. The awakened conscience, alarmed by disobedience, is not so easily quieted as was once thought. The shame and guilt of rebelling against a loving Father is felt deeply. To aggravate matters, the heart may prove sluggish, unresponsive, or plagued by paralyzing doubts, inhibiting genuine efforts to return to God. Those who love God find that true repentance is costly.

It is precisely at this point that we discover an unexpected source of hope in the immutability of God. Immutability, an unexpected source of hope? Yes! Consider how often you have been tempted to think that repentance would be easier if God were a little more like us, if He were not so unchanging, a bit less morally rigid.

READ HOSEA 11:1-9.

Describe the people's actions and God's response to them.

_____

_____

_____

_____

Notice the reason He gives for this response in verse 9:

For I am _____, and not _____ .

For a closer look at the immutability of God as a motive for repentance, we need to jump forward to the final book of the Old Testament.

MALACHI'S UNCHANGING GOD

After generations of idolatrous hearts, stiff necks, and deaf ears, the children of Israel are exiled. Seventy years later, Cyrus, the king of Persia, allows them to return. They begin to rebuild Jerusalem but become discouraged. The prophets Haggai and Zechariah encourage the people with promises of prosperity, peace, and the return of God's glorious presence to the new temple. Ezra and Nehemiah come to spur them on. A century later, the temple is finished, but the people are still far from God and despairing. The covenant promises of God seem to mock them in their present distress.

Dire circumstances touch every area of their lives. Economically, they are poor. Crops have failed, and there has been a long drought. Politically, they live in a twenty by twenty-five mile plot of land. The population is 150,000—one-sixth the number that left Egypt. They are under the authority of a foreign king. What has become of David's line? Spiritually, the restored temple is unimpressive in appearance and there is no visible evidence of God's manifest presence. Where is He? Has He changed His mind? They slog on in an apparently hollow religion with a distant God!

THE SIN OF MALACHI'S DAY

Although the exile had brought about the permanent removal of open idolatry, the people became accustomed to an offended and distant God. Instead of idolatry, a type of dead orthodoxy was embraced and flourished. Instead of repenting, the children of Israel began to shift the blame to God.

Here are six accusations that the Israelites level against God during the days of the prophet Malachi:

1. We don't believe God loves us as He said He would. (1:2)

2. We don't believe that we need to be so particular in our worship of God. (1:6-8, 13)

3. Because God is not faithful, we don't believe it is necessary to keep faith with others. Example: divorce. (2:14)

4. God doesn't seem to care about good and evil anymore. Maybe He has changed His views on these things. (2:17)

5. Because God doesn't care for us, we don't believe that we owe God anything. Example: robbing Him of tithes. (Remember: sin can be giving to God in part what we owe Him in whole.) (3:7-8)

6. Because of the way He has treated us, we think it is really useless to serve God. We will do okay without Him. (3:13-15)

Time flaps a ceaseless wing, and from the wings decay and death drop down. "I AM THAT I AM" sits high above all this. He is "the same yesterday and to-day and forever."

— Henry Law

Friendship only flourishes in the atmosphere of confidence, suspicion is deadly to it: shall the Lord God, true and immutable, be day after day suspected by his own people?

— C. H. Spurgeon

SELF-EXAMINATION

This is what the church attenders were saying in Malachi's day.

But what about you? Have any of these attitudes ever shown themselves in your life? What about now? Are any of these accusations being harbored in your heart and mind?

WRITE any of the above that you have believed.

_____

_____

_____

THE HEART OF THE BOOK: THE UNCHANGED GOD IS COMING IN THE PERSON OF THE MESSIAH

READ MALACHI 3:1-6.

God calls His people "sons of Jacob." Do you remember Jacob—that shifting, sly swindler? They are following in his footsteps. They too are treacherous, unfaithful, continually shifting. We have heard the six accusations against God from Jacob's descendants, six evidences that they are capable of change. But God is not. God's immutability is the reason why these people were not consumed. Not only did He not destroy them, but He promised to send the Messiah. The activity of the coming Messenger in Malachi 3:1-5 shows us that God has not changed.

God does not change in His ways:

* He always opposes sin, and He always rescues His people—even if by refining fire.

God does not change in His plans. From Genesis forward we have promises of a coming redemption:

* Adam was promised that the serpent would be crushed by Eve's offspring.

* Abraham was promised that the entire world would benefit through one of his offspring.

* David was promised a king that would rule without borders and without end.

> *The unchangeableness of Jesus is the unchangeableness of His attributes.*
>
> — Henry Law

God remains unaltered throughout the centuries. He does all that is necessary to fulfill these promises:

- Eve's line brings forth the babe called Jesus, who crushes the enemy.

- Abraham's family becomes the cradle of Christ and the gospel.

- David's line produces a king who rules from heaven, whose rule knows no end.

Because God does not change, His plans do not change, and His promises are fulfilled. That is why He can call Jacob's children to return.

> Malachi 3:7
> *"From the days of your fathers you have turned aside from My statutes and have not kept them. Return to Me, and I will return to you," says the LORD of hosts.*

There is no love, too, so gentle, so patient, so enduring, as Christ's love. Again and again you have questioned it, wounded it, forsaken it; again and again you have returned to it with tears, confession, and humiliation, and have found it as unchilled and unchanged as his nature . . . .

— Octavius Winslow

God freely chose Israel, He freely made promises to them, and He freely keeps those promises. The unworthiness of Jacob's unfaithful people will not prevent God's faithfulness. Don't miss this: God's people are Jacob's sons, Jacob's family—always changing—but God made promises to that family. Nothing they do, right or wrong, can alter the covenant-faithfulness of God. Not only can nothing outside of God change His plans for His people, nothing inside of Him can change them either. This is not merely because of His integrity to His word; it is because of His immutable love. God's unchanging love for His people calls them to repentance. He doesn't say, "Okay, I will let you return." No, He longs for their return. He cares for them, and like the father of the prodigal, He promises to meet His returning people—"I will return to you."

APPLICATIONS

Like the Israelites of Malachi's day, we also are being given a chance to reform our lives according to Scripture. We are daily given the opportunity to return to the God of the Bible.

Do you value this opportunity, one that is rooted in God's unchanging character? What practical evidences are there in your life that you really value the call to return to God?

_____

_____

_____

Does your present situation cause you, like those in Malachi's day, to doubt Christ's promises to His followers? How does the immutability of God counteract the doubts you have formed?

_____

_____

_____

Think biblically. If you are a follower of Christ, none of God's plans for you have changed, and no change in situation—your family, your job, your home, your health, your church, or your nation—can alter these plans. Through "all the changing scenes of life," the unchangeableness of our God offers hope to the Christian. It also calls for an unfaltering allegiance to Christ's immutable call, "Follow Me," and all that is included in that command.

FOR REFLECTION

How will God's unchanged purpose alter the way you live this week?

DAY 3: IMMUTABLE PURPOSES

As you learned yesterday, God's unchanging nature prevented the people of Malachi's day from being consumed. Instead of destroying them, God called them to return, promising the covenant-Redeemer. Exactly who that Redeemer would be and how their redemption would be accomplished was not fully explained. The New Testament, however, unfolds many of the mysteries of this redemption. God, in His unchanging purposes, has given His unchanging Son to be our Savior.

The immutable plans of God for redemption were mentioned in HEBREWS 6:17-20:

> *In the same way God, desiring even more to show to the heirs of the promise the* unchangeableness *of His purpose, interposed with an oath, so that by two unchangeable things in which it is impossible for God to lie, we who have taken refuge would have strong encouragement to take hold of the hope set before us. This hope we have as an anchor of the soul, a hope both sure and steadfast and one which enters within the veil, where Jesus has entered as a forerunner for us, having become a high priest forever according to the order of Melchizedek.*

To get the big picture, let's consider the unchanging purposes of God that provided our Savior. Because God's plans are founded upon all His other perfections, they do not change. He is all-knowing, all-wise, all-powerful, and utterly righteous. What could cause such a being to change course? No new information, opposition, or obstacle can hinder the plans of the Almighty. No error on His part could necessitate a "Plan B."

To change His purposes in anything, God would have to undergo one of the following:

He is as constant as He is great. As surely as He ever lives, so surely He ever lives the same. He is one expanse of never-varying oneness. He sits on the calm throne of eternal serenity.

— Henry Law

- A CHANGE OF MIND – For God to rethink His plans would require some information or circumstance of which God was unaware to be brought to His attention. To entertain such a thought, we must assume that God has limited knowledge—and that is a false assumption. He not only knows what has happened and is happening, He knows exactly what will happen. Nothing new can arise that might change His mind.

- A CHANGE OF HEART – The passing of time changes people and nations. Those who were once close friends are now distant. Allies become enemies. Enemies become allies. How we feel about a person may change significantly, but God is unchanging with respect to the objects of His love, and His plans are not altered by a cooling affection.

- A CHANGE OF WILL – Since God cannot change His mind or His affections, no reason exists for Him to change His will. Why would He alter His course if nothing new has occurred to Him? Why would He adjust His plans when there has been no change of heart?

As God's children, our obedience and disobedience receive differing responses from Him. Yet regardless of how He responds (blessing or judgment), every response flows from the same unaltered purpose—to bring His children to be conformed to the moral image of His Son.

Are you wrestling with the reality of God's immutable purposes and plans? Does the Bible back up the claim that God's purposes are immutable?

FILL IN THE BLANKS in the passages below.

HIS UNALTERED PURPOSES INCLUDE ALL OF HIS WORKS

Acts 15:18
. . . says the LORD, who _____
_____.

Ecclesiastes 3:14

I know that everything God does _____;
there is nothing to add to it and there is nothing to take from it, for God
has so worked that men should fear Him.

Numbers 23:19

God is not a man, that He should lie, nor a son of man, that He should
repent; has He said, and _____?
Or has He spoken, and will He not make it good?

Isaiah 46:10

Declaring the end from the beginning, and from ancient times things
which have not been done, saying, "My purpose _____
_____, and I _____
all My good pleasure . . . ."

HIS UNALTERED PURPOSES INCLUDE THE NATIONS

Isaiah 14:24, 26-27

The LORD of hosts has sworn saying, "Surely, just as I have intended
_____, and just as I have planned so it will
stand . . . . This is the plan devised against the whole earth; and this
is the hand that is stretched out against all the nations. For the LORD
of hosts has planned, _____?
And as for His stretched-out hand, who can turn it back?"

Psalm 33:10-11

The LORD nullifies the counsel of the nations;
He frustrates the plans of the peoples.
_____ stands forever,
The plans of His heart from generation to generation.

HIS UNALTERED PURPOSES INCLUDE INDIVIDUALS

Proverbs 16:9

The mind of man plans his way, but the LORD _____
_____.

Job 23:13-14

But He is unique and who can turn Him?
And what His soul desires, _____.
For He performs what is appointed for me,
And many such decrees are with Him.

Daniel 4:35

All the inhabitants of the earth are accounted as nothing, but He

_____

in the host of heaven and among the inhabitants of earth; and no one can ward off His hand or say to Him, "What have You done?"

HIS UNALTERED PURPOSES INCLUDE THE WORK OF SALVATION

Ephesians 1:9

He made known to us the mystery of His will, according to His kind intention which _____ in Him.

Ephesians 1:11-12

. . . also we have obtained an inheritance, having been predestined according to His purpose who works all things _____ _____, to the end that we who were the first to hope in Christ would be to the praise of His glory.

2 Timothy 1:9

[God] who has saved us and called us with a holy calling, not according to our works, but according to _____ and grace which was granted us in Christ Jesus from all eternity . . . .

Once a Father, always a Father; once a Friend, always a Friend. His providences may change but His heart does not.

— Octavius Winslow

When nothing in us will furnish Him with a reason for His favors, He furnishes Himself with one [His name and glory].

— Matthew Henry

These passages reveal that the loving counsels of God stand firm, as immutable as His person. He drew all His reasons for loving and saving His people from within His own person, so His love is unchanging.

The Father, Son, and Spirit have taken counsel and have determined to rescue a multitude of sinners by the Son's gospel labors. Nothing in humanity or in this fallen universe will thwart that purpose.

What is the appropriate response to this immutable God who has set in motion purposes of mercy that can never be modified?

READ ISAIAH 25:1 and write out Isaiah's response.

_____

_____

_____

DAY 4: IMMUTABILITY: A REASON TO RESIST TEMPTATION

Do you recall Timothy Dwight's definition of immutability mentioned in Day 1? Please copy his definition from this week's first day.

_____

_____

God's immutability is essential to who He is. His person and purposes are not maintained by any effort on His part. He is who He is, always and effortlessly, and everything that He does is consistent with His perfect, unchanging nature.

Do you remember the goal of our study? Our purpose is to learn how to live unto God. We want our minds to be enlightened by scriptural doctrine, our hearts enlivened with love to God, and our wills moved to a new obedience.

This world is not conducive to obedience. It constantly strives to lure us away from God and into sin. Lies regarding who God is, who we are, and what sin is relentlessly bombard us. Our enemy seeks to destroy us, and we are susceptible to his lies. Therefore, to live unto God we must know how to deal with sin's attraction; we must know how to resist temptation.

It should encourage us that when James wrote to early churches about how to live unto God, he included the truth about our ongoing struggle with sin and instructions for dealing with temptation. Notably, James points us once again to the immutability of God.

Our main business with any doctrine of religion is, not to prove it, but to proceed upon it—not to understand it, but to apply and employ it.

— Ichabod Spencer

THE BLAME GAME

Sin is not a topic we like to consider, particularly when our sin is being exposed by God. When our sin is bared, our first reaction is often to blame someone. We come from a long line of blame-shifters. Sometimes we blame other people, but often we blame God for our sin, much like Adam who said, "This woman that *You* gave me tempted me and I sinned."

Blaming God for our sin may sound like this:

* "God knows that I have trouble with that particular sin, and He put me in that situation."

* "God made me like this."

* "My upbringing and my past are causing me to sin. It's my parents' fault, and God gave them to me."

Sometimes we don't accuse God directly, but we blame Him nonetheless. When we attribute our sin to the internal or external circumstances of our lives, we are indirectly placing blame on God.

Have you ever used any of the following?

- *My spouse*: "Other people in the church have good marriages. My spouse is impossible."

- *My work*: "No one could work with my boss and co-workers without sinning."

- *My church*: "If only I were in a good church, then I could be obedient. I need Christian friends and someone to disciple me."

- *The present time*: "This day and age is so wicked. We have temptation at our fingertips constantly."

In reality, none of these is the source of temptation.

READ JAMES 1:12-15.

What is the source of temptation?

_____

_____

"Lust" in this context refers not only to sexual desire but to any strong desire or craving for something (e.g., power, security, money, control, pleasure, recognition).

What two things does James tell us about the immutability of God in this passage?

_____

_____

_____

We cannot rightfully blame God for even one sinful thought, word, or deed. We cannot rightly accuse Him of failing to provide sufficient help. We cannot say, "I was confused, and He did not give wisdom. I was weak, and He did not give strength." Nor can we justly blame God by saying, "He didn't keep me from sin. He is sovereign. He is in control. Why didn't He stop me?"

Paul said the following to the Corinthian church:

No temptation has overtaken you but such as is common to man; and God is faithful, who will not allow you to be tempted beyond what you are able, but with the temptation will provide the way of escape also, so that you will be able to endure it. (1 Corinthians 10:13)

And Peter wrote:

. . . His divine power has granted to us everything pertaining to life and godliness, through the true knowledge of Him who called us by His own glory and excellence. (2 Peter 1:3)

So, temptations will come, but God will always provide all we need to escape their snare. Part of the provision for life and godliness is received through a true knowledge of God.

GOD CAN NEVER BE THE SOURCE OF TEMPTATION

Let's consider what we are told about God and sin.

James 1:13
Let no one say when he is tempted, "I am being tempted by God"; for God cannot be tempted by evil, and He Himself does not tempt anyone.

God's character makes it impossible for Him to be the source of temptation. He can neither be enticed by sin, nor can He entice someone to sin. He is morally perfect, pure, upright, righteous, and holy, and He is immutably so. Because of His immutable holiness and moral perfection, God is incapable of being the author of sin or temptation.

God's holiness is perfect moral separation from all that is contaminated with sin. He does not approve of sin and has no desire to sin. He is not morally pure because He makes good choices or has a pattern of behavior maintained by perfect willpower. He is holy and morally pure by nature. This is as effortless to Him as being human is to us. He is holy in His essence, and as we have seen, His essence cannot be changed. Thus, there is no possibility of Him sinning.

It is a less injury to him to deny his Being than to deny the purity of it. The one makes him no God, the other deformed, unholy, and detestable.

— Stephen Charnock

1 John 1:5
This is the message we have heard from Him and announce to you, that God is Light, and in Him there is no darkness at all.

God is described here as moral light. No darkness can proceed from Him in the form of temptation. God may and does use the sin of His enemies for His own purposes, but He is never the source or origin of sin. We see this very clearly in the book of James.

THE PATTERN OF SIN AND TEMPTATION

The source of our sin is our lusts (our inordinate and selfish desires). Trace the development of sin as described in JAMES 1:12-18.

_____

_____

_____

_____

Sin goes in a disguise, and thence is welcome; like Judas, it kisses and kills; like Joab, it salutes and slays.

— George Swinnock

Temptation does not lead to sin unless we let it. Luther said that we cannot prevent birds from flying over our heads, but we can prevent them from building a "nest" in our hair. Before temptation becomes sin, we must first allow it to "nest" in our mind and heart. When we choose to believe sin's lies, it is because our desires are twisted around self, our mind is absorbed with thinking only of self, and our choices are guided by self-gratification.

Sin comes to our door like a clever salesman pitching wonderful offers to us. Our selfish desires make us susceptible to its lies. We can shut the door and turn temptation away, or we can invite it in for a conversation. Once inside the door, sin proves to be quite persuasive, and we succumb to its requests. Outside the door, sin's child (death) lies in wait, for death always accompanies sin. Death waits to show its face until we have given into sin's lies, yet we can be sure that death will always follow sin's entrance into our lives.

Death is separation from God. God told Adam that if he sinned, he would surely die. When Adam sinned, he did not immediately die physically, but the effects of death immediately entered his life. Adam died spiritually and needed redemption. If sin is our pattern of life, eternal death will be our end.

For a Christian, sin results in death to fellowship with God. It brings with it spiritual callousness, famine, drought, and purposelessness. Sin is misery for the believer. Sin brings separation from the one source of life. So, whether a temporary separation from the face of God for the believer or an ongoing and eventually eternal separation for the unrepentant sinner, do not be deceived— sin brings death!

And who is to blame for your sin? YOU! According to what you have been studying today, why is this true?

_____

_____

_____

THE TRUTH ABOUT GOD'S GIFTS

Satan wants us to think that his gifts are good and God's gifts are not. He assures us that he has what we want and that God's goal is to spoil all our fun. His lies appeal to our selfishness and our innate desire to be independent of God. But Satan is a liar—the father of lies, in fact. Never forget that he earnestly desires to "kill, steal, and destroy."

Satan's gifts, which we obtain through sin, are like poisoned candy—sweet on the tongue but bitter in the stomach. Inevitably and invariably, his gifts bring death. God's gifts are completely different.

> James 1:16-17
> *Do not be deceived, my beloved brethren. Every good thing given and every perfect gift is from above, coming down from the Father of lights, with whom there is no variation or shifting shadow.*

One of the keys to resisting temptation is to believe that God loves us and wants what is best for us. He doesn't withhold anything from His children that is good for them. "Every good and perfect gift" is from Him, and like Himself, His gifts do not change. They do not start good and turn bitter. His gifts are sweetness through and through. They are like Him, who does not change like "shifting shadows."

Think of how much sin we would avoid if we would believe this one simple truth: God is immutably good, and He alone can provide what satisfies. Every good and every perfect gift is from Him.

FOR REFLECTION

Are there areas in your life in which you are failing to trust Him to give you what is good? Will you determine today to trust the God who changes not?

The grand sin of the human race is their continual endeavor to live independently of God.

— Adam Clarke

Where the things of God are concerned, acceptance always means the happy choice of mind and heart of that which He appoints, because (for the present) it is His good and acceptable and perfect will.

— Amy Carmichael

DAY 5: LIVING ON THESE TRUTHS

During the twelve weeks of this study, nothing will prove a deadlier enemy than a religion made only of new concepts. You can work hard at gathering truths about God in your mind, intellectually understanding them, and even being emotionally moved by them, yet never live on them. If you desire to live unto God, having simple aids for applying truth to your life will be of great benefit.

In the first week's video sermon we looked at a passage taken from Paul's letter to the Colossian church. This passage contains five metaphors of Christian progress. You will be encountering this passage and the accompanying exercises numerous times throughout the workbook. The exercises will be identical, but your focus will be different each time you work through the questions, depending upon which aspect of God's character you studied that week. Some of your answers may overlap. The goal is to give you an opportunity to stop and deal honestly with yourself, applying the truths of that week to your life in practical ways. In case you have forgotten the lesson, or were unable to watch it, here are a few reminders to help you with this task.

Remember that Paul, in the book of Colossians, addressed young Christians who were on the verge of being taken captive by the lies of false teachers. The exact nature of these lies is not stated. However, it is clear that the false teachers believed that something must be added to Jesus Christ in order to have a holy and happy life. Paul refutes the lies by displaying the incomparable Christ (1:15-18). He then helps believers see how to apply these truths about Christ in practical ways (2:8 to the end of the letter). But before Paul explains some of the common ways that Christ must be applied to life, he gives five word pictures that illustrate how to live on these truths. Paul uses things with which everyone is familiar, which should prove helpful to us.

In the passage below, the five word pictures are in bold print:

> *Therefore as you have received Christ Jesus the Lord, so **walk** in Him, having been firmly **rooted** and now being **built up** in Him and **established** in your faith, just as you were instructed, and **overflowing with gratitude**.* (Colossians 2:6-7)

Let's consider how the truths we have studied this week can be lived upon by using these five pictures.

HAVING RECEIVED CHRIST JESUS THE LORD . . .

1. Walk in Him

The word "walk" shows us two things about Christian living.

First, walking is an everyday activity that does not seem significant. We take thousands of steps in a day, and very few steps would be looked back upon as particularly noteworthy, much less spiritually meaningful. Our little, common choices each day may also seem insignificant, but like our steps, they do matter—because they add up to be the stuff of life. For this reason, truths about God must affect our common choices in everyday life.

Second, when a person in the ancient world walked, he or she almost certainly had a destination in mind. Today people often walk for exercise, and in that case the destination isn't important. You may walk on a treadmill or in circles around a track. That is not what Paul has in mind when he says "walk." Christians should be walking toward a definite destination: complete conformity to Christ's character. The little choices of each day, guided by the truths you are studying, should be aiming at that destination—Christlikeness. But why? Not for self-improvement, but for the pleasure and honor of our God.

With these things in mind, go back and review this week's lessons. Below, write some of the ways you can apply these truths about God's immutability in even seemingly insignificant ways that lead to the destination of Christlikeness.

_____

_____

_____

_____

_____

_____

_____

2. Sink Your Roots in Him

Paul says that God has rooted every believer in Christ. Following Christ means daily sinking the roots of your life into the truths of God. Roots gain nutrients from the soil. Your soul may find temporary satisfaction in the junk food of our culture, or it will find lasting satisfaction in the feast of the immutable realities of God.

> *. . . each day we must submit afresh to Him and walk in humble dependence. Being yoked to Christ speaks of a relationship in which we learn to walk in the way He walked with the Father.*
>
> — Clyde Cranford

> *Root yourselves in God, making Him your truest treasure, and nothing can rob you of your wealth.*
>
> — Alexander MacLaren

Go back and review this week's lessons. Below, write some of the truths that you feel are the most nourishing food for your soul. What must you feed upon if you are to live out the Christian life? Is there "junk food" that you should put away?

_____

_____

_____

_____

_____

_____

3. Build a Life on Truth

Each truth you learn in this study can be seen as a brick. Combined with other truths, each brick will be an essential part of building a life with Christ as the foundation. Coming to Jesus in repentance and faith is the only place to begin, but good beginnings are not all there is to Christianity. Paul knew that the Colossian Christians needed more than a foundation built on Christ; they also needed a life built by His grace with His biblical truths. To leave the truths you are studying piled like bricks in a corner of your life would be a grave mistake. You don't want to look back in twelve weeks and see a pile of bricks! You need a life that is a true dwelling place for God Himself.

Review this week's lessons and ask yourself, "In what ways can I build my life (my marriage, my family, my friendships, or my work) on the realities of the immutable God?"

_____

_____

_____

_____

_____

_____

4.   **Become Established in Your Faith**

Paul used a word, translated in the NASB as "established," which conveys the idea of firming something up, making something stable, solid. In spiritual life, we might use the word *maturity*. You must grow to maturity in your faith (your grasp of the great realities of God); in part, so that you will not be easily shifted by false teaching or half-truths.

CONSIDER HEBREWS 5:12-14.

> *For though by this time you ought to be teachers, you have need again for someone to teach you the elementary principles of the oracles of God, and you have come to need milk and not solid food. For everyone who partakes only of milk is not accustomed to the word of righteousness, for he is an infant. But solid food is for the mature, who because of practice have their senses trained to discern good and evil.*

Here the writer is speaking to people who have heard the truth many times but have remained immature in their faith. He tells us that maturity comes from a life that applies and practices what it is learning. Through application, you are established, or matured, in the great realities of God.

Review this week's lessons. How does God's immutability help your faith to be established, solid, and unwavering? In what ways have you failed to put the truths of His immutability to practical use?

_____

_____

_____

_____

_____

_____

With these four pictures as guides, we never want to settle for new Bible-truths which are undigested, unapplied, unsettled, and sitting like a wasted pile of bricks.

There is one more picture we need to employ. Without this final metaphor our Christianity will not reflect God.

What is the reason there is so much preaching and so little practice? For want of meditation . . . . Constant thoughts are operative and musing makes the fire burn.

— Thomas Manton

5. **Do All of These with an Overflow of Gratitude to God**

You can attempt to apply 1-4, but without a grateful heart, how can you honor God?

In the Old Testament Moses warned the people before they entered the Promised Land:

> *Because you did not serve the LORD your God with joy and a glad heart, for the abundance of all things; therefore you shall serve your enemies whom the LORD will send against you, in hunger, in thirst, in nakedness, and in the lack of all things; and He will put an iron yoke on your neck until He has destroyed you.* (Deuteronomy 28:47-48)

Surely that is a shocking message for us as well. If we go about our Christian lives trying to walk in truth, sink roots in truth, build upon truth, and be established in truth, but we do so with ungrateful hearts, we can expect divine discipline.

Review this week's lessons. What reasons for gratitude toward God arise from the study of His immutability?

_____

_____

_____

_____

_____

_____

May the God who cannot be altered in His perfect character and purposes grant you such a sight of His immutability that you can live out your faith with joy and thanksgiving for His eternal love and provision.

KNOWING THE GOD WHO IS INFINITE AND ETERNAL

DAY 1: THE INFINITE GOD

One of the most mystifying aspects of God's perfection is His infinitude. How do we describe a God who is infinite? God's infinitude means that His perfection is unlimited, immeasurable, and incapable of either increasing or decreasing.

GOD IS UNLIMITED

God is all that He is, essentially and without limitation. God does not *do* anything to be without limits; He simply *is* limitless. He may limit the expression of His attributes (He may choose to pour out His love or to restrain His strength), but in their essence all His attributes are unlimited.

GOD IS IMMEASURABLE

If there are no limits to God's attributes, then there is no way they can be measured.

READ ▷ PSALM 145:3.

> *Great is the LORD, and highly to be praised,*
> *And His greatness is unsearchable.*

The greatness (immensity, largeness) of God is unsearchable (cannot be measured). This ought to provoke every Christian to praise. Every aspect of God is so immense that only He knows the measure of His greatness.

GOD CAN NEITHER INCREASE NOR DECREASE

This great God cannot grow bigger or better. Because He is infinite, He cannot shrink. He cannot increase or decrease in any way.

The unity of His character means that every attribute is connected to His infinity. God's attributes are never at odds with one another, because God is a perfect being. In fact, His attributes are not really separate. They might

There is something exceedingly improving to the mind in a contemplation of the Divinity—it is a subject so vast, that all our thoughts are lost in its immensity; so deep, that our pride is drowned in its infinity.

— C. H. Spurgeon

Thou art a sea without a shore,
A sun without a sphere;
Thy time is now and evermore,
Thy place is everywhere.

—John Mason

be understood individually as we study them, but in truth they are perfectly united to each other. This means that every attribute of God is affected by and in harmony with every other attribute. In other words, all that God reveals about His character is infinite, and everything about His person is without limitation.

READ the verses and fill in the blanks in the headings. The first one has been done for you.

1. His *sovereign rights* are unlimited.

   Daniel 4:34b-35
   For His dominion is an everlasting dominion,
   And His kingdom endures from generation to generation.
   All the inhabitants of the earth are accounted as nothing,
   But He does according to His will in the host of heaven
   And among the inhabitants of earth;
   And no one can ward off His hand
   Or say to Him, "What have You done?"

2. His _____ is without limit.

   Psalm 147:5
   Great is our Lord and abundant in strength;
   His understanding is infinite.

3. His _____ is infinite: filling all creation.

   Jeremiah 23:23-24
   "Am I a God who is near," declares the LORD,
   "And not a God far off?
   Can a man hide himself in hiding places
   So I do not see him?" declares the LORD.
   "Do I not fill the heavens and the earth?" declares the LORD.

   Job 34:21-22
   For His eyes are upon the ways of a man, and He sees all his steps.
   There is no darkness or deep shadow where the workers of iniquity may hide themselves.

God is . . . goodness, beauty, power, wisdom, justice, mercy, and love itself! . . . God is one infinite perfection in Himself!

— Thomas Brooks

4. His _____ and _____ are infinite.

    Psalm 40:5
    Many, O LORD my God, are the wonders which You have done, and Your thoughts toward us; there is none to compare with You. If I would declare and speak of them, they would be too numerous to count.

    Job 9:10
    Who does great things, unfathomable, and wondrous works without number.

So the Scripture confirms what we understand to be true of God: all of His person, all of His attributes, are without measure. Not one can be limited. Not one can be reduced. Not one can be measured. There is none like our God; for us there is none but God! No wonder the Psalmist wrote:

> *Great is the LORD, and highly to be praised,*
> *And His greatness is unsearchable.* (Psalm 145:3)

Tomorrow you will be looking at the infinite God as He reveals Himself through His Son.

DAY 2: THE FULLNESS OF THE GOD-MAN

John, the disciple whom Jesus loved, one of the privileged inner three, is the last of the Gospel writers to take up his pen. John's Gospel is different from the others. He expects us to have read the accounts of the other three Gospel writers and he does not include many of the narratives found there. Instead, he gives us details that the others do not. The Gospel of John is contemplative and deep. For many decades he has walked by faith and paid a terrible cost to take the good news of Christ to the nations. He has seen the destruction of Jerusalem that Christ foretold. What does John say of Jesus now, nearly half a century after the ascension? He remembers back to those early days when he first met the Son of God and records:

> *And the Word became flesh, and dwelt among us, and we saw His glory, glory as of the only begotten from the Father, full of grace and truth.*
> (John 1:14)

Glory! Not a shining halo, but the display of God's moral perfections reflected in the life of the God-Man. How did this glory manifest itself? In fullness. The kind of fullness that belongs only to God, that overflows the boundaries of description—infinite fullness, without limit or measure. Amazingly, it was a fullness that showed itself in two great ways: grace and truth.

The incarnation of God is the greatest wonder in the countless wonders that crowd the universe.

— Octavius Winslow

Now it is very important that we understand what John was describing. This is a fullness that the Father placed in the Son as the Mediator. That is important, because it was not a fullness for Himself, but for those whom He would save. Listen to Paul speak about this:

> *For it was the Father's good pleasure for all the fullness to dwell in Him, and through Him to reconcile all things to Himself . . . .* (Colossians 1:19-20)

> *For in Him all the fullness of Deity dwells in bodily form, and in Him you have been made complete . . . .* (Colossians 2:9-10)

Now listen to John again:

> *For of His fullness we have all received, and grace upon grace.* (John 1:16)

There is certainly enough in our Savior, if only we open our eyes that we may see it, to solve every doubt and satisfy every longing of the heart; and He is willing to give it in full measure.

— Elizabeth Prentiss

What a truth for needy people like us! It pleased God the Father to send His Son to us in human form. But this stooping down of the Son does not mean that He is less God than He was in eternity past. As the Son of God, all the fullness of God truly dwells in Him. As the Son of Man, this fullness is poured out to His followers so that everyone might be made complete. We might ask, "how full?" Infinitely full! Take all that you learned of God's infinity yesterday, apply it to the person of Jesus of Nazareth, and you will begin to see what John saw.

John helps us get a sense of that fullness by looking at it from different angles.

1. John tells us of the type of fullness he experienced in following the Son of God.

COPY ▷ JOHN 1:14.

_____

_____

HE IS INFINITELY FULL OF TRUTH

He is the truth.

John 14:6
Jesus said to him, "I am the way, and the truth, and the life; no one comes to the Father but through Me."

He brings us the truth about the Father.

> John 1:18
> *No one has seen God at any time; the only begotten God who is in the bosom of the Father, He has explained Him.*

He opens our eyes to receive the truth.

> Matthew 11:27
> *All things have been handed over to Me by My Father; and no one knows the Son except the Father; nor does anyone know the Father except the Son, and anyone to whom the Son wills to reveal Him.*

How urgently we need the truth. It is a beautiful and alarming thing. Sin is a blinding enemy. It thrives on false advertising about itself, and it lies to us about God and about us. Because we are sinners, we love to be lied to, and we prefer not to get too close to the light. Listen again to John:

> *This is the judgment, that the Light has come into the world, and men loved the darkness rather than the Light, for their deeds were evil. For everyone who does evil hates the Light, and does not come to the Light for fear that his deeds will be exposed.* (John 3:19-20)

CONSIDER the following statements.

- We like to be lied to in a way that fits our self-centered choices.

- We like to be told things that agree with our proud views of ourselves.

- We like to be told that our particular sins are justifiable.

Can you think of lies that you are believing, areas of pride that you are harboring, or sins and doubts that you are justifying?

_____

_____

_____

If we are to be rescued from ourselves, we will need someone who brings us the truth. Paul went further to say that Jesus Himself was made to be our wisdom; that is, God gave us Christ to bring us the truth and rescue us from our spiritual ignorance. Jesus is the storehouse of all God's wisdom (Colossians 2:3). He has been given to us to deliver us from our soul-destroying spiritual stupidity.

HE IS INFINITELY FULL OF GRACE

What good would the truth be if God did not also give His Son infinite love to bring to those who could not deserve it? The unearned favor (grace) of the Most High is in Jesus of Nazareth, to be given to His enemies when they turn to Him in repentance and faith. Think of the people He loved in the gospel accounts: a prostitute, an embezzling tax-collector, a political revolutionary, a misguided Bible teacher, and a thief. Consider also that Jesus did not love any of these people because of what they offered Him or His kingdom. He, being infinite God, did not love them for what He could get from them (for He needed nothing), but for what He could give them (they needed everything).

We need both truth and grace, and we need them from a source that cannot be depleted.

- Without truth, grace would be turned into a sentimentalized religion in which we use God's love for self-indulgence.

- Without grace, truth would present us with an unbearable reflection of our spiritual pollution and God's relentless rage against every sin.

2. John tells us the measure by which we receive Christ's fullness.

COPY JOHN 1:16.

_____

_____

How many millions of dazzling pearls and gems are at this moment hidden in the deep recesses of the ocean caves. Likewise, unfathomable oceans of grace are in Christ for you. Dive and dive again—you will never come to the bottom of these depths.

— Robert Murray

"Grace upon grace"—how are we to understand this phrase? The preposition John uses is only found here in the Bible. In the original Greek, it described the exchange that took place in a sale. One thing was given (money) in the place of another thing (the item purchased). Here the idea is that one expression of undeserved favor from God is given in exchange for another. It shows the continual refreshing of the believer's life as God sends fresh grace each moment. The reality is something like the waves of the sea: one rolls up on the sandy beach and washes it, and as it recedes another follows and replaces it. Grace after grace, grace in the place of grace, grace on the heels of grace—the fullness of God in Jesus brings this to every genuine Christian. There can be no mistaking John's meaning: for the followers of Jesus, the undeserved expressions of divine friendship will never grow stale, never come to an end. Why? Because it was the Father's pleasure that all the fullness of God would be united to Jesus' humanity.

Describe the "grace upon grace" that you receive from Christ.

_____

_____

_____

3. John gives a contrast to the fullness of Christ.

COPY JOHN 1:17.

_____

_____

_____

In order to understand this aspect of Christ's fullness for His people, we must think like a first-century Jew. John contrasts the fullness of Jesus Christ with that of Moses. For the Jews, Moses was the figurehead of the Old Covenant and so one of the great channels of God's fullness. He was the chosen instrument to deliver God's people from Egypt. God used him as the one through whom His law would be revealed. But Moses, as the representative of the Old Covenant, is nothing compared to Jesus, who ushered in the New Covenant. John is not comparing these two as men. He is not saying that Moses was good, but he was not as righteous as Jesus. He is saying that God gave us a great deal through Moses, but nothing compared to the fullness that He gives us through His Son, Jesus.

The law is a window through which we see the perfect righteousness of God, as well as a mirror in which we view our unrighteousness. But the law can only expose; it cannot heal (like a spiritual MRI). The Old Covenant only contained pictures and shadows of what Jesus would actually provide. Jesus fulfilled the law with His life and death. He was raised from the grave and declared ruler over all. Now seated at the right hand of His Father, He distributes every possible spiritual blessing to His people (Ephesians 1:3). There is no comparison between the benefits of Moses' labors and the benefits of union with Jesus.

The infinite God has come to us in the person of Jesus Christ. He has come with all the fullness of His deity. He has become a fountain of never-ending grace and truth to everyone who follows Him.

DAY 3: THE ETERNAL GOD

We have spent a few days being introduced to God's infinity. Now we need to see how it is connected with the duration of God's existence. God is infinite with regard to time. God's eternal existence has three distinguishing characteristics:

1. He has no beginning.

2. He has no end.

3. He does not experience time as a succession of moments as we do.[20]

Let's take a look at the Scriptures in which God reveals His eternal existence.

THE ANCIENT OF DAYS

Immortal, invisible, God only wise,
In light inaccessible hid from our eyes,
Most blessed, most glorious, the Ancient of Days,
Almighty, victorious, Thy great name we praise.

— Walter Chalmers Smith

In the 7th chapter of Daniel, we find the man of God in a state of deep spiritual concern. The nation's idolatry has led to a Babylonian captivity. The world seems to be ruled, not by the God of Abraham, but by arrogant regional empires. God's promises made to Daniel's forefathers regarding His people seem a distant memory that only causes heartache. At a time like this, Daniel sets his face toward the Lord. In a vision, God answers Daniel's questions and calms his fears. He shows Daniel Himself.

READU DANIEL 7:1-10.

The world powers, here portrayed symbolically as four mythical beasts, are taken in hand by the true king of heaven and earth. He deals with them exactly as He wishes. That is surely comforting to Daniel. Yet it is the sight of God Himself that forms the foundation of hope. God is enthroned. He is dressed in white (a symbol of His purity), and fire (righteous judgment) flows from His throne. For our purposes today, the name of God in this passage is significant—the Ancient of Days.

What are we to make of this title? Clearly, this king predates all others and will outlast all others. This is what the Bible means when it says He is the Alpha and Omega. He is the A and Z of life. He is the first and the last. He comes before all others (having no beginning), and He will have no end.

CONSIDER the following passages.

Revelation 1:8
"I am the Alpha and the Omega," says the Lord God, "who is and who was and who is to come, the Almighty."

Psalm 102:24b-27
Your years are throughout all generations.
Of old You founded the earth,
And the heavens are the work of Your hands.
Even they will perish, but You endure;
And all of them will wear out like a garment;
Like clothing You will change them and they will be changed.
But You are the same,
And Your years will not come to an end.

Psalm 93:2
Your throne is established from of old;
You are from everlasting.

Job 36:26
Behold, God is exalted, and we do not know Him;
The number of His years is unsearchable.

Psalm 90:2
Before the mountains were born
Or You gave birth to the earth and the world,
Even from everlasting to everlasting, You are God.

Without beginning or decline,
Object of faith and not of sense;
Eternal ages saw Him shine,
He shines eternal ages hence.

— William Cowper

He is first and last. He is the one whose life spans every generation of humanity, ruling on a throne that is from everlasting. If we were to attempt to calculate His years we could not, because there is no limit or measure to an infinite lifespan. According to A. W. Tozer, we worship the God who exists from "vanishing point to vanishing point." Tozer explained our dilemma thus:

> *The mind looks backward in time till the dim past vanishes, then turns and looks into the future till thought and imagination collapse from exhaustion; and God is at both points, unaffected by either.*[21]

As Creator, He predates all others. As the Everlasting One, He will outlast the physical creation. A being that existed before all things and will endure after all things we see are gone—that is a concept we can somewhat understand. But there is another aspect to eternity which bewilders us.

THE BEING WHO TRANSCENDS TIME

There never was nor shall be time wherein God could not say of himself, "I am."

— Thomas Brooks

Time is the measurement of existence by a succession of events. Events that are in the near future soon become events in the present and then events in our past. They pass like a stream. We measure our existence by the passage of these events. We experience life in time, or in other words, we experience things in a consecutive order. But God is not part of this creation and He is not affected by time's influences. He is not subject to time's constraints, and He doesn't have to experience things one at a time in a consecutive order. God lives above time.

> Isaiah 57:15 (NKJV)
> *For thus says the High and Lofty One*
> *Who inhabits eternity . . . .*

Eternity is not just long life; it is timelessness. We must not think that God dwells in the distant past and far off future. Eternity means that He inhabits all moments at once. Listen to what He reveals of Himself in the 41st chapter of Isaiah:

> . . . *"I, the Lord, am the first, and with the last. I am He."* (Isaiah 41:4)

Did you notice the strange statement? Elsewhere He tells us He is the first and the last, but here He says that He is the first, and at the very same moment He is *with* the last. How can this be? He interacts with time differently than we do. Take a look at what Peter tells us:

> *But do not let this one fact escape your notice, beloved, that with the Lord one day is like a thousand years, and a thousand years like one day.* (2 Peter 3:8)

Take a few moments to think about this verse and write your thoughts.

_____

_____

_____

_____

It is easy to understand how a being who has existed for millions of years would consider the passage of a thousand years to be like the passing of a day. But only a being who lives above time's influence could experience one day in such a way as to make it seem like a thousand years.

We can say that all times are *now* to God. When the Bible describes God as the one "who is and who was and who is to come" (Revelation 1:4), it is only using words of time that refer to our experience of Him. In reality, all times are "now" and all places are "here" to our God.

He knows no past. He knows no future. He lives unmoved in one unmoving present. He stretches through all the ages which are gone and which are yet to come. His only bounds are immeasurable boundlessness.

— Henry Law

PRACTICAL APPLICATIONS

FILL IN THE BLANKS in the passages below.

When you call upon the living God, you are calling upon the same God that Abraham called upon.

> Genesis 21:33
> *Abraham planted a tamarisk tree at Beersheba, and there he called on the name of the LORD, _____*
>
> *_____.*

Every time you take shelter in God, you are finding refuge in the same God that Moses did.

> Psalm 90:1
> *Lord, You have been _____*
> *in all generations.*

Being above the effects and limits of time does not mean that He is uncaring about what happens to those who live within time.

> Isaiah 57:15
> *For thus says the high and exalted One*
> *Who lives forever, whose name is Holy,*
> *"I dwell on a high and holy place,*
> *And also with the contrite and lowly of spirit*
> *In order _____*
> *And to _____."*

As beings created in the image of God, we hunger for something more permanent than what this life offers. This longing is satisfied only when we are brought into union with the Ancient of Days through the redemptive labors of His Son, applied to us by His Spirit.

Because God is in all times at once, there can never be any legitimate reason for the Christian to pine for the "good-ole-days." Looking back in history and wishing we lived during the days of the New Testament, or the Reformation, or the First Great Awakening is proof that we have failed to understand the eternity of God. We would not be closer to Him in the first century than we are now. We do not need to look toward the future and wish we lived in some time yet to come when things will be better.

There is another way that God's eternality should affect our lives. Christians often recall with thanksgiving what God has done in the past. We often think hopefully about what God will do in the future, those things He has promised. But do you think often about the fact that God is here NOW, with you in this present moment? We cannot relive the past and we cannot live in the future, but then we do not need to—He is here and now for every follower of Christ.

How does the fact that God is always here now affect your life?

_____

_____

_____

Sometimes we forget God when we think about our personal past or future. When you replay your life's history in your mind, do you forget God? Do you ever allow your mind to dwell on a fearfully imagined future? How can the truth of God's eternality help with these thoughts?

_____

_____

_____

DAY 4: THE PSALM OF MOSES, PART 1

Each time you encounter a description of God's character in Scripture, stop and ask yourself two questions:

1. What does this passage tell me about my God?

2. Why does God reveal Himself in this way and at this point in human history?

We should use the first question to help us determine whether or not we have embraced the truth about God. If our thoughts of God differ from what Scripture says, we need to turn from our inadequate ideas of Him (repent) and submit our minds to His self-revelation (faith). The second question is not always answerable due to the fact that some passages do not tell us the specific historical context in which they were written. Yet often a passage does have a specific context, and it is helpful to see why God reveals certain things about Himself at a particular time, related to certain circumstances in human history. It improves our understanding of how we must apply the same truth to our circumstances.

One of the most helpful passages for applying God's eternity is Psalm 90, written by Moses.

MOSES' SITUATION

The content of the Psalm suggests that Moses wrote it during the forty years in which Israel was wandering in the wilderness. Due to their unbelief, the older generation forfeited the right to enter the Promised Land. Moses was given the unenviable task of leading them in the wilderness until that generation died. These people were faced with a monotonous journey that ended in death. Days, months, and years passed while the land was being filled with their graves. We imagine that Moses would have been tempted with a sense of purposelessness and despair.

This is a significant help for us. The Christian life is often overrun with sorrows. Life can at times seem like a relentless march of mundane tasks with little hope of better days. How do you live with the eternal God at such times?

The unbeliever finds refuge in the world. This world's way of living seems to provide for the unbeliever's perceived needs. But the Christian, like David in Psalm 63, cannot find a true resting place in this world's supply.

> *O God, You are my God; I shall seek You earnestly;*
> *My soul thirsts for You, my flesh yearns for You,*
> *In a dry and weary land where there is no water.* (Psalm 63:1)

This world is not a safe refuge; its promises are empty, and it leaves us thirsty and worn out. Where did Moses find hope, happiness, and a refuge?

COPY ▷ PSALM 90:1.

_____

_____

Moses' hope is that God has always been, is now, and will always be the safe refuge of His people. In fact, he goes on to say that every generation of believers has found the same God to be their hiding place. How can that be true? Moses explains in the next verse:

> *Before the mountains were born*
> *Or You gave birth to the earth and the world,*
> *Even from everlasting to everlasting, You are God.* (Psalm 90:2)

All earthly things are as salt water, that increases the appetite, but satisfies not.

— Richard Sibbes

*Art thou afraid His power
shall fail
When comes the evil day?
And can an all-creating
arm
Grow weary or decay?*

*Mere human power shall
fast decay,
And youthful vigor cease;
But they who wait upon
the Lord
In strength shall still
increase.*

— Isaac Watts

God exists from the everlasting past to the everlasting future. In every moment, He is God. As we mentioned yesterday, eternity is a difficult concept for time-bound people. Moses gives us some help by contrasting God with the passage of a thousand years of human history.

Stop and consider all that has changed in the past one thousand years: the rise and fall of nations, the introduction of countless new inventions, the passing of families, etc.

WRITE some of the key events which have occurred in the last one thousand years.

_____

_____

_____

_____

_____

Consider the many small events that occur in one year, in one person, that never make it to the history books. Even if you could gather every event that occurred in the span of a thousand years, from every individual and nation, from every corner of the earth, what would that be to an eternal God?

> *For a thousand years in Your sight
> Are like yesterday when it passes by,
> Or as a watch in the night.* (Psalm 90:4)

Think back on yesterday. It might have been a difficult day that seemed to last forever, but as you look back, how long does it feel now?

Think back on last night. If you worked a night shift, or if you were having trouble sleeping, last night probably felt very long. But for the rest of us, last night seems to have passed in the blink of an eye.

The point of these comparisons is simple: a thousand years of human history do not merely pass quickly when you are a God who is eternal. A thousand years is as nothing—it doesn't really even register. The eternal God watches a thousand years pass on planet earth, and they seem to Him as if they took no time at all.

In PSALM 90:5-6 we find the description of the lives of men:

> *You have swept them away like a flood, they fall asleep;*
> *In the morning they are like grass which sprouts anew.*
> *In the morning it flourishes and sprouts anew;*
> *Toward evening it fades and withers away.*

We are not like God. We are creatures of time, and our lives come and go quickly, like debris swept away by flood waters. Our short lives are like grass. We grow and flourish. We achieve things. We finish school, find a spouse, start a family. Perhaps we gain a certain amount of success in our businesses. But in a few short years we begin to decline. Our bodies and minds start to fail us. Life begins to take back: parents, friends, even our children are buried. We all fade like grass. Moses does not paint an encouraging picture, but who would blame him for writing like this as he watched the Israelites slowly dying for forty years?

Are your thoughts clear regarding the frailty of human life? Do you think the history of great men, great nations, great families, or even great denominations is the history of mighty oaks? It is not. The history of the greatest people and organizations on earth is the history of withering grass!

Tomorrow you will study the second half of Psalm 90 and see how sin is to be viewed in light of the eternal God. You will also see where hope is to be found during difficult years like the ones Moses faced.

Time, like an ever-rolling stream,
Bears all its sons away;
They fly forgotten, as a dream
Dies at the opening day.

Our God, our help in ages past,
Our hope for years to come,
Be Thou our guard while troubles last
And our eternal home.

— Isaac Watts

DAY 5: THE PSALM OF MOSES, PART 2

Moses has shown us that our short lives pass as quickly as fading grass. A spiritual cause is behind this sad state of things, this lack of permanence that we all feel.

COPY PSALM 90:7-8.

_____

_____

_____

_____

The Lord of hosts is on our side,
Our safety to secure;
The God of Jacob is for us
A refuge strong and sure.

— The Psalter #46 [22]

Death is one of God's judgments on sin. His wrath dismays us. Why? Because every sin you have ever committed has been done before the face of the one being who lives in every moment. He was there with you when you sinned as a child. He was there when you sinned as a young adult. He was there when you sinned this week. And if you have more years of life ahead of you, every sin you commit will be carried out before His eyes. He has put every one of your iniquities before Himself.

We often mistake a bad memory for a clear conscience. God does not suffer from this problem. Not only does He *know* all things—past, present, and future—He has *witnessed* all things. Apart from the work of a mediator, all your sins remain as a barrier between you and God. He views them all in the present moment, and His wrath is terrible.

Moses continues his psalm by describing the effects of sinning against an eternal God.

FILL IN THE BLANKS below from PSALM 90:9-11.

For all our days have _____ in Your fury;
We have finished our years like a _____.
As for the days of our life, they contain seventy years,
Or if due to strength, eighty years,
Yet their pride is but _____;
For soon it is gone and we fly away.
Who understands the power of Your anger
And Your fury, according to the fear that is due You?

Life declines and it finishes, not with a shout of triumph, but with a sad sigh. For those who have the strength to make it eighty years, their reward is extended labor and sorrow. The anger of a God who lives in every moment at once is beyond comprehension. After all, how can you really measure the anger of a person who, from everlasting to everlasting, has been viewing the repeated acts of rebellion in the people He created?

The human condition is a difficult one to face honestly. We prefer the made-for-television version with the happy ending. Moses doesn't have any time for polite self-deception. He needs a solid hope that can sustain hundreds of thousands of Israelites whose lives are doomed to death in the wilderness. He finds that hope and explains it in verses 12-17.

THE PARADOX OF HOPE

Moses' hope is paradoxical; that is, it seems contradictory. He has told us that the offended eternal God is behind our fading lives. Now Moses tells us that the cure for our condition is to have this eternal God come close to us and work in our lives! In this section Moses lays a number of requests before the eternal God.

READ PSALM 90:12-17 below.

UNDERLINE Moses' requests.

> *So teach us to number our days,*
> *That we may present to You a heart of wisdom.*
> *Do return, O LORD; how long will it be?*
> *And be sorry for Your servants.*
> *O satisfy us in the morning with Your lovingkindness,*
> *That we may sing for joy and be glad all our days.*
> *Make us glad according to the days You have afflicted us,*
> *And the years we have seen evil.*
> *Let Your work appear to Your servants*
> *And Your majesty to their children.*
> *Let the favor of the Lord our God be upon us;*
> *And confirm for us the work of our hands;*
> *Yes, confirm the work of our hands.*

Moses understands that the brevity of human life requires that we be taught by God how to live wisely. But what is the wisest life? It is a life that seeks the things that are best, of real value, essential.

Moses desires that God Himself might return to the people who have offended Him. It may seem strange, but Moses wants the one person who knows all their sins to come close to them. He desires that God would satisfy them with His love and that they might have songs of joy in their hearts for the remainder of their days. How much joy? He desires that the happiness the Jews have from God's loving return would far outweigh the sorrow they have had from His disciplinary absence. Moses is not willing to only ask for the present generation; he also includes the next generation. He pleads with God to work in such a way that the young people can see it.

And finally, knowing the frailty and weakness of human efforts, he asks the eternal God to grant them His favor by confirming, or giving permanence to, their spiritual labors.

APPLICATION

When you look around within your church, or home, or your own soul, do you feel the vapor-like quality of life? Do you see how insignificant the most impressive people really are? Do you feel the weight of your sins because they are committed before the face of the God who lives in every moment of your life? Now Christian, it is important that you feel the truths that Moses felt. The people you live among need you to feel it because you, through Jesus Christ, have access to the courts of the everlasting king. What will you plead for? What can you not bear to be without? What is so spiritually necessary that it is not optional?

Do you plead that God would return? Do you even notice that He has withdrawn His noticeable and active presence from so many who claim to trust Christ?

If you ask Him to return, what is it you are asking Him to do when He comes close? Do you ask Him to captivate His church once again with His soul-satisfying kindness? Are you pleading that He would revive His people in such a way that the joy they have in Him for years to come would far outweigh the sorrows they have experienced from their lives of compromise? Do you ask Him to come back and work in such a manner that the young people would see things about God that they could never forget, no matter how long they live? Do you look at your hands, young or old, strong or weak, and realize that you simply do not have what it takes to rescue people from self-destruction? In your powerlessness, do you beg Him to take your weak labors for His kingdom and give them permanence?

Permanence in things that matter ought to be of great consequence for every true Christian. Do you want the labors of your church to last only a few years? Are you satisfied to see the converts in your church fall away after baptism? Do you want the efforts you have made to point others to Christ to fade as soon as your life ends? Don't you want something of permanence to be added to your efforts? Moses did. Most of the people he was leading could not go into the Promised Land. He would not be allowed to enter the Promised Land. He longed that his efforts might outlast his 120 years on earth.

There is only one person who can satisfy the soul that longs for something that lasts. There is one person who can work through us so that our labors will make a permanent impact. He is the Ancient of Days, the king who is from everlasting to everlasting, and He is the only God there is.

This is what we live for, and die for: to make much of Jesus Christ and his glorious, universe-encompassing kingdom.

— John Piper

God is the only desirable good, nothing without Him is worthy of our hearts . . . . The life, the glory, the blessedness, the soul-satisfying goodness that is in God is beyond all expression.

— John Bunyan

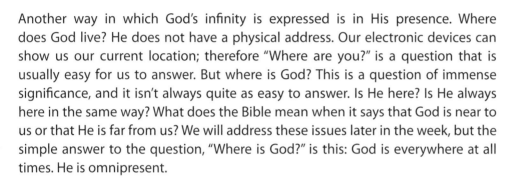

KNOWING THE GOD WHO IS EVERYWHERE

DAY 1: THE GOD WHOSE PRESENCE IS INFINITE

Another way in which God's infinity is expressed is in His presence. Where does God live? He does not have a physical address. Our electronic devices can show us our current location; therefore "Where are you?" is a question that is usually easy for us to answer. But where is God? This is a question of immense significance, and it isn't always quite as easy to answer. Is He here? Is He always here in the same way? What does the Bible mean when it says that God is near to us or that He is far from us? We will address these issues later in the week, but the simple answer to the question, "Where is God?" is this: God is everywhere at all times. He is omnipresent.

A heathen philosopher once asked, "Where is God?" The Christian answered: "Let me first ask you, where is He not?"

— John Arrowsmith

Of the many realities God has revealed regarding His majesty, His all-presence has significant potential to alter everything about the way we live. Believing this truth should strike us with despair, or fill us with hope—God, the God I read about in the Bible, is here with us! We could say that He calls all places "here." God's omnipresence is perhaps the attribute most often mentioned and least often lived upon. Remember the words of Jacob in Genesis 28:16. After he awoke from his sleep, he exclaimed: "Surely the Lord is in this place, and I did not know it." Too many of us would have to say the same about our lives. We have lived every moment in the presence of the Most High, and we did not know it. We have lived as if He were not here with us.

This week we will consider this aspect of God's perfection, and how we should live in light of it.

Timothy Dwight wrote of God's presence:

> *He dwells throughout the known universe, and the uninhabited regions of immensity.*[23]

Hildebert of Lavardin wrote:

> *God is over all things, under all things; outside all; within but not enclosed; without but not excluded; above but not raised up; below but not depressed; wholly above, presiding; wholly beneath, sustaining; wholly within, filling.*[24]

In the Bible, we read David's testimony of God's presence:

> *Where can I go from Your Spirit?*
> *Or where can I flee from Your presence?*
> *If I ascend to heaven, You are there;*
> *If I make my bed in Sheol, behold, You are there.*
> *If I take the wings of the dawn,*
> *If I dwell in the remotest part of the sea,*
> *Even there Your hand will lead me,*
> *And Your right hand will lay hold of me.*
> *If I say, "Surely the darkness will overwhelm me,*
> *And the light around me will be night,"*
> *Even the darkness is not dark to You,*
> *And the night is as bright as the day.*
> *Darkness and light are alike to You.* (Psalm 139:7-12)

God dwells in His creation and is everywhere indivisibly present in all His works. He is transcendent above all His works even while He is immanent within them.

— A. W. Tozer

COPY the following passages.

Jeremiah 23:23-24

_____

_____

_____

Acts 17:27-28

_____

_____

_____

WHAT DOES THIS TELL US ABOUT GOD?

Below are six statements that summarize what God's all-presence signifies:

1. God is in every place, yet He cannot be contained within any one place.

2. God is in every place at once, rising above all limitations of place in the same way that He rises above all limitations of time. He fills all places with His presence as He fills all times.

3. Terms of distance mean nothing to God. When speaking of His essential presence, nothing can be far from Him. He has never travelled.

4. All places are *here* to God, as all times are *now*.

5. God is solitary and unique in this perfection; no other being is omnipresent.

6. God's infinite presence is essential to His nature. It comes as "naturally" to God as being human comes to us. He does not need to exert effort to extend His presence to all places at once.

These six statements are fundamental to the biblical portrait of God. Accepting them as true does not change much in a person's life. Living on them is a wonder-filled and life-changing undertaking. We will see these truths again as the week progresses. For now, let's think about the implications that these truths hold for us.

IMPLICATIONS FOR THOSE WHO WOULD LIVE WITH GOD

1. God is the unchanging environment of every person.

In the Old Testament the patriarch Jacob blessed his son Joseph. He referred to God as "the God before whom my fathers Abraham and Isaac walked, the God who has been my shepherd all my life to this day" (Genesis 48:15). Later, the prophets Elijah and Elisha both spoke of God as the Lord of Hosts "before whom I stand" (1 Kings 18:15; 2 Kings 3:14). Paul told the Athenians that all people, not just believers, "live and move and exist" in God's presence (Acts 17:28).

Here is a truth that brings a great deal of stability and comfort to the Christian. In the nineteenth century the Scottish missionary to China, William Burns, was leaving his friend and co-worker, Hudson Taylor. Burns faced this hardship with unshaken hope. He gave his reason. He wrote that, though he was losing the companionship of a friend and moving to a new part of China, God remained his unaltered environment. That was enough for William Burns.

The omnipresence of God— gracious antidote to every earthly sorrow!

—John MacDuff

Can you think of a time in your life when the fact that God is your unaltered environment was a particular comfort to you?

_____

_____

_____

2. God is present, observing all events in all places at once.

God does not merely know about, but also attends all events: the motions of an insect, the rotation of a planet, the crawling of a worm, and the labors of an archangel. He is present at the birth of every star in the galaxy, and He is with every graveside mourner. He is filling all these places and observing all events.

God does not merely know all; He is the eye-witness of all. This is a sobering thought. Whether we invite Him or not, He is with us. Whether we agree to the fact of His presence or not, He is present.

CONSIDER the following verses carefully.

Hosea 7:2
And they do not consider in their hearts
That I remember all their wickedness.
Now their deeds are all around them;
They are before My face.

Ezekiel 9:9
Then He said to me, "The iniquity of the house of Israel and Judah is very, very great, and the land is filled with blood and the city is full of perversion; for they say, 'The LORD has forsaken the land, and the LORD does not see!'"

Job 22:12-13
Is not God in the height of heaven?
Look also at the distant stars, how high they are!
You say, "What does God know?
Can He judge through the thick darkness?"

We may ignore, but we can nowhere evade, the presence of God.

— C. S. Lewis

Do you see that every sin, in some measure, is born out of the practical denial of God's presence? These verses represent people who wish to devote their lives to selfishness. They comfort themselves with a number of lies regarding God's all-presence.

What are some of these lies?

_____

_____

Are you tempted to believe these or similar lies about God's presence?

Each of us will come to grips with the unalterable truth that the judge of all the earth has been an eye-witness to every action. He was with me when I did, thought, and said them all. There is no hope of offering Him false evidence to justify my treason.

Consider the omnipresent God sitting on the throne to judge all peoples as you read the following passage.

> Revelation 20:11-15
>
> *Then I saw a great white throne and Him who sat upon it, from whose presence earth and heaven fled away, and no place was found for them. And I saw the dead, the great and the small, standing before the throne, and books were opened; and another book was opened, which is the book of life; and the dead were judged from the things which were written in the books, according to their deeds. And the sea gave up the dead which were in it, and death and Hades gave up the dead which were in them; and they were judged, every one of them according to their deeds. Then death and Hades were thrown into the lake of fire. This is the second death, the lake of fire. And if anyone's name was not found written in the book of life, he was thrown into the lake of fire.*

3. God is present, acting in all things.

We must not think of God as being passively present, like air or water, merely filling a place. God is acting, not only observing but also governing and providing. Let's look at these three activities of the God who is everywhere.

GOD IS EVERYWHERE, GOVERNING

Everywhere that God is, He is king. He is essentially sovereign (that is, it is His essence). God is ruling every place that He inhabits. The older writers called this God's providential rule. God's providence is His governance of all things, people, and events. He guides and uses these for His glory and His people's good.

Think of how this reality is foundational to what Paul says in Romans 8.

> *And we know that God causes all things to work together for good to those who love God, to those who are called according to His purpose.* (Romans 8:28)

Only a God who is filling all places at once could be trusted to rule over all events for the good of His church.

Do nothing that you would not like God to see. Say nothing you would not like God to hear . . . . Go no place where you would not like God to find you . . . . Never spend your time in such a way that you would not like God to say, "What are you doing?"

—J. C. Ryle

Do you believe that God is ruling over all things for His glory *and* for your good (if you are a Christian)? List circumstances in your life where this is hard to believe. Will you trust Him with those?

_____

_____

_____

GOD IS EVERYWHERE, PROVIDING

Creation is not self-sustaining. Though God has established observable laws of nature, nature requires God to continually sustain it. Listen to a poetic description of God providing for all of His creation.

> Psalm 104:24, 27-30
> *O LORD, how many are Your works!*
> *In wisdom You have made them all;*
> *The earth is full of Your possessions . . . .*
> *They all wait for You*
> *To give them their food in due season.*
> *You give to them, they gather it up;*
> *You open Your hand, they are satisfied with good.*
> *You hide Your face, they are dismayed;*
> *You take away their spirit, they expire*
> *And return to their dust.*
> *You send forth Your Spirit, they are created;*
> *And You renew the face of the ground.*

Our God is present with all creation, and He alone is capable of sustaining all life. He alone does sustain everything. God is in all places observing, governing, and sustaining. In Him "we live and move and exist" (Acts 17:28). This fact can bring great rejoicing or dreadful despair, but it must not be ignored.

DAY 2: THE RELATIONAL PRESENCE OF GOD

> *So He drove the man out; and at the east of the garden of Eden He stationed the cherubim and the flaming sword which turned every direction to guard the way to the tree of life.* (Genesis 3:24)

For though the LORD is exalted, yet He regards the lowly,
but the haughty He knows from afar. (Psalm 138:6)

Then He will also say to those on His left, "Depart from Me . . . ."
(Matthew 25:41)

These will pay the penalty of eternal destruction, away from the presence
of the Lord and from the glory of His power. (2 Thessalonians 1:9)

Alienated. Withdrawn. Distant. How can these words accurately describe the one being who dwells in all places at all times? If we all "live and move and exist" in His presence, how can He be further from, or closer to, any of us? The answer lies in the fact that the Bible speaks of God's presence in more than one way. There is the *essential presence* of God—the fact that He *essentially* fills all of creation. We looked at that in yesterday's lesson. There is also the *relational presence* of God—the fact that He is *relationally* involved with His creation in varying degrees.

When the Bible speaks of God being near or far from people, it is referring to a *relational* distance, not an *essential* distance. His essence fills every place, but He does not interact with all people in the same manner. With some He describes Himself as distant, and with others as near—revealing His relationship to them and His activity in their life using the metaphor of distance. This is the aspect of God's presence that we will be studying the remaining days of this week. Sadly, many have often treated this truth carelessly, acting as if God's relational distance is universally the same regardless of the kind of life a person leads. A biblical understanding of the relational distance has the potential to fundamentally change our lives.

In the Old Covenant provision of the tabernacle and temple, the distance between mankind and God played a significant part in religion. There was an outer court, an inner court, a holy place, and a most holy place—access to these places was restricted to different groups of people. The point of it all was clear to the worshipper: there is a distance between the Holy One and humanity.

In the New Covenant, the great promises have been fulfilled at the cross, and the gospel brings us to God in a way that no Old Covenant believer could experience. When there is an offense between two people, the offense must be removed to restore the relationship. Sin, the offense that exists between God and mankind, must be removed in order to restore our relationship with God.

2 Corinthians 5:18-19, 21
Now all these things are from God, who reconciled us to Himself through
Christ and gave us the ministry of reconciliation, namely, that God was
in Christ reconciling the world to Himself, not counting their trespasses

In Eden—sad indeed that day—
My countless blessings fled away,
My crown fell in disgrace . . . .

— William Williams

. . . But on victorious Calvary
That crown was won again for me
My life shall all be praise.

— William Williams

73

*against them, and He has committed to us the word of reconciliation . . . .
He made Him who knew no sin to be sin on our behalf, so that we might
become the righteousness of God in Him.*

How did God accomplish reconciliation? How was the offense removed? How
can a holy God not count our trespasses against us?

_____

_____

_____

In Ephesians, Paul speaks to the Gentiles about the removal of this distance.

COMPLETE EPHESIANS 2:12-13.

*. . . remember that you were at that time separate from Christ, excluded
from the commonwealth of Israel, and strangers to the covenants of
promise, having no hope and without God in the world. But now in
Christ Jesus you who formerly were* _____
_____
_____
_____.

Christ's death has brought every believer near to God because by it the
alienating guilt and offense of sin has been legally removed. Humanity could
not climb up to God and remove this offense. Likewise, this rescue could not be
accomplished from heaven's heights. In order for the distance between us and
God to be eliminated, God had to come to us in the person of His Son, Jesus
Christ.

READ the following passages.

Isaiah 7:14b
*Behold, a virgin will be with child and bear a son, and she will call
His name Immanuel.*

Hebrews 2:14-17
*Therefore, since the children share in flesh and blood, He Himself
likewise also partook of the same, that through death He might render
powerless him who had the power of death, that is, the devil, and
might free those who through fear of death were subject to slavery all*

their lives. For assuredly He does not give help to angels, but He gives help to the descendant of Abraham. Therefore, He had to be made like His brethren in all things, so that He might become a merciful and faithful high priest in things pertaining to God, to make propitiation for the sins of the people.

Philippians 2:6-8
[Christ Jesus,] who, although He existed in the form of God, did not regard equality with God a thing to be grasped, but emptied Himself, taking the form of a bond-servant, and being made in the likeness of men. Being found in appearance as a man, He humbled Himself by becoming obedient to the point of death, even death on a cross.

What do we learn from these verses? In order for mankind to be brought to God, God must come to us. He did so by sending His Son, who is called Immanuel (God with us). He came to save fallen humans, so He had to be one of them. As God and man, Jesus is the perfect mediator between God and mankind. To come to us He emptied Himself of His glory (by taking on our humanity) and took the role of a servant in the work of our salvation, even to the point of death on the cross. This is the only way to change our being "far off" from God to being "near" to Him.

A SONG OF NEARNESS

In Psalm 68 we find a song written to commemorate the carrying of the Ark of the Covenant up the temple mount to be placed in the Holy of Holies. The coming of this Ark, with its mercy-seat and all it represented of God's mediated presence with His people, was something that made all other mountains (though greater in stature) jealous of the mountain on which the temple was built.

> *Why do you look with envy, O mountains with many peaks,*
> *At the mountain which God has desired for His abode?*
> *Surely the LORD will dwell there forever.* (Psalm 68:16)

It is a striking picture—the higher mountains of the earth look with envy upon the smaller mountain in Jerusalem. Why? Because the living God has come to manifest His presence there. Of all places in the universe, this lonely hill will be the place where the people of God will find God near in that relational way.

The Psalm goes on to portray the triumph of Christ. Read the following verse:

> *You have ascended on high,*
> *You have led captive Your captives;*

Christ stood not upon His greatness, but, being equal with God, He became a servant. Oh, we should dismount from the tower of our conceited excellency.

— Richard Sibbes

75

You have received gifts among men,
Even among the rebellious also,
That the LORD God may dwell there. (Psalm 68:18)

Perhaps you recognize this verse? Paul quoted it in Ephesians 4:8 to describe one of the benefits of Christ's ascension. In this verse we see a foreshadowing, a prophetic pencil-sketch, of the results of Christ's finished work as He ascends back to His Father in heaven.

Let's list them:

1.   He led captive His captives.

2.   He received gifts *among* (other translations say "*for*") men, even those who were rebels.

3.   He did this so that the LORD God might dwell among these rescued people.

Do you see it in the third benefit mentioned above? The nearness of God to His people is as much a result of the labors of Jesus as the freeing of spiritual captives and the giving of spiritual gifts. What we could never have achieved by all our spiritual efforts, Jesus accomplished by obeying the Law and suffering its full penalty for those who were His enemies. When God came to us in Immanuel, He made a way for us to be brought near to Him. Apart from a true union with Christ, all talk of God's nearness is religious fiction or madness—the unmediated presence of God is not something we can bear.

Before we go further, it would be helpful to stop and answer some questions.

If you are a Christian, what did you hope would bring you near to God *before* you came to Christ?

_____

_____

_____

_____

_____

If the Ark of the Covenant could make the world's mountains jealous, would the nearness of God to your life make the great people of this world envious?

DAY 3: THE ANCIENT IDOL OF A LOCALIZED GOD RETURNS TO CHURCH, PART 1

Remember that superb description of God's omnipresence by Hildebert of Lavardin from Day 1:

> *God is over all things, under all things; outside all; within but not enclosed; without but not excluded; above but not raised up; below but not depressed; wholly above, presiding; wholly beneath, sustaining; wholly within, filling.*

Recall also Timothy Dwight's description of God:

> *He dwells throughout the known universe, and the uninhabited regions of immensity.*

Only Christians have a living God, and that God is infinite in His location, effortlessly dwelling in all places at once. Man-made idol-gods are limited. For example, one was thought to be the god of the mountains, another the god of the rivers and lakes, and another was said to ride upon the clouds of the storms. Limited in place, they were also thought to be limited in activity. Each idol was said to have a specific task that is connected to its specific environment. One was thought to bring rain, another to give good crops, another to help in war. Thankfully, the living God is not like the idols that we make.

God's omnipresence is a reality that is easy to study but difficult to apply in our daily choices. In fact, you may find that your life resembles that of the ancient idolaters who served a localized god, a god who is only effective in certain places.

Views of God that limit Him to certain places and activities are apparent among many who claim to follow Christ. They may think, "He is near me at church on Sunday, but not so near at work on Monday." Perhaps this stems from the desire to protect the truth that God is transcendent and not like anything in His creation. Of course, a flippant, "God-is-my-co-pilot" attitude towards His presence is not one we want to develop. Yet the answer is not to limit God to certain places and activities. An effective way to combat a superficial view of God's nearness is to understand and apply the biblical realities connected to God's omnipresence.

> *We need never shout across the spaces to an absent God. He is nearer than our own soul, closer than our most secret thoughts.*
>
> — A. W. Tozer

An example of the localized views of ancient idolaters can be found in 1 Kings 20.

READ 1 KINGS 20.

It is not merely pagan kings who misunderstand the location of our God. We might find evidence that this view of God has crept into our homes and churches as well.

A SIMPLE TEST

Below is the summary of the biblical testimony regarding God's unlimited presence.

1. God dwells in all places at once, effortlessly.

2. There is no place from which He can be excluded.

3. There is no place that can fully contain Him.

4. As regards His essential presence, there is no place that has more, or less, of God.

5. God's essential presence is our one unchanging environment or circumstance.

6. God is not merely existing everywhere, He is observing, governing, and sustaining all things.

ASK yourself: Am I living as if God were a local deity, limited to certain places?

- Am I living as if God is only present in religious buildings, attending religious events?

- Do I tell myself that He is not active in my home because I am the only believer in my family?

- Do I believe the lie that God is not ruling over my workplace because it is anti-Christian?

- Do I believe that Sundays are lived near God, and Mondays are lived far from Him?

- Do I believe that He is "over there" and "back then" instead of "here" and "now"?

Which of the things mentioned above do you find most difficult to live upon?

_____

_____

_____

ASK yourself: Am I living as if God is limited to certain tasks?

Some religions taught that their idol-god controlled an aspect of nature—brought in spring rains, produced harvests, blessed with children, etc.

Idolatrous ideas of the true God may manifest themselves today in our lives. You may believe that God's real work is limited to religious tasks, but the non-spiritual and mundane activities that fill your day are left to you.

Can you list some areas of life in which you feel God is not as active, areas in which you feel He has left you to do the best you can on your own?

_____

_____

Will you determine to root out all idolatrous views of God which make Him appear like the idols of the ancient cultures, limited only to certain religious places and tasks?

Our great sin is limiting God, the Holy One of Israel. We measure His infinity by a finite scale.

— Octavius Winslow

DAY 4: THE ANCIENT IDOL OF A LOCALIZED GOD RETURNS TO CHURCH, PART 2

Yesterday you began to consider the ancient lie that God is limited in His presence and activity. We have referred to this as the idol of a localized god. This is a theme that needs further development. As we continue this theme, we will attempt to identity the ways the localized god resurfaces in the twenty-first century.

One reason that a localized god appears so reasonable to us is that we often find ourselves living at a distance from the true God. If we are suffering the effects of God's absence relationally, we find it easy to misinterpret the reason for this absence and to believe that God is localized, and we cannot expect Him to work here and now. Throughout Scripture God has made it very clear that He will not allow those who embrace sin to enjoy the experience of His nearness. The Christian remains a son or daughter of God, but the experience of that familial closeness is lost. This is found in both the Old and New Covenants.

READ the following passages and describe the conditions that will forfeit God's nearness.

Isaiah 59:1-2

_____

Hosea 5:15

_____

Revelation 3:14-20

_____

When this loss of God's nearness is experienced for extended periods of time, the church may be susceptible to the lie that God is not really capable of being here and now. Instead of repenting and seeking the covenanted nearness of God, the believer may accept a life with God at a distance, hiding behind the lie that God is limited to certain places, people, or events.

There are a number of ways that the lie of a localized god can manifest itself in your life and in the life of your church. These may be things which you have become accustomed to in religion. It takes a careful look to see these for what they really are: attempts to live the Christian life with a localized god.

SUBSTITUTING FOR AN ABSENT GOD

A pinch-hitter in baseball takes another player's at bat in hopes that he has a better chance of getting a hit under the circumstances. This might be a wise tactic in baseball, but it is a deadly choice in our relationship with God. When God has withdrawn His relational presence due to cherished sin in us, we are faced with the temptation to pinch-hit for Him. We substitute for the God who feels distant and inactive. One very practical problem with this approach is that we are completely incapable of accomplishing anything of eternal value without God. Actually, we couldn't even take our next breath without Him. Instead of trying to substitute for an absent God, we must turn from our offending sin and seek His nearness. To many in the church, however, it appears easier to find a substitute who might fill in for God rather than to set ourselves earnestly to return to Him regardless of the cost.

How might that look in your life and your church?

- Your church might say that God is an all-present king, but in practice it makes decisions as if God were away in a foreign country and no one knows when or if He will return, leaving the church body to rule by its own preferences. You elect capable businessmen to run your church committees in the place of the rule of the divine king.

- You may find Christianity sadly lacking with a localized God. Sundays are bearable; but since God does not live in the weekdays, at work, or in the home, you are left to fill the emptiness of your life with the world's offers.

A. W. Tozer noted the consequences of going on in religion with God at a distance:

> *The tragic results of this spirit are all about us: shallow lives, hollow religious philosophies, the overwhelming element of fun in gospel meetings, the glorification of men, trust in religious externalities, salesmanship methods, and the mistaking of dynamic personality for the power of the Spirit.*[25]

In short, when God seems distant and we believe the lie that He is limited in His presence, we tend to become little gods that attempt to substitute for the true God—*we* provide, *we* plan, *we* govern. Allowing a religion with a localized god is a terrible burden.

It is our honour that we are made capable of this acquaintance [with God], our misery that by sin we have lost it; our privilege that through Christ we may return to it; and our unspeakable advantage to renew and cultivate it.

— John Wesley

LIVING WITHOUT PURPOSE OR MEANING

Another symptom of the localized god lie is that you begin to view most of life's events as without spiritual purpose or meaning. We have all felt this at times; but have you seen how a misunderstanding of God's presence can contribute to the problem?

If God only lives in religious places, and only attends religious events, then most of your life (which is made up of non-religious things) will be viewed as spiritually meaningless and without purpose. The all-presence of God guarantees that all of life has value because all of life is lived before His face. Mundane tasks may be done with Him as near to you as He is when you are reading your Bible.

A localized god is at the heart of what we will call the *sacred-secular* lie—the idea that only religious things (sacred activities) have spiritual value. If God is not present when we are busy doing the daily tasks that He has given us, tasks which aren't particularly religious (like housework, or driving home from work), then we may feel that these are of little worth. You may apologize to God for all the

How little time or thought we give to the character of God as revealed in Jesus Christ! We must be on intimate terms with Him. To know God, as to know a man, we must "live with" Him, must summer and winter with Him, must bring Him into the pettinesses of daily life, must let our love set to Him, must be in sympathy with Him, our wills being tuned to make harmony with His, our whole nature being in accord with His.

— Alexander MacLaren

time you are spending on work, on your studies, mowing the grass, or preparing meals and cleaning up after them.

When we think that God is not near to us in these non-religious activities, we believe a lie rooted in the false view of a localized god. In reality, the all-presence of God means that everything a Christian does can be done with God and for God. God can be as near when you wash the dishes or drive to work as when you sit and read your Bible. Not all tasks are equally important (mowing the grass is not as significant as gathering to worship God), but all tasks can be equally holy if you refuse to believe the lie of a localized god and do everything in a Godward manner.

Make a list below of the things you do each week that are religious.

_____

_____

_____

Make a list below of some of the things you do each week that do not seem religious.

_____

_____

_____

Can you see that the all-presence of God means that the second list can be as holy as the first? God can be as close to you when you are doing the things in the second list as when you are doing the things in the first. The lie of a localized god, a god that is only involved with religious events in religious places, will rob your everyday tasks of meaning.

CONSIDER the following passages.

Ecclesiastes 9:10
Whatever your hand finds to do, do it with all your might . . . .

1 Corinthians 10:31
Whether, then, you eat or drink or whatever you do, do all to the glory of God.

Colossians 3:17, 23-24

Whatever you do in word or deed, do all in the name of the Lord Jesus, giving thanks through Him to God the Father . . . . Whatever you do, do your work heartily, as for the Lord rather than for men, knowing that from the Lord you will receive the reward of the inheritance. It is the Lord Christ whom you serve.

The prophet Zechariah speaks of the changes that will accompany the New Covenant.

In that day there will be inscribed on the bells of the horses, "HOLY TO THE LORD." And the cooking pots in the LORD's house will be like the bowls before the altar. Every cooking pot in Jerusalem and in Judah will be holy to the LORD of hosts . . . . (Zechariah 14:20-21)

The bells on the farm animals and the pots in the kitchen will be holy to God because the New Covenant has provided a nearness to Him that is extraordinary. Everyday things—working, eating, drinking . . . whatever—can be done in the presence of the one God who is everywhere. For the Christian, this changes everything.

WHAT CAN BE DONE FOR THOSE WHO HAVE LIVED WITH A LOCALIZED GOD?

Earlier this week you studied Psalm 68, which spoke of the effects of Christ's labors. These effects included the nearness of God to His people in a relational manner. But if we desire the nearness of God in our daily lives, we must do more than merely believe; we must live in constant awareness of His presence.

Consider this quote from A.W. Tozer:

That we see this truth is not enough. If we would escape from the toils of the sacred-secular dilemma, the truth must "run in our blood" and condition our thoughts. We must practice living to the glory of God, actually and determinedly. By meditation upon this truth, by talking it over with God often in our prayers, by recalling it to our minds frequently as we move about among men, a sense of its wondrous meaning will begin to take hold of us . . . . We must offer all our acts to God and believe that He accepts them. Then hold firmly to that position and keep insisting that every act of every hour of the day and night be included

To live all of life coram Deo *is to live a life of integrity. It is a life of wholeness that finds its unity and coherency in the majesty of God.*

— R. C. Sproul

in the transaction. Keep reminding God in our times of private prayer that we mean every act for His glory; then supplement those times by a thousand thought-prayers as we go about the job of living. Let us practice the fine art of making every work a priestly ministration. Let us believe that God is in all our simple deeds and learn to find Him there.[26]

Christian, will you determine, based on the labors of Jesus Christ, to live the rest of your days before the face of this God, dedicating all to Him, doing all with Him?

DAY 5: THE NEARNESS OF GOD: THE DISTINGUISHING PRIVILEGE OF THE CHURCH

If you don't feel strong desires for the manifestation of the glory of God, it is not because you have drunk deeply and are satisfied. It is because you have nibbled at the table of the world so long. Your soul is so stuffed with small things, and there is no room for the great.

— John Piper

Letters, texts, phone calls, and pictures of distant loved ones—all are appreciated in their way. And yet, there are times when the longing for those we love cannot be satisfied with anything less than their personal presence. The same could be said of a Christian's longing for God. The yearning for the experience of God's presence, not merely a grasp of the doctrine of His omnipresence, is normal for the Christian. In fact, it is an expression of healthy Christianity when a person is no longer satisfied to read about God's mediated presence and sets his or her heart to pursue it. The Bible provides ample proof of this assertion.

CONSIDER the following passages.

Psalm 27:4, 8
One thing I have asked from the LORD, that I shall seek:
That I may dwell in the house of the LORD all the days of my life,
To behold the beauty of the LORD
And to meditate in His temple . . . .
When You said, "Seek My face," my heart said to You,
"Your face, O LORD, I shall seek."

Psalm 42:1-3
As the deer pants for the water brooks,
So my soul pants for You, O God.
My soul thirsts for God, for the living God;
When shall I come and appear before God?
My tears have been my food day and night,
While they say to me all day long, "Where is your God?"

Psalm 63:1
O God, You are my God; I shall seek You earnestly;
My soul thirsts for You, my flesh yearns for You,
In a dry and weary land where there is no water.

Psalm 73:28
But as for me, the nearness of God is my good;
I have made the Lord GOD my refuge,
That I may tell of all Your works.

These prayers reveal that the believer longs to experience God's nearness in a manner that no second-hand account can satisfy. We are grateful for stirring biblical records and Christian biographies that tell of how others walked with God, but we desire something of that for our own life.

We find ourselves asking:

- Have not believers been promised this nearness of God through the work of His Son?

- Why then should I be satisfied only to hear reports of God's nearness?

There is good news for every follower of Christ who has asked those questions and echoed the words of the psalmists above: God is pleased to distinguish His people by His nearness.

God delights to draw His people to Him and to dwell among them. In the following passage we see this theme pictured in the priesthood and the tabernacle.

COMPLETE ▶ the following passages.

Leviticus 26:11-12
. . . I will make My dwelling among you, and My soul will not reject you. I will _____
_____.

We also see this intimate nearness fully realized in the eternal life that believers enjoy near their God in the new creation.

Revelation 21:2-3
And I saw the holy city, new Jerusalem, coming down out of heaven from God, made ready as a bride adorned for her husband. And I

Faith is our walk, but fellowship sensibly felt is our rest. Faith is the road, but communion with Jesus is the well from which the pilgrim drinks.

— C. H. Spurgeon

heard a loud voice from the throne, saying, "Behold, the tabernacle of God _____

_____

_____

_____.*"*

Exodus 33 speaks of God's nearness to His people and the practical implications of this reality. It falls in the midst of the sad account of Israel's sin in building a golden calf, immediately following their miraculous exodus from Egypt. Following the destruction of the idol, God meets with Moses and explains the consequences of their actions.

READ EXODUS 33:1-16.

Did you notice that one of the consequences of their idolatry was that they would lose the presence of God (verse 3)? The fact is that they could not, nor can we, embrace sin and enjoy the experience of God's relational nearness. Moses argues that he cannot lead the people if God does not go with them. His argument is immensely important here. He does not tell God that Israel desires to experience His presence; rather, He argues on the basis of what the world would think when the nation that claimed to belong to the living God could offer no evidence of His presence.

COPY EXODUS 33:16.

_____

_____

_____

The logic of Moses' argument might be stated thus:

- There is only one God, and He is unlimited in His location.

- This God has chosen Israel as His special people.

- The nearness of God to His people is unique, and therefore distinguishes them from all the other nations.

Israel had proof that they were God's people—they were distinguished by His very real presence.

Oh to be so filled with the presence of the Lord Jesus, so one with Him, that His life may flow through our veins; that He may borrow our lips to speak His messages, borrow our faces to look His looks of patience and love, our hands to do His service and our feet to tread His weary journeys.

— Hudson Taylor

Later, in Deuteronomy, Moses reminds Israel of the privilege that is theirs alone as they walk with God.

READ DEUTERONOMY 4:1-8.

In verses 7 and 8 Moses tells the people that they have two distinguishing traits, things which set them apart from all other nations. They have the word of God, and they have the nearness of God. These are employed as motivations to walk obediently with their God in the Promised Land.

APPLYING THIS TO YOUR CHURCH TODAY

Write below the things that distinguish the church you attend. Perhaps you might consider honestly what things would come to the mind of those in your community if your church were brought up in a conversation.

_____

_____

_____

_____

As in Moses' day, we too may claim two things that distinguish a true church from all other religious gatherings: the word of God and the presence of God. Have you considered that the real nearness of God, a nearness that includes both intimacy and activity, is still a distinguishing mark of a church that walks in harmony with her Lord?

Have you considered that, as with Israel, the church today can forfeit God's nearness (intimacy, activity) by embracing sin? If you are under the assumption that this is a strictly Old Covenant kind of problem, read the following New Covenant passages.

READ REVELATION 3:14-22 and answer the questions.

Where is Christ?

_____

Upon what grounds will Christ return or draw near again to His people?

_____

_____

READH JAMES 4:7-10 and answer the question.

God is speaking here of His people drawing near to Him after a period of spiritual adultery (James 4:1-6). What is expected of these believers if they are once again to be distinguished by God's nearness?

_____

_____

_____

PERSONAL REFLECTION

Have you considered that the church's ineffectiveness in evangelism might be related to the fact that, in times of spiritual decline, she no longer possesses one of the distinguishing marks of God's people?

Is it enough to point to our Bibles and tell the world that we are the people of the living God, if we have forfeited His presence and therefore are not distinguishable from other religions?

Would you be content to attend a church that no longer had the word of God as its guide and foundation? Would you be content to attend a church without the relational presence and activity of God to distinguish it?

Other than religious language, what distinguishes your church from humanitarian groups if you do not enjoy the distinguishing nearness of God?

My goal is God Himself....
At any cost, dear Lord,
by any road.

— John Owen

The experiential, relational presence of God that results in a degree of intimacy between the believer and God as well as a degree of God's activity—both of which visibly distinguish the true followers of Christ from the world—is a reality that has been purchased by Jesus' redemptive labors. Will you determine not to be at ease in a Christianity that lacks His presence?

Behold your God

KNOWING THE ALMIGHTY

DAY 1: THE BIBLICAL TESTIMONY REGARDING THE FULLNESS OF GOD'S POWER

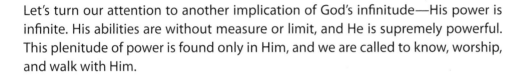

Let's turn our attention to another implication of God's infinitude—His power is infinite. His abilities are without measure or limit, and He is supremely powerful. This plenitude of power is found only in Him, and we are called to know, worship, and walk with Him.

The Latin word for infinite power is *omnipotence* (all-potency). The Bible describes this omnipotence simply and profoundly:

> *Once God has spoken; twice I have heard this: that power belongs to God.* (Psalm 62:11)

Stephen Charnock writes:

> *The power of God is that ability and strength whereby He can bring to pass whatsoever He pleases, whatsoever His infinite wisdom may direct, and whatsoever the infinite purity of His will may resolve . . . . God's power is like Himself: infinite, eternal, incomprehensible; it can neither be checked, restrained, nor frustrated by the creature . . . . As His essence is immense, not to be confined in place; as it is eternal, not to be measured in time; so it is almighty, not to be limited in regard to action.* [27]

Power is that quality by which someone is *able* to do what he wishes. This is different than sovereignty, which describes a person's *right* to do what he wishes. Of course power is something with which we are acquainted. We see power in nature, in nations, and in a lesser degree in individuals. But let's stop and consider how very different God's power is from all other powers.

GOD'S POWER IS ESSENTIAL TO HIS BEING

God does not have to do anything in order to maintain His omnipotence. As with His other attributes, power is not merely what God possesses; it is *who* He

Come then, and with such loving teachableness let us take our seat beside this sea of truth, and strive with reverence to touch the spray that sparkles on the shore.

— Henry Law

is. To think of God as if there is any limitation to His ability to do all He pleases is to embrace a life of idolatry, not Christianity. It is to build a life upon a god that does not exist. A.W. Pink wrote: "He who cannot do what he will and perform all his pleasure cannot be God." [28]

GOD'S POWER IS SELF-EXISTING

The origin of God's power is found in Himself. He has not received it from another. Remember David's statement: "power belongs to God." All other beings that have power, whether angels or insects, have a power that has been given to them. Its origin lies in God. A simple comparison might help us understand the uniqueness of God's power. When we think of powerful men, we think of men who are wealthy or who wield political power. They can create jobs, buy influence, or command armies. Yet what is the source of their power? It is in others—their employees, subjects, or soldiers. In themselves they do not have the ability to accomplish their desires. Imagine the most distinguished general facing the enemy alone on the battlefield with no army to command. He will be defeated because he is dependent upon others as the source of his power. God is in a different category, for He alone possesses a power that finds its existence in Himself.

GOD'S POWER IS INFINITE, HAVING NO LIMITATION, MEASURE, OR BOUNDARY

Paul asks that God would show the believers in Ephesus "what is *the surpassing greatness of His power* toward us who believe" (Ephesians 1:19). What Job's friend, Zophar, says about God's immensity could be applied to the attribute of His power. He asks:

> *Can you discover the depths of God?*
> *Can you discover the limits of the Almighty?* (Job 11:7)

The power of God has depths that cannot be discovered and limits that will never be reached.

The greatness (immensity) of God's power is included in David's statement:

COPY PSALM 145:3.

_____

_____

Finally, Paul is building all of his hopes for the church in Ephesus upon the bigness of God's power.

COPY EPHESIANS 3:20-21.

_____

_____

_____

_____

God may limit the expressions of His power, but His power is essentially infinite. We tend to measure the power of God by our experiences, by what we have seen Him do or not do, especially in the churches we have attended. But the only safe description of the infinite power of God is found in the Bible. Consider what the Scripture tells us about the power of God. Truly it has no limit. Yet there are certain things that God cannot do. He cannot sin. He cannot lie or contradict Himself. He cannot fail in His purposes. He cannot be tempted nor can He tempt others with sin. These divine limitations are not an expression of weakness, but are the proof that His power is united to His moral perfection.

GOD'S POWER IS IMMUTABLE

What a source of strong comfort for every Christian—the God whose power called the universe into being, who sent His Son to redeem us, who raised Him from the grave, who prospered His church in the book of Acts, who has often visited His church with seasons of reformation or revival, is the same God we wake up and walk with today.

CONSIDER the prophet Isaiah's words.

> *Do you not know? Have you not heard? The Everlasting God, the LORD, the Creator of the ends of the earth does not become weary or tired . . . .* (Isaiah 40:28)

His power cannot be depleted. He cannot become tired at the end of a day, or a century. His power is unchanging; therefore it does not increase, either. How can the one who possesses all power increase in power? Others increase in power and then begin to fail. Athletes, scholars, businessmen, politicians—they achieve a certain level of ability, and then slowly begin to lose it. They rise, only to gradually decline. God alone remains unalterably omnipotent.

GOD'S POWER EXISTS
ABOVE THE LIMITS OF TIME AND PLACE

God's power is eternal. It exists in the past, present, and future simultaneously.

Romans 1:20
For since the creation of the world His invisible attributes, His eternal power and divine nature, have been clearly seen, being understood through what has been made, so that they are without excuse.

The power of God is also all-present. It exists in all places at once. Everywhere you travel, every house you enter, every nation or city we call home is a location of His omnipotence. All sin is committed in the presence of His omnipotence. All prayers are offered in the presence of His omnipotence. All child-like efforts to live a Godward life are exerted in the presence of His omnipotence.

GOD'S POWER IS SOVEREIGN

He not only possesses the ability to do all He desires; He also possesses the right to do all He desires. Some men have the power to rule but not the right (they have usurped the seat of power). Some men have the right to rule but not the ability. God alone possesses all power and all rights. In fact, He has always possessed all power and all rights in all places, without ever trying. He is who He is—the almighty king.

God is infinite in power, and therefore it is impossible for any to withstand His will, or resist the outworking of His decrees! Such a statement as that is well calculated to fill the lost sinner with alarm— but from the believer, it evokes nothing but praise.

— A. W. Pink

CONSIDER the following passages and fill in the blanks.

Job 36:22-23
Behold, God is exalted in His _____;
Who is a teacher like Him?
Who has appointed Him His way,
And who has said, "You have done wrong"?

Psalm 135:5-6
For I know that the LORD is great
And that our Lord is above all gods.
Whatever the LORD _____, _____.
In heaven and in earth, in the seas and in all deeps.

Isaiah 46:10
Declaring the end from the beginning,
And from ancient times things which have not been done,
Saying, "My purpose will be established,
And I _____ all My good pleasure."

GOD'S POWER IS UNITED
TO ALL HIS OTHER ATTRIBUTES

God is undivided. He cannot find certain attributes at odds with others (e.g., mercy and justice). Consider how tragic it would be if we belonged to a God who possessed all power but not purity, wisdom, and compassion. What if He were all powerful but not eternal? What if His power could change?

Consider also the joy it is to a believer to realize that God's goodness is all-powerful, His wisdom is all-powerful, His patience and faithfulness are all-powerful, His zeal is all-powerful, His justice is all-powerful! Every perfection of God is forever endowed with the ability to do all He desires to do.

GOD'S POWER IS INCOMPARABLE

This ought to be obvious to us at this point in our study. No one can fully grasp what it means when we say our God is almighty, or that there is no one like Him in power. He remains forever unique and in a category all to Himself.

READ PSALM 89:6, and summarize it in your own words below.

_____

_____

_____

_____

_____

_____

God's power is like Himself: infinite, eternal, incomprehensible; it can neither be checked, restrained, nor frustrated by the creature.

— Stephen Charnock

CONCLUDING THOUGHT

When you consider the biblical testimony regarding God's ability to do all His pleasure, you are immediately confronted with a choice: will you lay aside all inferior views of God's power and make room for the truth?

This is not an easy choice. You will find in your studies this week that it will cost you something to believe that God is almighty; but believing is the only path for followers of Christ.

DAY 2: THE HIDING OF GOD'S POWER

Yesterday we began to consider the infinite power of God. Below is the definition given by Stephen Charnock.

FILL IN THE BLANKS using yesterday's lesson. *p 89*

> *The power of God is that _____ and _____ whereby He can bring to pass _____ He _____,*
> *whatsoever His infinite _____ may direct, and whatsoever the infinite _____ of His _____ may resolve . . . . God's power is like _____: infinite, eternal, incomprehensible; it can neither be checked, restrained, nor frustrated by the creature . . . .*
> *As His essence is immense, not to be confined in place; as it is _____, not to be measured in time; so it is _____, not to be limited in regard to action.*

> *Where is the hope? I meet millions who tell me that they feel demoralized by the decay around us. Where is the hope? The hope that each of us have is not in who governs us, or what laws are passed, or what great things that we do as a nation. Our hope is in the power of God working through the hearts of people, and that's where our hope is in this country; that's where our hope is in life.*
>
> — Charles Colson

Today we will look at the power of God applied to the perplexing problems and internal struggles that believers often face, particularly in times of spiritual decline among God's people. Is there real value in contemplating the power of God? Is it self-indulgent religion to contemplate the attributes of God when people are telling you that there are more "practical" issues facing the believer? The prophet Habakkuk shows us how to live upon the reality of God's power even in the midst of deep grief and confusion.

THE CAUSE OF THE PROPHET'S GRIEF

The northern ten tribes that made up Israel have already been carried into exile by Assyria for their idolatry. Babylon, by military conquest, has now become the dominant empire of the region, gradually consuming smaller nations. Judah has refused to learn from the mistakes of Israel; instead, she increases her rapid descent into idolatry and rebellion.

It is during this decline that the prophet enters into a conversation with the Almighty, and through his little book we are allowed to listen in on what is said.

READ HABAKKUK 1:1-4 and list some of the symptoms of Judah's rebellion that the prophet mentions.

_____

_____

READx HABAKKUK 1:5-11 for God's astonishing response to the prophet's first complaint.

Do you see the answer?

God is going to raise up a pagan nation, full of violence, and use it to discipline His idolatrous people. If the prophet were alive today, he might object: "The cure is worse than the disease!" (If you would like to better understand the discipline prophesied here, read the book of Lamentations.)

READx HABAKKUK 1:12-2:1 and record the prophet's second complaint.

_____

_____

Difficulties afford a platform upon which He can show Himself. Without them we could never know how tender, faithful, and almighty our God is.

— Hudson Taylor

After giving a warning to the arrogant Chaldeans (Babylonians) in Habakkuk 2:2-20, Habakkuk records his ultimate hopes in a prayer found in the third chapter. He now knows what to ask for—that God would revive His powerful work during these dark times.

> *LORD, I have heard the report about You and I fear.*
> *O LORD, revive Your work in the midst of the years,*
> *In the midst of the years make it known;*
> *In wrath remember mercy.* (Habakkuk 3:2)

After composing a song on this theme, Habakkuk comes to his conclusion.

READx HABAKKUK 3:16-19.

How can a man who cares about God's honor see the decline in God's people and find hope? How can a man who cares about God's people see the coming judgment and still sing?

The answer lies in WHO God is:

- God is Habakkuk's salvation (3:18).

- God is Habakkuk's strength (3:19).

These realities become more encouraging when the prophet considers God's power.

READ HABAKKUK 3:3-15.

In this passage the prophet mentions six ways that God has displayed His power in Israel's history. And yet, Habakkuk tells us that these displays of power might be more accurately described as the "hiding of His power" (3:4). The Jews would have recognized each of these events. Let's consider the ways God displayed His omnipotence, and why Habakkuk sees in these a veiling of God's strength.

HIS GLORIOUS COMING WHEN HE GAVE THE LAW AT SINAI (3:3-4)

Teman and Paran are mountains in the Sinai region. Listen to Moses' description of the display of God's all-power in EXODUS 19:16-20:

> *So it came about on the third day, when it was morning, that there were thunder and lightning flashes and a thick cloud upon the mountain and a very loud trumpet sound, so that all the people who were in the camp trembled. And Moses brought the people out of the camp to meet God, and they stood at the foot of the mountain. Now Mount Sinai was all in smoke because the LORD descended upon it in fire; and its smoke ascended like the smoke of a furnace, and the whole mountain quaked violently. When the sound of the trumpet grew louder and louder, Moses spoke and God answered him with thunder. The LORD came down on Mount Sinai, to the top of the mountain; and the LORD called Moses to the top of the mountain, and Moses went up.*

Who can think of His power so mighty, so irresistible—a power which is able to crush us into atoms with infinitely greater ease than we can tread the crawling worm beneath our feet—and not fear Him?

— John MacDuff

What a display! The earth was full of His praise! God's glory shone forth like the rays of the noon-day sun. His splendor terrified the people; even Moses trembled. There were flashes of lightning from God's hand. Surprisingly, Habakkuk says this is an event that hid, or veiled, God's power!

How are we to understand this statement at the end of verse 4? The Bible commentator Matthew Henry writes regarding this passage:

> *The operations of his power, compared with what he could have done, were rather the hiding of it than the discovery of it.*[29]

In other words, there will always be more hidden of God's power than there is revealed, in any of His works. The most you can see is the edge of His ways. His power, like Himself, is incomprehensibly great and even His coming to Mount Sinai hid more than it revealed.

Let's look at five more examples, all of which reveal God's power; and yet, in each one more is hidden than manifested.

HIS DELIVERANCE OF ISRAEL FROM EGYPT BY THE TEN PLAGUES (3:5)

The Exodus record contains these acts of all-power:

- Waters turned to blood (7:20)

- Frogs (8:6)

- Lice (8:17)

- Beetles, flies (8:24)

- Cattle disease (9:3)

- Boils (9:10)

- Hail (9:24)

- Locusts (10:13)

- Darkness (10:22)

- Death of the firstborn (12:29)

Each of these shows God's ability to do all that He pleases with His creation; yet these were hiding more of God's power than they revealed.

HIS DIVIDING UP THE LAND AND GIVING IT TO ISRAEL AS HE PROMISED (3:6-7)

God is pictured as looking over all the vast land of Canaan, surveying it for the purpose of dividing it up to give to the twelve tribes of Israel. The nations realize this and are startled, appalled. Even the nations of Cush and Midian are distressed by God's activity (and they are not part of God's gift to Israel). Nothing is beyond His mighty reach. Even the ancient mountains and hills bow before God's power. All that went into the giving of Canaan to Israel is thus portrayed in this song. Yet even here we have a hiding of God's power.

HIS REMOVAL OF THE NATURAL OBSTACLES TO RESCUE ISRAEL (3:8-10)

God's activity in the miraculous rescue of Israel makes it appear as if He is angry with earth's waters. Stop and consider this. The Red Sea and later the river Jordan stand before Israel and block their way. Then God acts. In this song the waters are personified as raising up their hands and complaining to God of the manner in which He has dealt with them. The Red Sea and the river Jordan flee before God's omnipotence when He determines to save His people. And yet, even these miraculous events are hiding more of God's strength than they reveal.

Who can enumerate all the beings and events, which are incessantly before His eye, adjusted by His wisdom, dependent on His will, and regulated by His power!

— John Newton

This may remind you of another time when the Lord commanded the waters and displayed His power for the comfort of His disciples (Matthew 8:23-27). The disciples' response was: "What kind of a man is this, that even the winds and the sea obey Him?"

In Habakkuk 3:9, the prophet mentions the dividing of the land with rivers. When hundreds of thousands of Israelites travelled for forty years in a wilderness, God continually supplied them with water to drink. Twice He gave it by cleaving a rock! When God rescues His people by creating a river from a rock, more power is being hidden than revealed.

HIS RESTRAINT OF EARTH'S ROTATION FOR JOSHUA AND THE ARMIES OF ISRAEL (3:11)

READ JOSHUA 10:1-15.

Here is a miracle that baffles the mind! In response to Joshua's prayer, God stopped the rotation of the earth so that Israel might utterly defeat her enemies in battle. Yet holding earth in its place so that the sun and moon remained in the sky, and doing so in a miraculous manner so that this world suffered no harm, was a veiling of the power of the God who called all the galaxies into being and determined their laws of operation.

HIS CONQUEST OF CANAAN (3:12-15)

This part of the song uses various expressions to describe God's conquest of Canaan for Israel. He unsheathed His bow, marched through the land in fiery anger, trampled the nations, wounded the leaders of His enemies, and pierced with spears the heads of the armies.

You can take time to read the accounts found in Joshua. And yet as you read of His mighty deeds, remind yourself—more of God's power was hidden in these events than was revealed!

PRACTICAL APPLICATIONS FOR YOU TODAY

1. Are you grieved by the spiritual decline of those who claim to know Christ? These passages offer hope!

Look again at these six poetic descriptions of His activity. Don't stop there— read the New Testament, the Gospels, and the book of Acts. See His power displayed, and each time remind yourself: more is still hidden than has been revealed.

My need now is great and urgent; God is greater and more near: and because He is, and is what He is, all must be, all is, all will be well.

— Hudson Taylor

2. Each of the six displays of incomprehensible and infinite power was given at a time when God's people needed deliverance.

God had made promises to Israel. He worked mightily to keep those promises. In the New Covenant the Christian finds astonishing promises. In contrast to those, the Christian finds countless enemies within and without. Where will you look for real hope? Why not despair and lie down, paralyzed with gloom? Like Habakkuk, you must remember the deeds of the Almighty. He will continue to save His people according to the integrity of His character. He will keep His word. He will do it by a mighty display of His power. When you fear it will not be sufficient for the present crisis, remind yourself: all the displays of God's power from the beginning of creation until now have hidden more of His might than they have revealed.

That is a truth to keep the Christian going!

With the goodness of God to desire our highest welfare, the wisdom of God to plan it, and the power of God to achieve it, what do we lack? Surely we are the most favored of all creatures.

— A. W. Tozer

DAY 3: MIGHTY TO SAVE: THE POWER OF GOD SEEN IN THE PERSON AND WORK OF JESUS

Endless gratitude is due to our God because He has chosen our rescue as the chief display of His immense power. The person and work of His Son, Jesus Christ, is the premier showcase of God's power.

Today you will have the opportunity to study and meditate on the power of Almighty God as you consider some of the most precious aspects of our salvation.

A SOBERING REALITY-CHECK

We can all agree upon a basic truth: all religion reflects the God or gods it serves. Therefore, if the false god is morally polluted and cruel, then we would expect the religion it creates to be morally polluted and cruel. In the case of Christianity, the realities of God's character are reflected in His deeds. Because God is all-powerful, then those who worship Him in truth must also be distinguished by His power. The idols mentioned in the Old Testament all share one thing in common: they are powerless. They have no real abilities. They boast various benefits but never actually do anything, good or bad.

What do we want? What would we be at? What do our souls desire? Is it not that we might have a more full, clear, stable comprehension of the wisdom, love, grace, goodness, holiness, righteousness, and power of God, as declared and exalted in Christ unto our redemption and eternal salvation?

—John Owen

READA PSALM 115:2-8 below, and notice the strange contrast between what an idol appears to be able to do and what it actually can do.

*Why should the nations say,
"Where, now, is their God?"
But our God is in the heavens;
He does whatever He pleases.*

Their idols are silver and gold,
The work of man's hands.
They have mouths, but they cannot speak;
They have eyes, but they cannot see;
They have ears, but they cannot hear;
They have noses, but they cannot smell;
They have hands, but they cannot feel;
They have feet, but they cannot walk;
They cannot make a sound with their throat.
Those who make them will become like them,
Everyone who trusts in them.

Mouths, eyes, ears, noses, hands, feet . . . they certainly look like they are able to speak, see, hear, smell, handle, and walk—yet they never do. Instead, they are created and carried about by their worshippers. So much for the power of idols. But the living God is not like this. He possesses all-power, and when He does something, it reflects that power.

If this is true, then Christianity (what God has done) should reflect the reality of God's power. It will be distinguished by a real ability to accomplish what it promises. Any religion that claims to be the result of an almighty God yet lacks power is not being honest about itself.

If you were to stop and look at your Christianity and the Christianity of your church, could you see the power of God reflected in your religion?

If you only kept those aspects of religion which demonstrated the working of an almighty God, what would you keep?

We must refuse to lean upon the broken staff of human wisdom and cling to the gospel alone as the power of God to save a hardened humanity.

— Paul Washer

_____

_____

_____

What would you remove?

_____

_____

_____

How long will we settle for a type of religion that fails to reflect the God of the Bible? What if our religion, personal or corporate, does not reflect the God of the Bible because it is not a religion about Him? What if it reflects the best *we* can do, because it is a religion by *us* and for *us*?

Paul was convinced of this basic principle. Accordingly, when he approaches the problem of false teachers in Corinth he takes an unusual approach.

In 1 Corinthians 2 Paul gives us an insight into how his view of the power of God guided the way he approached preaching.

The more you trust in the arm of the flesh, the less you're going to see of the power of God.

— Paul Washer

READ 1 CORINTHIANS 2:1-5 and write in your own words how Paul's preaching demonstrated that he spoke on behalf of an all-powerful God.

_____

_____

_____

_____

READ 1 CORINTHIANS 4:18-20 below and see how this guides Paul's dealing with the false teachers.

> *Now some have become arrogant, as though I were not coming to you. But I will come to you soon, if the Lord wills, and I shall find out, not the words of those who are arrogant but their power. For the kingdom of God does not consist in words but in power.*

What would Paul demand as evidence from the false teachers to prove they truly spoke on behalf of an omnipotent God? He wanted to see what power there was in their teaching. Why? Paul understood that those who falsely claimed to represent God would lack any real power in their words. They might entertain and dazzle, they might stir up the emotions, but their teaching would have no power to bring about real change in their hearers. Paul explains that because God's kingdom is not made up of words only (though doctrine was certainly important to Paul), but of power, then the truths of God have this distinguishing mark—they have power.

THE GREAT DISPLAY OF POWER IN JESUS' PERSON

It's time now to take a quick look at just a few places that we see the power of God reflected in the God-Man.

1. Christianity began with a great display of God's power.

Think of the person God sent to rescue you.

- To rescue you, He must be as strong as *God*.

- To represent you, He must be like you, truly *human*.

- He must be truly God and truly man, two natures in one person.

This is an important point. God might have created a body for His Son from the dust of the earth, as He did for Adam. In that case Jesus would have been truly human, but not a representative of Adam's race—not our kinsman. So God must bring Him into the fallen race of Adam, yet without the pollution of Adam's sin passed on to Him, nor the guilt (how could a polluted, guilty man help us?). In Jesus we have unspotted and genuine humanity, from the family of Adam, united to the unaltered fullness of God.

How could this union be? Listen to the angel's announcement to Mary and note the display of God's power in the Incarnation.

> *The angel answered and said to her, "The Holy Spirit will come upon you, and the power of the Most High will overshadow you; and for that reason the holy Child shall be called the Son of God."* (Luke 1:35)

Have you ever stopped to consider the measure of that power which overshadowed Mary in order to unite two things so vastly different as humanity and deity? We have such falsely inflated views of humanity and such small views of God; we need to rethink this union.

To get some idea of the difference between humanity and God, try to think of the distance between other created things and God:

• a moment in your day	vs.	• eternity (timelessness)
• a square foot on earth	vs.	• a presence that fills and overflows all creation
• death	vs.	• immortality
• ignorance	vs.	• all-knowledge
• helplessness	vs.	• all-power
• limitation	vs.	• infiniteness

Can you think of other things that show the distance between mankind and God?

- _____ VS. - _____

- _____ VS. - _____

- _____ VS. - _____

Imagine taking all of the energy of our sun and packing it into a clod of dirt the size of your fist. Imagine the clod containing all of that energy without being consumed, and yet remaining a true clod of dirt. These comparisons and illustrations may help us begin to rightly think of the difference between the eternal Son of God and a human body and soul. But in truth, a clod of dirt is much closer to the sun (both are created things) than the uncreated Creator is to a human being.

It is a greater miracle to take all the fullness of the perfections of God (Colossians 2:9) and unite them to a human body and soul in the womb of Mary. That is the first display of God's power in Jesus Christ.

2.   The labors of Jesus Christ continued to display God's power.

IN HIS OBEDIENCE

You might compare the tasks of Adam and the "Last Adam" (1 Corinthians 15:45).

Adam was given one command: Do not eat of the tree of the knowledge of good and evil (Genesis 2:17). This one command was given to him in a perfect environment. He was surrounded with all he needed for perfect happiness. He and Eve had the only perfect marriage, and, if we might say so, they attended the only flawless church. Yet, with all of these advantages, Eve and then Adam chose self above God. They sinned, and with their sin came shame and death to all of us.

Jesus was required to perfectly obey every command of God, always doing everything the Father desired, in His thoughts and words and actions, and never once doing anything that displeased God. He was required to perfectly reveal God to people that did not desire the truth. He was required to endure the infinite wrath of His Father, thus satisfying the Law's just penalty for those sinners He came to save. Moreover, He had this task in an environment that was constantly opposing Him. He grew up in a family in which every person needed saving. His church was full of those who hated His task (His own church leaders called for His crucifixion). The power of God is seen in the fact that Jesus was able to present Himself as a perfectly righteous and obedient sacrifice on the cross. Jesus Christ never failed to obey.

IN HIS RESURRECTION

To raise the dead is as unique an expression of omnipotence as to create in the first place. But the resurrection of Jesus was much more than a physical miracle over the grip of the grave. It is the spiritual reality behind the need for Jesus' death and resurrection that greatly enlarge our view of God's power at the empty tomb. Jesus was subjected to the grave because He became the sin bearer on the cross. The penalty for each sin, every sin, is death. Each sin is an offense against the infinite God who made us; therefore each sin carries an infinite penalty.

There is nothing left to us but to see how we may be approved of Him, and how we may roll the weight of our weak souls in well-doing upon Him, who is God omnipotent.

— Samuel Rutherford

Paul tells us in 2 Corinthians 5:21, "He made Him who knew no sin *to be* sin on our behalf, so that we might become the righteousness of God in Him." Thus, for Jesus to be raised from such a death meant that He had satisfied all the just wrath of God against all the sin of His people. He not only escaped the grave; He endured infinite divine wrath. Hence, the resurrection of Jesus, unlike the resurrection of others (Lazarus, for example), was a much greater display of the power of God. No wonder Paul says that it was the strength of God's might that was displayed in the resurrection of Jesus (Ephesians 1:19-20).

We have only glanced quickly at a few of the examples of God's power as displayed in the person and labors of Jesus Christ. You can take all the Gospel accounts of Christ's life and see in them some measure of the power of God being revealed.

Tomorrow we will consider the power of God in the ongoing work of the resurrected Christ.

DAY 4: THE POWER OF GOD DISPLAYED IN THE CONTINUING CONQUESTS OF JESUS

The continued labors of Jesus from His throne in glory demonstrate the power of God. When we think of God's power, we often think of His victories over His enemies. The power of God is viewed in Christ's many victories and conquests as He continues His work as our Redeemer.

Our rescue began with a mighty victory. Do you remember the words of Paul to the Colossians?

When you were dead in your transgressions and the uncircumcision of your flesh, He made you alive together with Him, having forgiven us all our transgressions, having canceled out the certificate of debt consisting of decrees against us, which was hostile to us; and He has taken it out of the way, having nailed it to the cross. When He had disarmed the rulers and authorities, He made a public display of them, having triumphed over them through Him. (Colossians 2:13-15)

Triumphed over them! Jesus, having done all the Father required of Him, prevailed over sin, death, and the devil; thus, He is free to take His people from the enemy's prison. That is what Jesus was alluding to in the following parable:

When a strong man, fully armed, guards his own house, his possessions are undisturbed. But when someone stronger than he attacks him and overpowers him, he takes away from him all his armor on which he had relied and distributes his plunder. (Luke 11:21-22)

That is a display of power every believer ought to treasure. But do you only notice the defeat of external enemies when you think of the power of God in our rescue? There is another aspect of victory in the beginning of our rescue. Have you ever thought deeply on the great power of God required in the conquest of your own heart in true conversion?

THE POWER OF GOD DISPLAYED IN A TRUE CONVERSION

Conversion, the turning of a soul in faith and repentance toward God, is the beginning of the conquest. It takes an almighty act of God to lead us to believe, love, and choose Him above the false advertisements of self and sin. Because sin has invaded our nature through Adam's rebellion, we are born opposing God. If that seems hard to believe, listen to the biblical testimony.

READyy ROMANS 3:10-11. This is a description of all of humanity.

For a further description, read ROMANS 5:6-10 and list the four descriptions of humanity prior to God's work within them.

_____

_____

_____

_____

Sin is what you do when your heart is not satisfied with God. No one sins out of duty. We sin because it holds out some promise of happiness. That promise enslaves us until we believe that God is more to be desired than life itself (Psalm 63:3). Which means that the power of sin's promise is broken by the power of God's.

—John Piper

This does not mean that all people act as badly as they can at all times. It does mean that the inner person, the soul, is permeated by sin's influence.

Regardless of how admirable people may appear outwardly, the Bible explains that no one understands God, seeks God, or truly obeys God. Sin causes the minds of all mankind to prefer lies rather than God's word. Sin predisposes our hearts to love selfishness rather than God and His ways. Sin enslaves our wills, our volition, and our desires to serve every master but the one who deserves our allegiance.

This spiritual condition is summarized by Paul in EPHESIANS 2:1-2:

> *And you were dead in your trespasses and sins, in which you formerly walked according to the course of this world, according to the prince of the power of the air, of the spirit that is now working in the sons of disobedience.*

Dead! Unresponsive to God, as unresponsive as a corpse. It takes a work of infinite power to alter our condition—to give us:

- a mind that loves God's truth

- a heart that loves God's ways

- a will that loves God's rule

This mighty work is described in the Bible as a new birth, a new creation, a quickening. No matter what we do, we cannot do this for ourselves, nor can we accomplish it in those we love. Every true conversion is an act of divine power.

THE POWER OF GOD SEEN IN A CHRISTIAN'S PERSEVERANCE

The good news includes more than a fresh start. The new birth is just the beginning of God's work within the Christian. What was begun by infinite power will be sustained by that same power. Think of the power of God seen in the perseverance and preservation of every Christian, without exception, regardless of enemies without or within.

This is evident in Paul's prayers for the young churches. In COLOSSIANS 1:11, Paul prays that they would be:

> *. . . strengthened with all power, according to His glorious might, for the attaining of all steadfastness and patience . . . .*

We are dependent on the power of God to convert us and give faith in Jesus Christ and the new nature . . . . The fallen creature cannot attain to true holiness, but by being created again. 'Tis a raising from the dead. Yea, 'tis a more glorious work of power than mere creation, or raising a dead body to life, in that the effect attained is greater and more excellent.

—Jonathan Edwards

Again, in EPHESIANS 1:18-20 Paul writes:

> *I pray that the eyes of your heart may be enlightened, so that you will know . . . what is the surpassing greatness of His power toward us who believe. These are in accordance with the working of the strength of His might which He brought about in Christ, when He raised Him from the dead and seated Him at His right hand in the heavenly places . . . .*

Paul expects that the new believers will continue to be strengthened by God. Then he gives the measure of this help. Write below Paul's measure of that strengthening we receive.

_____

_____

Yesterday and today we have mentioned:

- The power of God in the person and work of Christ

- The power of God in the conquering of a soul

- The power of God in the perseverance of a Christian

THE FUTURE DISPLAYS OF GOD'S POWER

Now let's consider the power of God yet to be displayed in the fulfilling of His promises. We only have time to consider two.

First, the completion of His work in all believers. This is what theologians call glorification. It includes the completion of all spiritual changes begun in the new birth, as well as the transformation of our mortal bodies into the same kind of body that Christ had after His resurrection.

READ PHILIPPIANS 3:20-21 below.

> *For our citizenship is in heaven, from which also we eagerly wait for a Savior, the Lord Jesus Christ; who will transform the body of our humble state into conformity with the body of His glory, by the exertion of the power that He has even to subject all things to Himself.*

Do you see it? The power that will subdue all creation, all nations and peoples, to the rule of Jesus is the power that will transform the Christian's body and complete the work of redemption.

When it is all finished, the Christian will be a marvel to behold: given a new body, clothed in the righteousness of Christ, and made perfect with His moral perfection. It is a change that requires the all-power of God.

Second, there is one more promise, the fulfillment of which will vividly display God's power. It is the Day of Judgment, when Jesus returns for His church. He will come in power. It is a terrible and beautiful scene to contemplate.

> 1 Corinthians 15:24
> *. . . then comes the end, when He hands over the kingdom to the God and Father, when He has abolished all rule and all authority and power.*

> 2 Thessalonians 1:7-10
> *. . . when the Lord Jesus will be revealed from heaven with His mighty angels in flaming fire, dealing out retribution to those who do not know God and to those who do not obey the gospel of our Lord Jesus. These will pay the penalty of eternal destruction, away from the presence of the Lord and from the glory of His power, when He comes to be glorified in His saints on that day, and to be marveled at among all who have believed—for our testimony to you was believed.*

God has promised that His unique and immeasurable power will be displayed in the judgment of those who have refused to "obey the gospel of our Lord Jesus."

CONCLUDING THOUGHTS

Because all power belongs to God, life includes certain inescapable realities, and it would benefit us to consider two of them now.

1. There can be no reason for the believer to despair.

The work of salvation by the Jesus of Scripture is a thing of infinite power from beginning to end. He to whom power belongs has engaged Himself by a covenant to finish what He has started. Christian, your weakness does not enter into this equation. It is the strength of God that you must live upon. In the descriptions of the past two days you have only glanced at the edges of His ways. You have only seen examples of God "hiding" more of His power than He reveals. The power of God counteracts two temptations that face Christians: the temptation to despair, and the temptation to indulge in the fiction of personal self-sufficiency. An almighty God is behind the rescue of every true Christian—from beginning to end. Learn to live in that reality.

2.   There can be no reason for those who refuse the claims of Jesus to hope.

Jesus of Nazareth is God, and as God, power belongs to Him. He will effortlessly crush all opposition to His rule. No one has the ability to escape Him when He comes in the Day of Judgment, provoked to a terrible wrath.

Every element of our own self-reliance must be put to death by the power of God.

— Oswald Chambers

DAY 5: LIVING ON THESE TRUTHS

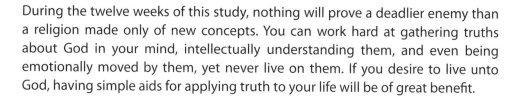

During the twelve weeks of this study, nothing will prove a deadlier enemy than a religion made only of new concepts. You can work hard at gathering truths about God in your mind, intellectually understanding them, and even being emotionally moved by them, yet never live on them. If you desire to live unto God, having simple aids for applying truth to your life will be of great benefit.

In Week 2, Day 5, the five metaphors in Colossians 2:6-7 were used to aid us. Today, you will have an opportunity, using those five simple pictures, to contemplate how to apply your studies regarding God's power.

In the passage below, the five word pictures are in bold print:

> *Therefore as you have received Christ Jesus the Lord, so **walk** in Him, having been firmly **rooted** and now being **built up** in Him and **established** in your faith, just as you were instructed, and **overflowing with gratitude**.* (Colossians 2:6-7)

Let's consider how the truths we have studied this week can be lived upon by using these five pictures. [Please note that your answers to today's questions may overlap to some degree.]

HAVING RECEIVED CHRIST JESUS THE LORD . . .

1.   **Walk in Him**

The word "walk" shows us two things about Christian living.

First, walking is an everyday activity that does not seem significant. We take thousands of steps in a day, and very few steps would be looked back upon as particularly noteworthy, much less spiritually meaningful. Our little, common choices each day may also seem insignificant, but like our steps, they do matter—because they add up to be the stuff of life. For this reason, truths about God must affect our common choices in everyday life.

We may search long to find where God is, but we shall find Him in those who keep the words of Christ. For the Lord Christ saith, "If any man love me, he will keep my words; and we will make our abode with him."

— Martin Luther

Second, when a person in the ancient world walked, he or she almost certainly had a destination in mind. Today people often walk for exercise, and in that case the destination isn't important. You may walk on a treadmill or in circles around a track. That is not what Paul has in mind when he says "walk." Christians should be walking toward a definite destination: complete conformity to Christ's character. The little choices of each day, guided by the truths you are studying, should be aiming at that destination—Christlikeness. But why? Not for self-improvement, but for the pleasure and honor of our God.

With these in mind, go back and review this week's lessons. Below, write how you can apply the truths about God's omnipotence in seemingly insignificant choices that lead to the destination of Christlikeness.

_____

_____

_____

_____

2.   Sink Your Roots in Him

Paul says that God has rooted every believer in Christ. Following Christ means daily sinking the roots of your life into the truths of God. Roots gain nutrients from the soil. Your soul may find temporary satisfaction in the junk food of our culture, or it will find lasting satisfaction in the feast of the immutable realities of God.

Go back and review this week's lessons. Below, write some of the truths that you feel are the most nourishing food for your soul. What must you feed upon if you are to live out the Christian life? Is there "junk food" that you should put away?

_____

_____

_____

_____

3. Build a Life on Truth

Each truth you learn in this study can be seen as a brick. Combined with other truths, each brick will be an essential part of building a life with Christ as the foundation. Coming to Jesus in repentance and faith is the only place to begin, but good beginnings are not all there is to Christianity. Paul knew that the Colossian Christians needed more than a foundation built on Christ; they also needed a life built by His grace with His biblical truths. To leave the truths you are studying piled like bricks in a corner of your life would be a grave mistake. You don't want to look back after twelve weeks and see a dusty pile of bricks! You need a life that is a true dwelling place for God Himself.

Review this week's lessons and ask yourself, "In what ways can I build my life (my marriage, my family, my friendships, or my work) on the realities of the all-powerful God?"

Our high and privileged calling is to do the will of God in the power of God for the glory of God.

— J. I. Packer

_____

_____

_____

_____

_____

4. Become Established in Your Faith

Paul used a word, translated in the NASB as "established," which conveys the idea of firming something up, making something stable, solid. In spiritual life, we might use the word *maturity*. You must grow to maturity in your faith (your grasp of the great realities of God), in part, so that you will not be easily swayed by false teaching or half-truths.

CONSIDER HEBREWS 5:12-14.

> *For though by this time you ought to be teachers, you have need again for someone to teach you the elementary principles of the oracles of God, and you have come to need milk and not solid food. For everyone who partakes only of milk is not accustomed to the word of righteousness, for he is an infant. But solid food is for the mature, who because of practice have their senses trained to discern good and evil.*

Here the writer is speaking to people who have heard the truth many times but have remained immature in their faith. He tells us that maturity comes from a life that applies and practices what it is learning. Through application, you are established, or matured, in the great realities of God.

Review this week's lessons. How does God's omnipotence help your faith to be established, solid, and unwavering? In what ways have you failed to put the truths of His omnipotence to practical use?

_____

_____

_____

_____

_____

With these four pictures as guides, we never want to settle for new Bible-truths which are undigested, unapplied, unsettled, and sitting like a wasted pile of bricks.

There is one more picture we need to employ. Without this final metaphor our Christianity will not reflect God.

5. Do All of These with an Overflow of Gratitude to God

Praise the Lord; 'tis good to raise
Our hearts and voices in His praise:
His nature and His works incite
To make His duty our delight.

— Isaac Watts

You can attempt to apply 1-4, but without a grateful heart, how can you honor God?

In the Old Testament Moses warned the people before they entered the Promised Land:

> *Because you did not serve the LORD your God with joy and a glad heart, for the abundance of all things; therefore you shall serve your enemies whom the LORD will send against you, in hunger, in thirst, in nakedness, and in the lack of all things; and He will put an iron yoke on your neck until He has destroyed you.* (Deuteronomy 28:47-48)

Surely that is a shocking message for us as well. If we go about our Christian lives trying to walk in truth, sink roots in truth, build upon truth, and be established in truth, but we do so with ungrateful hearts, we can expect divine discipline.

Review this week's lessons. What reasons for gratitude toward God arise from the study of His omnipotence?

_____

_____

_____

_____

_____

May the God who cannot be altered in His perfect character and purposes grant you such a sight of His omnipotence that you can live in nearness to Him, with grateful hearts and growing faith.

Because God cares for us, our desire should not be to keep the law, but to please the Father. There is nothing that promotes holiness as the realization that we are "heirs of God and joint-heirs with Christ," that our destiny is certain and secure, that nothing in all creation can prevent it.

— Martyn Lloyd-Jones

KNOWING THE GOD WHO KNOWS ALL

DAY 1: THE ALL-KNOWING GOD

Great is our Lord and abundant in strength; His understanding is infinite.
(Psalm 147:5)

We now turn our attention to a sobering fact: God knows all. *Omniscience* is the term for God's all-knowledge. But what exactly does omniscience mean? Consider the following definition:

> *He knows instantly, and with a perfection of fullness that includes every possible item of knowledge concerning everything that exists or could have existed anywhere in the universe at any time in the past or that may exist in the centuries or ages yet unborn.*[30]

Here is one of those truths that we find impossible to fully grasp. Perhaps it would help us if we thought of how God's all-knowledge makes certain things impossible for Him, which are common for us.

Who can enumerate all the beings and events, which are incessantly before His eye, adjusted by His wisdom, dependent on His will, and regulated by His power!

—John Newton

GOD:	THEREFORE:
knows all things and cannot add new knowledge.	He cannot learn.
knows all things instantly, effortlessly.	He does not reason through matters.
knows perfectly the present situation.	He does not need advising.
does not forget past events.	He does not need reminding.
is flawlessly aware of all future events.	He does not need warning.
cannot be mistaken.	He does not need correcting.

These statements ought to help us understand the difference between being brilliant and being all-knowing. God's knowledge is in a different category than ours. It is not simply like ours but multiplied beyond description. Though we cannot fully comprehend this type of knowledge, by God's help we can bow before it in astonishment and adoration.

Let's consider the key ways the Bible speaks of the omniscience of God.

GOD'S KNOWLEDGE IS INFINITE

> Psalm 147:5
> *Great is our Lord and abundant in strength; His understanding is infinite.*

Possessing an infinite understanding, God knows all things in their immensity as well as in their microscopic detail. He knows all facts about all created things on our planet, in our galaxy, and in every other galaxy. He knows the constantly shifting circumstances of every human life, the number of water molecules in the oceans, and the growth of every blade of grass. He knows the position of every star; in fact, He has named them all. He knows all of this and much more, not merely in the present, but in every moment of time since creation. He knows all past, present, and future facts at once. To Him, the incomprehensible complexity of creation is simple. Every actuality and every possibility are known to Him. He knows the activity of every subatomic particle. He knows the fluctuations within the cells of your body and the bodies of all people on the planet throughout time. He observes and perfectly understands all of this without feeling overwhelmed and without even the possibility of confusion.

Because God's knowledge is unlimited, other things follow.

GOD KNOWS HIMSELF

As big and complex as the universe is, there is a limit to its facts. Although we could never calculate the amount even if we employed every human and every computer, there is still a limit. And there is a knowledge that far exceeds the knowledge of this vast creation—God knows Himself! God knows every fact about His perfect person and His unparalleled activity throughout His timeless existence. God is infinite, having no limitations. And God alone, with His infinite knowledge, fully knows Himself.

COPY ROMANS 11:34.

_____

_____

No one else fully knows God, but He knows all things, including Himself.

GOD KNOWS ALL THINGS IN ALL TIMES

In chapter 41 of Isaiah, the prophet contrasts the living God with the dead idols Judah was embracing. One of the distinguishing marks of God is that He possesses knowledge of the future as easily as He does the present, and He reveals this knowledge in prophecies. The idols described in Isaiah, however, are incapable of knowing and declaring things to come. God summons the idols to a legal hearing, calling upon them to prove themselves by demonstrating their knowledge of future events.

> _Let them bring forth and declare to us what is going to take place; as for the former events, declare what they were, that we may consider them and know their outcome. Or announce to us what is coming; declare the things that are going to come afterward, that we may know that you are gods; indeed, do good or evil, that we may anxiously look about us and fear together. Behold, you are of no account, and your work amounts to nothing; he who chooses you is an abomination._
> (Isaiah 41:22-24)

GOD KNOWS ALL ABOUT YOU

We would all agree that we do not know all the immense or microscopic details of this universe. We would agree that our knowledge of the past is limited, and apart from God's word we would have no knowledge of the future. But we feel that if there is one thing we do know, it is ourselves; we boast that no one can know us as well as we do. Yet the Bible paints a different picture. We do not really understand ourselves, but God does.

Jeremiah 17:9-10
The heart is more deceitful than all else and is desperately sick; who can understand it? I, the LORD, search the heart, I test the mind, even to give to each man according to his ways, according to the results of his deeds.

Psalm 19:12a
Who can discern his errors?

Since all our secret ways
Are marked and known by
Thee,
Afford us, Lord, Thy light
of grace,
That we ourselves may see.

— John Newton

1 Samuel 2:3
Boast no more so very proudly,
Do not let arrogance come out of your mouth;
For the LORD is a God of knowledge,
And with Him actions are weighed.

Job 31:4
Does He not see my ways and number all my steps?

Job 34:21-22
For His eyes are upon the ways of a man,
And He sees all his steps.
There is no darkness or deep shadow
Where the workers of iniquity may hide themselves.

Psalm 7:9b
For the righteous God tries the hearts and minds.

Psalm 33:14-15
From His dwelling place He looks out on all the inhabitants of the earth, He who fashions the hearts of them all, He who understands all their works.

Hebrews 4:12-13
For the word of God is living and active and sharper than any two-edged sword, and piercing as far as the division of soul and spirit, of both joints and marrow, and able to judge the thoughts and intentions of the heart. And there is no creature hidden from His sight, but all things are open and laid bare to the eyes of Him with whom we have to do.

Psalm 139:1-6
O LORD, You have searched me and known me.
You know when I sit down and when I rise up;
You understand my thought from afar.
You scrutinize my path and my lying down,
And are intimately acquainted with all my ways.
Even before there is a word on my tongue,
Behold, O LORD, You know it all.
You have enclosed me behind and before,
And laid Your hand upon me.
Such knowledge is too wonderful for me;
It is too high, I cannot attain to it.

Viewing ourselves as under the eye of God's omniscience, would cause reverence in the worship of God.

— Thomas Watson

Based on the passages above that speak of God's knowledge of humanity, write below the specific ways that the Bible says God knows you.

_____

_____

_____

_____

_____

God knows your past as well as your present. He does not forget with the passage of time. God knows your future as well as your past. Tomorrow you will be considering how God's perfect knowledge of you is interwoven with His judgment of those who reject Him and His rescue of those who follow Him.

DAY 2: GOD: JUDGING AND SAVING BY THIS KNOWLEDGE

Yesterday you began to reacquaint yourself with the God who knows all things. Isaiah emphasizes God's omniscience in his rhetorical questions:

> *Who has directed the Spirit of the LORD,*
> *Or as His counselor has informed Him?*
> *With whom did He consult and who gave Him understanding?*
> *And who taught Him in the path of justice and taught Him knowledge*
> *And informed Him of the way of understanding?* (Isaiah 40:13-14)

Or see God's omniscience in the question asked in JOB 21:22:

> *Can anyone teach God knowledge, in that He judges those on high?*

God cannot be taught, counselled, instructed, or shown the path of understanding. These are all clear implications of His omniscience. However, there are other implications, two in particular that touch directly upon our spiritual condition. The first regards God judging sinful humanity in light of His flawless knowledge of all our works, ways, words, and thoughts. The second regards God saving His people through His Son, a rescue rooted in the plans of the omniscient God.

BEING JUDGED BY THE ONE PERSON WHO KNOWS ALL ABOUT YOU

When you wish to do something evil, you retire from the public into your house where no enemy may see you; from those places of your house which are open and visible to the eyes of men you remove yourself into your room; even in your room you fear some witness from another quarter; you retire into your heart, there you meditate: He is more inward than your heart. Wherever, therefore, you shall have fled, there He is.

— Herman Bavinck

Let's start by reviewing the things the Bible says about God's perfect knowledge of you. Look back at the following verses you read in yesterday's lesson:

- 1 Samuel 2:3

- Job 31:4

- Job 34:21-22

- Psalm 7:9b

- Psalm 33:14-15

Now consider the following verses:

> Jeremiah 11:20
> *But, O LORD of hosts, who judges righteously, who tries the feelings and the heart . . . .*

> 1 Corinthians 4:5
> *Therefore do not go on passing judgment before the time, but wait until the Lord comes who will both bring to light the things hidden in the darkness and disclose the motives of men's hearts . . . .*

According to these verses, God uses His complete and flawless knowledge of you to search, test, weigh, and try your thoughts and desires. He sees, numbers, and judges your actions.

With these in mind, read the final scene in REVELATION 20:12:

> *And I saw the dead, the great and the small, standing before the throne, and books were opened; and another book was opened, which is the book of life; and the dead were judged from the things which were written in the books, according to their deeds.*

God is symbolically portrayed as the Judge who has recorded in a book the result of His searching, watching, knowing, numbering and weighing of your thoughts, words, and actions. From that book an indisputable assessment of your life will be formed and a righteous judgment will be pronounced upon you.

THE MEMORY OF THE OMNISCIENT GOD

One of the ways the Bible helps us to understand God's knowledge of our choices is to speak of God remembering all things. Unlike all other beings, God's knowledge of the past is as complete as His knowledge of the present. He has known our every thought, He has heard our every word, and He has observed our every choice. He cannot forget (hence the picture of a book in which He recorded our lives, in Revelation 20). For us, a bad memory may be mistaken for a clear conscience. This is never the case with the omniscient God.

Stop and think for a moment: how terrible would it be if we had a perfect memory? How haunted we would be by the inability to forget all the details of our selfish choices. We are glad that the years pile upon our past in order to separate us from the details and blur our memory of the shame. For sinners aware of the weight of their sins, possessing a perfect memory would be torment. Christ is truly the sinner's only resting place.

What is God's final assessment of humanity?

> Psalm 14:2-3
> *The LORD has looked down from heaven upon the sons of men*
> *To see if there are any who understand, who seek after God.*
> *They have all turned aside, together they have become corrupt;*
> *There is no one who does good, not even one.*

SIN: A LIFE BASED UPON THE DENIAL OF GOD'S UNLIMITED KNOWLEDGE OF US

If you consider that God knows everything about you (remembering effortlessly your thoughts, words, and actions), your fondness for sin is insanity! Read the following verses and consider how sin is portrayed as denying some aspect of God's omniscience:

> Psalm 10:11
> *He says to himself, "God has forgotten; He has hidden His face; He will never see it."*

> Hosea 7:2
> *And they do not consider in their hearts that I remember all their wickedness. Now their deeds are all around them; they are before My face.*

Men would strip Deity of His omniscience if they could—what a proof that "the carnal mind is enmity against God" (Romans 8:7)! The wicked do as naturally hate this Divine perfection as much as they are naturally compelled to acknowledge it. They wish there might be no Witness of their sins, no Searcher of their hearts, no Judge of their deeds. They seek to banish such a God from their thoughts.

— A. W. Pink

Ezekiel 9:9

Then He said to me, "The iniquity of the house of Israel and Judah is very, very great, and the land is filled with blood and the city is full of perversion; for they say, 'The LORD has forsaken the land, and the LORD does not see!'"

Job 22:12-14

"Is not God in the height of heaven? Look also at the distant stars, how high they are! You say, 'What does God know? Can He judge through the thick darkness? Clouds are a hiding place for Him, so that He cannot see; and He walks on the vault of heaven.'"

One implication of these verses is that every sin is in some measure a denial of God's omniscience. It is the activity of practical atheism: living daily as if God were not, or as if He were not as He has described Himself to be—in this case, all-knowing.

SEEING SIN IN THE LIGHT OF GOD'S ALL-KNOWLEDGE

Just as it was foolish for Adam to think a clump of trees could hide his shame, it is foolish for us to think that darkness or distance makes it difficult for God to know exactly what we are doing (Psalm 139). But isn't it equally foolish to hope that the guilt of our own sin might be hidden from God by the distance of years or the cloak of religious words? Nothing can cover us from the full knowledge of the omniscient Judge.

Another equally foolish thought is that it would be better for sinful humanity if God's knowledge of us were not so complete. Do we really want a God that knows the next unkind thing to come out of our mouth before we even say it? Do we want to live with a God who weighs our best actions and tests our motives, who observes each secret desire? If it were possible, would you banish God, the one everlasting witness of your sins, and the searcher of your heart? Here is the silent statement that lies at the root of every willful sin: we prefer that this all-knowing Judge did not exist. We think that if we could rid ourselves of this aspect of God's perfect character, then perhaps He would be easier to live with. If we could live without Him knowing everything about us, then we would have hopes of slipping past the judgment. These are impossible hopes.

Apart from the labors of Jesus Christ, all people face a continuing terror. They are exposed to an all-knowing God before whose face every one of their sins has been acted out.

Remember what the writer of Hebrews said about life outside of the shelter of Jesus Christ:

COPY HEBREWS 10:31.

_____

Anyone who takes the holiness, justice, and omniscience of God seriously would have to agree: without a mediator, the nearness of God would be a terrifying and crushing experience.

Moses wrote about this in his song, Psalm 90.

FILL IN THE BLANKS from PSALM 90:7-8.

For we have been _____ by Your anger
And by Your _____ we have been dismayed.
You have placed our _____ before You,
Our _____ in the light of Your presence.

Sin is always joined to stupidity—the stupidity of thinking you might dupe an all-knowing God. The Bible provides you with a healthy dose of realism. If you stand before this God without mediation, you have no reason to hope. If this God is "against you," what does it matter who is "for you"?

Since God is infinite in knowledge, we should always feel as under His omniscient eye. "I have set the Lord always before me." The consideration of God's omniscience would be preventive of much sin. The eye of man will restrain from sin; and will not God's eyes much more?

— Thomas Watson

DAY 3: THE ALL-KNOWING GOD AND OUR RESCUE

Now we have arrived at the bright dawn of hope. The all-knowing God has exercised all His knowledge in choosing, sending, and equipping His Son to be a perfectly suited rescuer of His enemies.

As we mentioned yesterday, when we think of a God who knows all about our failures and judges us accordingly, it is easy to fall into the trap of wishing that He did not know us so well. Yet today you will be considering how the omniscience and perfect memory of God are in truth strong comforts when they are viewed from within the refuge of the person and work of Jesus Christ. In fact, these qualities in God are part of every Christian's assurance.

Let's consider the various aspects of the believer's rescue and how God's perfect knowledge brings security.

"I have seen his ways and will heal him." (Isaiah 57:18)

Here is one of the most blessedly incomprehensible paradoxes of God's love, which fairly startles us by its excess of compassionate grace: "I have seen his ways and"—one would have thought the next sentence must be, "I will punish him," or at least, "I will rebuke him," but instead of wrath, here is pardon . . . .

— Susannah Spurgeon

GOD'S PERFECT KNOWLEDGE OF YOUR SIN AND A FULL PARDON

God's plan of salvation was formulated before He created this universe. Even then He was completely aware of all our sin, and this knowledge is at the root of our confidence that He is able to perfectly justify us. Only a person who knows with unfailing precision the number, immensity, and nature of every one of our offenses can offer a perfect payment for each one. If any sin in us was not known to God when He laid the plans for our redemption, then we would have reason to fear that perhaps one day we would commit a sin for which He had made no provision. Thus, we would be exposed to the Law's penalty.

Isaiah speaks of the coming of Christ and His work for sinners on the cross in this way:

> *As a result of the anguish of His soul, He will see it and be satisfied;*
> *By His knowledge the Righteous One, My Servant, will justify the many,*
> *As He will bear their iniquities.* (Isaiah 53:11)

Jesus alone understands everything that the Law requires of His people, as well as everything that you and I need in order to be brought to the Father in flawless righteousness. His cross was not some blind expression of sentimental pity for sinners. Rather, it was an exact payment of the debt, based upon a precise knowledge of what God desires and what we owe.

Think of this. God alone knows the extent of your sin. You have forgotten more sins than you remember. If it were left to you to say how much forgiveness you needed, you would never be able to give an accurate calculation.

Remember the complaint and request of David in PSALM 19:12?

> *Who can discern his errors? Acquit me of hidden faults.*

God alone can deal with those secret sins, many of which we ourselves are unaware. Think carefully—what is the result of the atoning death of Jesus when an all-knowing God is behind the payment? No talebearer can bring a secret sin before God, surprising Him. No enemy can make a new accusation against you that catches God off guard. Likewise, nothing foul or cowardly or rebellious in you can suddenly come to light and make God turn away from you. He has seen and known all your shame before you were born and has laid it all, without exception, upon your Savior.

Even when your own conscience rightly accuses you before God, and you feel that God would no longer accept you, remember what John wrote to the young believers in his first letter:

> *We will know by this that we are of the truth, and will assure our heart before Him in whatever our heart condemns us; for God is greater than our heart and knows all things.* (1 John 3:19-20)

GOD'S PERFECT KNOWLEDGE OF YOUR WEAKNESS AND A LIFE OF TRANSFORMATION AND PRESERVATION

No unsuspected weakness in your character can make God's plans for you fall short, for His omniscience has already provided for all weakness.

COPY PSALM 103:13-14.

_____

_____

_____

_____

Standing beneath the shadow of the cross, the weakest saint can confront his deadliest foe . . . "No condemnation to those who are in Christ Jesus," are words written as in letters of living light upon the cross.

— Octavius Winslow

Only God knows how to save people who are like "dust."

THE ISSUE OF GOD'S MEMORY AND OUR HOPE

Returning to the issue of God's memory, we find that it plays a key part in the Christian's hope. This is brought forth in two ways in the Bible:

- God's ability to "forget" our sins

- God's ability to remember things related to our rescue

First, God is able to "forget" our sin.

READ the following verses.

Jeremiah 31:33-34
"But this is the covenant which I will make with the house of Israel after those days," declares the LORD, "I will put My law within them

and on their heart I will write it; and I will be their God, and they shall be My people. They will not teach again, each man his neighbor and each man his brother, saying, 'Know the LORD,' for they will all know Me, from the least of them to the greatest of them," declares the LORD, "for I will forgive their iniquity, and their sin I will remember no more."

Isaiah 43:25
I, even I, am the one who wipes out your transgressions for My own sake, And I will not remember your sins.

Psalm 79:8
Do not remember the iniquities of our forefathers against us; Let Your compassion come quickly to meet us, for we are brought very low.

If God knows everything and He remembers everything without possibility of error, how are we to understand these passages? God is using the human metaphor of memory to emphasize how secure salvation is. It is built upon the determination of God never to remember the sins of His people against them. He forgives them in a manner which guarantees that their sins cannot be brought up and laid at their door. He who cannot forget chooses not to remember His people's offenses, for they have been remembered against their Savior at the cross (Colossians 2:14).

Second, God will remember things that are critical to the rescue of a Christian.

We often find the believer, aware of his or her sin, pleading that God would remember certain things.

UNDERLINE what God is asked to remember in the following passages.

Psalm 25:6-7
Remember, O LORD, Your compassion and Your lovingkindnesses, For they have been from of old. Do not remember the sins of my youth or my transgressions; According to Your lovingkindness remember me, for Your goodness' sake, O LORD.

Habakkuk 3:2
Lord, I have heard the report about You and I fear. O LORD, revive Your work in the midst of the years, In the midst of the years make it known; in wrath remember mercy.

---

*The terrors of law and of God
With me can have nothing
    to do;
My Saviour's obedience and
    blood
Hide all my transgression
    from view.
The work which His goodness
    began,
The arm of His strength will
    complete;
His promise is Yea and Amen,
And never was forfeited yet.
Things future, nor things that
    are now,
Not all things below nor above
Can make Him His purpose
    forgo,
Or sever my soul from His love.*

— Augustus Toplady

Psalm 105:8-9

He has remembered His covenant forever,
The word which He commanded to a thousand generations,
The covenant which He made with Abraham,
And His oath to Isaac.

Psalm 106:4

Remember me, O LORD, in Your favor toward Your people; visit me
with Your salvation.

Psalm 74:2

Remember Your congregation, which You have purchased of old . . . .

It is a great comfort for those united to Christ to plead God's memory, and a reason to hope for continued mercies. Even in wrath, we can ask Him to remember the mercies He has promised us through the work of Jesus Christ. Has not our God told His people, even in the dark days of Isaiah:

Can a woman forget her nursing child
And have no compassion on the son of her womb?
Even these may forget, but I will not forget you.
Behold, I have inscribed you on the palms of My hands;
Your walls are continually before Me. (Isaiah 49:15-16)

ONE FINAL WORD FOR THOSE WHO CLAIM TO KNOW AND BE KNOWN BY THE GOD OF THE BIBLE

It is an amazing fact that the God who knows everything about everyone would ever tell a person that He did *not* know them, that He *never* knew them.

COMPLETE MATTHEW 7:21-23 below.

"Not everyone who says to Me, 'Lord, Lord,' will enter the kingdom of heaven, but he who does the will of My Father who is in heaven will enter. Many will say to Me on that day, 'Lord, Lord, did we not prophesy in Your name, and in Your name cast out demons, and in Your name perform many miracles?' And then I will declare to them, _____
_____
_____."

The deep, universal sin does not lie in the indulgence of passions, or the breach of moralities, but it lies here—"thou hast left Me, the fountain of living water."

— Alexander MacLaren

This does not mean that God lacked knowledge of these people. Clearly in the passage above Jesus demonstrates that He knew that they practiced lawlessness, in spite of all their religious duties. The point is that Jesus did not know them as "His own." He did not know them in a relational manner. They were not His people.

On the other hand, we find God telling people that He *did* know them, and only them, of all the people on earth. This is repeatedly said to Israel, as in the Amos passage below.

COPY ▶ AMOS 3:2.

_____

_____

_____

And here in Amos we have a very important truth. Along with the privilege of being brought into a relationship with God comes greater accountability. If the Christian lives like those who were never known by God as His people, like those who have never been brought into a relationship with Him by Jesus Christ, then that Christian risks entering into the discipline of God. When the all-knowing God has used His perfect knowledge of your sin and helplessness to provide a Savior whose labors are guaranteed to rescue you; when this God has acted in such a way that you can be sure He will never remember your crimes against you; when this God has provided so fully for you that you can ask Him to remember His covenant and His mercies promised to you; when this God sets you apart from the whole world . . . to be known by God in this way, and yet to live as if it were a small matter, is a grievous sin. Christian, do not forget how amazing grace is.

DAY 4: THE GOD WHO ALONE IS WISE

No pretended god knows aught of us; but the true God, Jehovah, understands us, and is most intimately acquainted with our persons, nature, and character. How well it is for us to know the God who knows us!

— C. H. Spurgeon

We want to look at another aspect of God's character which has always produced hope in the lives of the believer—God's wisdom.

This attribute of God sustains His people even in the worst of circumstances. Consider how the contemplation of God's wisdom fills Daniel with praise for God even when living in a Babylonian exile.

> Daniel 2:20-22
> *Daniel said, "Let the name of God be blessed forever and ever,*
> *For wisdom and power belong to Him.*

It is He who changes the times and the epochs;
He removes kings and establishes kings;
He gives wisdom to wise men
And knowledge to men of understanding.
It is He who reveals the profound and hidden things;
He knows what is in the darkness,
And the light dwells with Him."

When writing to those about to enter into the Roman persecution under emperor Nero, Paul notes God's unique wisdom as a distinguishing mark of His character that calls for praise.

FILL IN THE BLANKS from the following passages.

Romans 16:25-27
Now to Him who is able to establish you according to my gospel and the preaching of Jesus Christ, according to the revelation of the mystery which has been kept secret for long ages past, but now is manifested, and by the Scriptures of the prophets, according to the commandment of the eternal God, has been made known to all the nations, leading to obedience of faith; _____
_____, through Jesus Christ, be the glory forever.

The victorious Lamb of God is attributed with all power and wisdom in the praises of heaven.

Revelation 5:12
. . . Worthy is the Lamb that was slain to receive power and riches and _____ and might and honor and glory and blessing.

Revelation 7:12
Saying, "Amen, blessing and glory and _____ and thanksgiving and honor and power and might, be to our God forever and ever. Amen."

We want to understand God's wisdom better and get a clearer view of how this is part of the weight of His majesty.

DEFINING GOD'S WISDOM

To search for wisdom apart from Christ means not simply foolhardiness but utter insanity.

— John Calvin

Knowledge is the foundation of wisdom, but they are distinct qualities. J.I. Packer defines wisdom as "the ability to see and choose the best and highest goal, along with the surest means of attaining it." [31]

Let's take that as our working definition and elaborate upon it.

Wisdom is:

- The ability to take knowledge and use it for the *best goal*.

- The ability to take knowledge and choose the *best means* for reaching the goal.

- The ability to take knowledge, having chosen the right goal and the right means for achieving this goal, and to do it in a morally *right way*.

So, a foolish person is one who:

- Uses his knowledge to set his heart upon an *unworthy goal*.

- Chooses an *inappropriate means* for reaching that goal.

- Goes about pursuing that goal in a morally *wrong way*.

The man who takes all he knows and devotes it to a goal that is unworthy of his life, utilizing means that are not fit for reaching that goal, and doing it in a way that cuts moral corners—that is a man that Scripture refuses to call wise.

The Hebrew word behind our English word "wisdom" was originally used to describe the skill of a craftsman or an artist. Later, this word came to describe a person who conducts his or her life with discretion and governs desires carefully, so as to live skillfully. Thus, wisdom became the skillful ordering of life based on right understanding.

Because God has shared wisdom with His creation, we have some experience of what it looks like in a human life. We all know people who we consider wise or foolish. However, when we turn our eyes upon the all-wise God, we have embarked on a study that is unique. God's wisdom is in a separate category.

GOD IS ESSENTIALLY, NECESSARILY WISE

God's wisdom is part of who He is. He did not gain it by observation or experience. He did not receive it through the help of another. He would cease to be God if He ceased to possess infinite wisdom.

God's wisdom is self-existing. It comes from within His uncreated perfection. What books would God study to gain wisdom? Who would He observe? Whose quotes would He memorize? If He took a test to determine how wise He was, who would be qualified to create such a test, and who would grade it? The source of His wisdom is His own deity.

GOD IS COMPREHENSIVELY WISE

God's wisdom is perfect, touching every area of His life and activity with equal fullness. We might say that His wisdom is universal. With the wisest people we often see that they are very skilled in one area, but completely helpless in another. A genius in mathematics or science might be hopeless at repairing his car. But God's wisdom affects every area of His person and work. He knows how to create a solar system, sustain all life on planet earth, raise a troubled child, convince an atheist, rescue a hypocrite, and build a genuine church. There isn't any area in which He is lacking wisdom, or skill.

God's wisdom does not merely touch every area of His life and activity; it is united to every other attribute. Every one of God's attributes is enriched with an unlimited wisdom. Each time they are exercised, they are done so with perfect skill.

GOD IS IMMUTABLY AND PERPETUALLY WISE

People can grow wiser as they grow older. We expect to grow wiser and hope that others would as well. We attempt to train our children to be wise. But we realize that no matter how wise a person becomes, a time will come when he will begin to lose his skill in the very areas in which they once were so notably effective. Time alters the wisdom of created beings.

God alone possesses an unchanging skill to make the best use of knowledge. He was not better at being God in the book of Exodus than He was when Lamentations was penned. He is not a wiser God in the New Testament than in the Old. His wisdom is ancient and cutting edge at the same time. He is as capable of making the best use of knowledge today as He was when He created all things by merely speaking them into existence and fashioning them according to His desire. His wisdom is beyond the reach of change. It has never been altered for the better or the worse. It is immutable.

Whatsoever God is he is infinitely so. He is infinite wisdom, infinite goodness, infinite knowledge, infinite power, infinite Spirit; infinitely distant from the weaknesses of creatures, infinitely mounted above the excellencies of creatures: as easy to be known that he is, as impossible to comprehend what he is.

—J. C. Ryle

GOD'S WISDOM IS INFINITE AND THEREFORE INCOMPREHENSIBLE

Every perfection of God shares in His infinity. This means that God's wisdom is not capable of being measured or limited. If His wisdom is infinite, then it is also incomprehensible to all but Himself. We can study the biblical testimony about God's wisdom, but we will never fully grasp its vastness, its depth and breadth, length or height. The term "philosopher" means "one who loves wisdom." Every Christian ought to be a type of philosopher: one who delights to watch the wisdom of God as we view it in His works.

No wonder Paul exclaims at the end of eleven chapters of theology:

> *Oh, the depth of the riches both of the wisdom and knowledge of God! How unsearchable are His judgments and unfathomable His ways!* (Romans 11:33)

DAY 5: LIVING ON THESE TRUTHS

You have had an opportunity this week to be reintroduced to the one person who has unlimited knowledge and wisdom. While these are facts commonly professed and agreed upon, they are not always applied. To leave these unapplied will not only give the world a distorted portrait of our God's majesty, it will also rob the believer of that glorious privilege of living unto the God who knows all things and has the skill to apply all He knows for good.

I pity all the wordlings' talk
Of pleasures that will
quickly end:
Be this my choice, O Lord,
to walk
With Thee my Guide, my
Guard, my Friend.

— Thomas Goodwin

Today, as in Weeks 2 and 5, you will be using the metaphors taken from Colossians 2:6-7 to help you find practical ways to apply this aspect of God's majesty in your life, your workplace, your home, and your church.

In the passage below, the five word pictures are in bold print:

> *Therefore as you have received Christ Jesus the Lord, so **walk** in Him, having been firmly **rooted** and now being **built up** in Him and **established** in your faith, just as you were instructed, and **overflowing with gratitude**.* (Colossians 2:6-7)

Let's consider how the truths we have studied this week can be lived upon by using these five pictures. [Please note that your answers to today's questions may overlap to some degree.]

HAVING RECEIVED CHRIST JESUS THE LORD . . .

1. Walk in Him

The word "walk" shows us two things about Christian living.

First, walking is an everyday activity that does not seem significant. We take thousands of steps in a day, and very few steps would be looked back upon as particularly noteworthy, much less spiritually meaningful. Our little, common choices each day may also seem insignificant, but like our steps, they do matter—because they add up to be the stuff of life. For this reason, truths about God must affect our common choices in everyday life.

Second, when a person in the ancient world walked, he or she almost certainly had a destination in mind. Today people often walk for exercise, and in that case the destination isn't important. You may walk on a treadmill or in circles around a track. That is not what Paul has in mind when he says "walk." Christians should be walking toward a definite destination: complete conformity to Christ's character. The little choices of each day, guided by the truths you are studying, should be aiming at that destination—Christlikeness. But why? Not for self-improvement, but for the pleasure and honor of our God.

With these in mind, go back and review this week's lessons. Below, write some of the ways in which you can apply these truths in everyday, apparently insignificant ways that lead to the destination of Christlikeness.

_____

_____

_____

_____

_____

2. Sink Your Roots in Him

Paul says that God has rooted every believer in Christ. Following Christ means daily sinking the roots of your life into the truths of God. Roots gain nutrients from the soil. Your soul may find temporary satisfaction in the junk food of our culture, or it will find lasting satisfaction in the feast of the immutable realities of God.

When you gaze upon the sun—it makes everything else dark; when you taste honey—it makes everything else tasteless. Likewise, when your soul feeds on Jesus—it takes away the sweetness of all earthly things; praise, pleasure, fleshly lusts, all lose their sweetness. Keep a continued gaze! Run, looking unto Jesus. So will the world be crucified to you—and you unto the world!

— Robert Murray M'Cheyne

133

Go back and review this week's lessons. Below, write some of the truths that you feel are the most nourishing food for your soul. What must you feed upon if you are to live out the Christian life? Is there "junk food" that you should put away?

_____

_____

_____

_____

_____

_____

3.   **Build a Life on These Truths**

Each truth you learn in this study can be seen as a brick. Combined with other truths, each brick will be an essential part of building a life with Christ as the foundation. Coming to Jesus in repentance and faith is the only place to begin, but good beginnings are not all there is to Christianity. Paul knew that the Colossian Christians needed more than a foundation built on Christ; they also needed a life built by His grace with His biblical truths. To leave the truths you are studying piled like bricks in a corner of your life would be a grave mistake. You don't want to look back after twelve weeks and see a dusty pile of bricks! You need a life that is a true dwelling place for God Himself.

Review this week's lessons and ask yourself, "In what ways can I build my life (my marriage, my family, my friendships, or my work) on the realities of the all-knowing and all-wise God?"

_____

_____

_____

_____

_____

4. **Become Established in Your Faith**

Paul used a word, translated in the NASB as "established," which conveys the idea of firming something up, making something stable, solid. In spiritual life, we might use the word *maturity*. You must grow to maturity in your faith (your grasp of the great realities of God), in part, so that you will not be easily swayed by false teaching or half-truths.

CONSIDER ▶ HEBREWS 5:12-14.

> *For though by this time you ought to be teachers, you have need again for someone to teach you the elementary principles of the oracles of God, and you have come to need milk and not solid food. For everyone who partakes only of milk is not accustomed to the word of righteousness, for he is an infant. But solid food is for the mature, who because of practice have their senses trained to discern good and evil.*

Here the writer is speaking to people who have heard the truth many times but have remained immature in their faith. He tells us that maturity comes from a life that applies and practices what it is learning. Through application, you are established, or matured, in the great realities of God.

Review this week's lessons. Below write some areas that the knowledge and wisdom of God need to be applied to your faith so you will be established, solid, unwavering in your grasp of biblical truth.

There is no knowing that does not begin with knowing God.

—John Calvin

_____

_____

_____

_____

_____

With these four pictures as guides, we never want to settle for new Bible-truths which are undigested, unapplied, unsettled, and sitting like a wasted pile of bricks.

There is one more picture we need to employ. Without this final metaphor our Christianity will not reflect God.

5. Do All of These with an Overflow of Gratitude to God

You can attempt to apply 1-4, but without a grateful heart, how can you honor God?

In the Old Testament Moses warned the people before they entered the Promised Land:

> *Because you did not serve the LORD your God with joy and a glad heart, for the abundance of all things; therefore you shall serve your enemies whom the LORD will send against you, in hunger, in thirst, in nakedness, and in the lack of all things; and He will put an iron yoke on your neck until He has destroyed you.* (Deuteronomy 28:47-48)

Surely that is a shocking word for us as well. If we go about our Christian lives, trying to walk, sink roots in, build upon, and be established in these truths, but we do so with ungrateful hearts, we can expect divine discipline.

Review this week's lessons. What reasons for gratitude toward God arise from the study of His knowledge and wisdom?

_____

_____

_____

_____

_____

_____

There is no such thing as genuine knowledge of God that does not show itself in obedience to His Word and will.

— Sinclair B. Ferguson

May the God who possesses infinite knowledge and wisdom give you such a sight of these perfections that you can:

* walk (go about the normal things of life) in its atmosphere . . .

* sink roots for nourishment in it . . .

* build a life with it . . .

* grow firm and be established in your grasp of God's truth because of it . . .

* do all of this with an overflowing sense of gratitude to Him.

Behold your God

— Week 7 —

KNOWING THE GOD WHO RULES ALL

DAY 1: THE DOMINION, AUTHORITY, AND SOVEREIGNTY OF OUR GOD

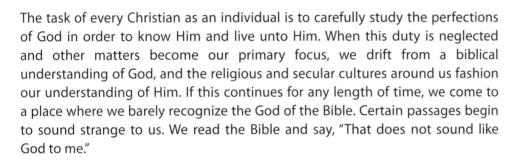

The task of every Christian as an individual is to carefully study the perfections of God in order to know Him and live unto Him. When this duty is neglected and other matters become our primary focus, we drift from a biblical understanding of God, and the religious and secular cultures around us fashion our understanding of Him. If this continues for any length of time, we come to a place where we barely recognize the God of the Bible. Certain passages begin to sound strange to us. We read the Bible and say, "That does not sound like God to me."

Nowhere is this more obvious than in the doctrine of God's sovereignty. We have wandered from a careful explanation of God's authority, settling for vague ideas that God is the boss of the universe. To make matters worse, most of us have grown up in a culture that reinforces the idea that no one has the right to rule over anyone else with an absolute and undisputed authority. Therefore, meeting a true king who has absolute authority over every aspect of our existence comes as quite a shock. It often appears that preachers are busy attempting to reinterpret certain passages to protect their people from just such an encounter, reducing God to a more manageable, cosmic elected official.

This week you will have an opportunity to return to the Bible and listen to its clear witness regarding the highest of kings, and His supreme rule over all He has made.

GOD, THE GREAT KING

In Malachi's day the drift was obvious. People continued to be involved with the temple and the worship of God, but their views of Him were inadequate. God intervenes in this situation, and of the many things He says to His people through His prophet the simplest and most significant is found in chapter 1.

> "... I am a great King," says the LORD of hosts, "and My name is feared among the nations." (Malachi 1:14)

The "god" of this generation is a helpless . . . being who commands the respect of no really thoughtful man. He no more resembles the Supreme Sovereign of Holy Writ, than does the dim flickering of a candle, the glory of the midday sun!

— A. W. Pink

We understand a little about kings, rulers, and authorities. We may have had good experiences with those who have authority over us, or we may have had bad experiences. But good or bad, we know something about authority. Yet we have never met any boss, master, ruler, or king like the one who is speaking to us through Malachi. Let's slow down now and take a serious look at the unique type of sovereignty that God alone possesses and exercises.

WHAT IS IT TO BE SOVEREIGN?

We need to be careful to distinguish between omnipotence and sovereignty. Omnipotence refers to God being unlimited in His actions because of His ability. Sovereignty refers to God being unlimited in His actions because of His moral right.

We will take the following as a working definition for God's rule, dominion, or sovereignty: God possesses and continually exercises the sole right to do all His pleasure with all His creation, without explanation or successful interference.

Now, upon what do we build such a statement?

1.　God's rule is unique because sovereignty is essential to His person.

Sovereignty is a part of God's perfect character. Only He is essentially authoritative. Only He is essentially royal. He cannot set this aside any more than He could His infinity, eternity, knowledge, or wisdom. He did not earn this right to rule as others have. It is based in who and what He is as the I AM. God was sovereign in Himself, even before He created anything to exercise this rule over.

2.　God's sovereignty is unique because it is self-existing and independent.

As He does not owe His existence to the activity of anyone else, so He does not receive His right to rule from anyone else. Earthly rulers owe their position to their armies or supporters or royal lineage. God establishes His rule over all without any aid. All other authorities have received their right to rule only by His permission. Theirs is a borrowed and limited sovereignty.

COPY PSALM 103:19.

The Lord has established His kingdom in the heavens & His kingdom rules over all.

1 Timothy 6:15-16

. . . He who is the blessed and only Sovereign, the King of kings and Lord of lords, who alone possesses immortality and dwells in unapproachable light, whom no man has seen or can see. To Him be honor and eternal dominion! Amen.

3. God's sovereignty is unique because it is eternal and enduring.

God's sovereignty is eternal, timeless, enduring. His rule never had a beginning; it will never have an end. Unlike all other kings, He had no predecessor, nor will He have any successors.

Consider what Daniel says of God's kingdom (seen here entrusted to the Messiah):

I kept looking in the night visions,
And behold, with the clouds of heaven
One like a Son of Man was coming,
And He came up to the Ancient of Days
And was presented before Him.
And to Him was given dominion,
Glory and a kingdom,
That all the peoples, nations and men of every language
Might serve Him.
His dominion is an everlasting dominion
Which will not pass away;
And His kingdom is one
Which will not be destroyed. (Daniel 7:13-14)

The prophet Isaiah speaks of the fragility of human rulers:

He it is who reduces rulers to nothing,
Who makes the judges of the earth meaningless.
Scarcely have they been planted,
Scarcely have they been sown,
Scarcely has their stock taken root in the earth,
But He merely blows on them, and they wither,
And the storm carries them away like stubble.
"To whom then will you liken Me
That I would be his equal?" says the Holy One. (Isaiah 40:23-25)

Thy names, how infinite
they be!
Great Everlasting One!
Boundless thy might and
majesty,
And unconfined thy throne . . . .

In vain our haughty reason
swells,
For nothing's found in thee
But boundless inconceivables,
And vast eternity.

— Isaac Watts

139

According to the psalmist, God's rule is different:

The LORD reigns, He is clothed with majesty;
The LORD has clothed and girded Himself with strength;
Indeed, the world is firmly established, it will not be moved.
Your throne is established from of old;
You are from everlasting. (Psalm 93:1-2)

GOD IS THE BEST OF KINGS

God was under no constraint, no obligation, no necessity to create. That He chose to do so was purely a sovereign act on His part, caused by nothing outside Himself, determined by nothing but His own mere good pleasure.

— A. W. Pink

We have seen that God's authority is based in who He is, not in anything He did to earn the right to rule. Even so, it might help us to consider a number of things about God which make Him, not us, the best choice for king.

1. God is the best of kings, having created all that He presently rules.

   Psalm 24:1-2
   The earth is the LORD's, and all it contains,
   The world, and those who dwell in it.
   For He has founded it upon the seas
   And established it upon the rivers.

   COPY COLOSSIANS 1:16.

   _____

   _____

   _____

   _____

   _____

He did not make creation out of basic materials which He received from someone else. All that God rules, God made. In the beginning He made all things from nothing. He called matter into existence and fashioned it in His perfect wisdom. No one else's lands, people, or resources were used to create His kingdom.

2. God is the best of kings, sustaining all He rules.

One might argue that if any aspect of creation were self-supporting, it could put forward a case for self-rule. Yet nothing is self-sustaining. God has not only created all things, He also continues to exert all the power required to sustain them. All that He rules is dependent upon Him for life.

COPY COLOSSIANS 1:17.

_____

_____

3. God is the best of kings, and the vastness of His realm includes all places and persons.

Simply consider *where* He rules:

He rules over all the universe. He rules over every galaxy in every corner of the universe effortlessly. God has no trouble ruling over our galaxy, the Milky Way, which is not particularly large as galaxies go. Our solar system is like many others, and God does not find it difficult to rule over it. Our planet is a speck of dust in this galaxy. Do we think God has any problem ruling over all that occurs on it? Now, consider how small your workplace is, your church, your home. When we speak of a God who is infinitely large, ruling over all places is not hard for Him.

Or, consider *over whom* He rules:

He rules over the angels, both holy and fallen. He rules over the great and the small people on this planet. He rules over every ethnic group and race. He rules over every empire, nation, and small village. He rules over young and old. He rules over Christians, Jews, Muslims, Hindus, Mormons, pagans, and atheists. Every person we have ever read about or met, rich or poor, great or small, is the proper subject of this one king.

4. God is the best of kings, being the reason for all things and persons.

No matter how strange it might sound to our ears, we do not exist for ourselves. Our pleasures, plans, pursuits—none of these is the reason for our being made and sustained. We exist for someone other than ourselves. We exist for someone whose worth is greater than ours, greater than all of humanity's. The purpose of our life is God.

If there be a God, a "King, eternal, immortal, and invisible," he cannot but be sovereign, and he cannot but do according to his own will, and choose according to his own purpose. You may dislike these doctrines, but you can only get quit of them by denying altogether the existence of an infinitely wise, glorious, and powerful Being. God would not be God were he not thus absolutely sovereign, in his present doings and his eternal pre-arrangements.

— Horatius Bonar

Listen again to the apostle Paul.

> Colossians 1:16
> *For by Him all things were created, both in the heavens and on earth, visible and invisible, whether thrones or dominions or rulers or authorities—all things have been created through Him and for Him.*

> Romans 11:36
> *For from Him and through Him and to Him are all things. To Him be the glory forever. Amen.*

5. God is the best of kings, possessing every perfection desirable in a ruler.

Just because a person has the ability to rule does not mean he has the right. Just because a person has the right to rule does not mean that he has the ability. In God, all the perfections of greatness and goodness are combined. In light of what you have read above, and in light of God's perfections you have been studying in these past weeks, it is clear that there is one and only one person who has the right to do all He desires with all His creation.

DAY 2: THE FREEDOM OF THE SOVEREIGN GOD, PART 1

Nebuchadnezzar was about to carry the Jews away from the land which flowed with milk and honey to his own far distant country; but the prophet consoled himself with the reflection that, whatever Nebuchadnezzar meant to do, he was only the instrument in the hands of God for the accomplishment of the divine purpose. He proposed, but God disposed.

— C. H. Spurgeon

We saw yesterday that God alone has both the power and the right to do all He desires with all He has created. These attributes are unique to God. All other monarchs and governors rule by the good pleasure of the only king whose authority is based in who He is.

One aspect of God's absolute authority is freedom. He is free to act as He sees best. When Christians come to grips with this reality, they are comforted by remembering that God is morally perfect, not merely immensely big! When we know this king, we are glad He is the only one who is free to do all His perfect will. This quality of freedom is demonstrated in God's interaction with an ancient king, Nebuchadnezzar.

Before you look at the passage in Daniel, let's consider some background.

Babylon, the kingdom over which Nebuchadnezzar ruled, was enjoying extraordinary glory. Having conquered the Assyrians and the Egyptians, Nebuchadnezzar led his armies to take Judah. This was exactly what God had foretold through the prophets. The Babylonians looted the palace and temple in Jerusalem and relocated the majority of the Jews in lands within the empire. Thus began the Babylonian exile that God brought against His own people to discipline them for generations of idolatry and hypocrisy.

The capital city, Babylon, was rebuilt by Nebuchadnezzar. He built a highway system to make it the center of commerce. It was surrounded by defensive walls of astonishing proportions, eighty-five feet thick and encircling an area of 200 square miles! The bricks that made up the great wall were covered in bright enamel and each one was inscribed with the statement, "I am Nebuchadnezzar, King of Babylon." He had a man-made mountain built in the city and covered with exotic vegetation from every corner of the empire. These gardens, rising high above the other buildings and watered by a type of reservoir system, appeared to be suspended in the air. The Hanging Gardens of Babylon became one of the wonders of the ancient world.

And yet, in spite of all its grandeur, thirty short years after the death of Nebuchadnezzar, the Babylonian empire fell to the Persian armies.

More importantly for our study is the fact that Nebuchadnezzar was the recipient of extraordinary encounters with the living God. God had judged His people and delivered them into Babylon, but He would still exalt His name. He raised a witness through the lives of Daniel and his three faithful friends. He also used Nebuchadnezzar, a proud pagan emperor.

READy the responses of this king as he witnessed the activity of the true God.

Daniel 2:46-47
Then King Nebuchadnezzar fell on his face and did homage to Daniel, and gave orders to present to him an offering and fragrant incense. The king answered Daniel and said, "Surely your God is a God of gods and a Lord of kings and a revealer of mysteries, since you have been able to reveal this mystery."

Daniel 3:26-30
Then Nebuchadnezzar came near to the door of the furnace of blazing fire; he responded and said, "Shadrach, Meshach and Abednego, come out, you servants of the Most High God, and come here!" Then Shadrach, Meshach and Abednego came out of the midst of the fire. The satraps, the prefects, the governors and the king's high officials gathered around and saw in regard to these men that the fire had no effect on the bodies of these men nor was the hair of their head singed, nor were their trousers damaged, nor had the smell of fire even come upon them. Nebuchadnezzar responded and said, "Blessed be the God of Shadrach,

Meshach and Abednego, who has sent His angel and delivered His servants who put their trust in Him, violating the king's command, and yielded up their bodies so as not to serve or worship any god except their own God. Therefore I make a decree that any people, nation or tongue that speaks anything offensive against the God of Shadrach, Meshach and Abednego shall be torn limb from limb and their houses reduced to a rubbish heap, inasmuch as there is no other god who is able to deliver in this way." Then the king caused Shadrach, Meshach and Abednego to prosper in the province of Babylon.

Nebuchadnezzar has one more encounter with God, one in which he will find himself laid low before the true king of kings. How this happens, and what Nebuchadnezzar says about our God after this encounter, are of real significance for our study.

The king has a dream in which he is warned that his pride will be brought down by God if he will not humble himself. Daniel explains the symbolism of this dream.

READD DANIEL 4:1-27 for the king's own account of this encounter.

He does all according to His own counsel and pleasure, in the armies of heaven, and among the inhabitants of the earth.

—John Newton

Proud Nebuchadnezzar ignores the warning, and the outcome is that God strikes him with insanity for seven years, during which time he is hidden away from the public eye.

READ DANIEL 4:28-33.

The wonderful part of this account is what Nebuchadnezzar says about our God at the end of the seven years.

READ DANIEL 4:34-37 below, and write Nebuchadnezzar's descriptions of the Sovereign God.

But at the end of that period, I, Nebuchadnezzar, raised my eyes toward heaven and my reason returned to me, and I blessed the Most High and praised and honored Him who lives forever;
For His dominion is an everlasting dominion,
And His kingdom endures from generation to generation.
All the inhabitants of the earth are accounted as nothing,
But He does according to His will in the host of heaven
And among the inhabitants of earth;
And no one can ward off His hand
Or say to Him, "What have You done?"

At that time my reason returned to me. And my majesty and splendor were restored to me for the glory of my kingdom, and my counselors and my nobles began seeking me out; so I was reestablished in my sovereignty, and surpassing greatness was added to me. Now I, Nebuchadnezzar, praise, exalt and honor the King of heaven, for all His works are true and His ways just, and He is able to humble those who walk in pride.

_____

_____

_____

_____

Surely it cannot escape our notice that this pagan king has clearer views of the sovereign rights of God to do as He wishes with all He has created than many who claim to believe the Bible. When was the last time you heard such an accurate description of God's rights from a church pulpit? Many sermons are taken up apologizing for God's lack of control over contemporary worldwide events.

There are two very clear applications for us today:

1. God is able to put down the proud of earth, whether a great monarch or a common worker.

The safest course is to recognize that there is only one who possesses the rights of a true king, and to humble yourself before His throne. We are all accounted as nothing before the Most High. We cannot ward off His hand, and we have no right to complain about His choices. All His ways are right, and He is able to humble the proud.

Consider how God's questions for Job demonstrate that God alone can humble the proud:

> *. . . do you have an arm like God,*
> *And can you thunder with a voice like His?*
> *Adorn yourself with eminence and dignity,*
> *And clothe yourself with honor and majesty.*
> *Pour out the overflowings of your anger,*
> *And look on everyone who is proud, and make him low.*

The great controversy between God and man has been, whether He or they shall be God; whether His reason or theirs, His will or theirs, shall be the guiding principle. If anything could frustrate God's will — then it would be superior to Him, God would not be omnipotent, and so would lose the perfection of the Deity, and consequently the Deity itself; for that which did wholly defeat God's will, would be more powerful than He. To be God and yet inferior to another, is a contradiction!

— Stephen Charnock

145

Look on everyone who is proud, and humble him,
And tread down the wicked where they stand.
Hide them in the dust together;
Bind them in the hidden place.
Then I will also confess to you,
That your own right hand can save you. (Job 40:9-14)

2.   Here is a right diagnosis of true insanity.

Think carefully: when was Nebuchadnezzar's insanity at its height? Was it when he thought he was an animal? Or was it when he thought he was like a god and the reason for Babylon's greatness? As shocking as it may seem to us to see an emperor running around the royal gardens and living like an animal for seven years, it ought to shock us more to see any human strutting around as if he were the ruler of his own life.

If one type of insanity is described as a person thinking he is someone he is not, then sin is insanity because sin is pretending we are little kings, self-ruled people in our own little kingdoms. We claim our rights at the workplace and in the home. We demand that others treat us with the honor we feel we deserve, even if we would not expect them to call us "your majesty." It is built into every human. And it is not removed until we meet the king of kings. That meeting might come through God's working in the heart and the preaching of the gospel, or else it will certainly come at the judgment.

DAY 3: THE FREEDOM OF THE SOVEREIGN GOD, PART 2

We can hold a correct view of truth only by daring to believe everything God has said about Himself. It is a grave responsibility that a man takes upon himself when he seeks to edit out of God's self-revelation such features as he in his ignorance deems objectionable.

— A. W. Tozer

As we saw yesterday, Nebuchadnezzar had to learn the hard lesson that God is not merely higher than he is; God is the Most High. As the Most High, the living God has the right to do all His good pleasure, and no one can restrain Him. And yet His works are true, and His ways are always just.

Because we do not find it easy to submit ourselves to someone else's complete authority over us, and we do not like to admit that any being, even God, has the freedom to do all He wishes with us and ours, it would be good to consider other passages of Scripture that speak clearly on this topic.

We must remind ourselves that God is wholly different from us. He is not merely a very big version of a human; He is the only one like Him. His rule, likewise, is not just a larger version of the kind of authority we see in our governments and nations. It is fundamentally different. There is no other rule that is exactly like His.

No earthly monarch, regardless of how absolute his authority may appear, has the right to do all his pleasure with all his subjects, but God does. Martin Luther's complaint against Erasmus in the sixteenth century is one we must guard against: "Your thoughts of God are too human."

We must also remind ourselves that God is not ruled by a higher moral law. God does not do right because there is a higher law of right and wrong that dictates to Him. The moral law of right and wrong is an expression of His perfectly righteous character. He is the foundation of all such law. He does right as a king with absolute authority and freedom, not because of a higher law but because of who He is: the Holy One who is at the same time the Most High God.

READ DANIEL 5:18-19 below.

> *O king, the Most High God granted sovereignty, grandeur, glory and majesty to Nebuchadnezzar your father. Because of the grandeur which He bestowed on him, all the peoples, nations and men of every language feared and trembled before him; whomever he wished he killed and whomever he wished he spared alive; and whomever he wished he elevated and whomever he wished he humbled.*

Nebuchadnezzar was a great king. He was the ruler over many nations, adding many smaller nations to his dominion as the Babylonian empire expanded. He possessed an earthly grandeur that few have attained. He was feared by all surrounding nations. He appeared to effortlessly decide the fate of lesser men—killing or sparing them as he wished, exalting or humiliating them according to his own desires. He appeared to have the freedom of an absolute monarch; but Daniel explains that in reality all of this was given to Nebuchadnezzar by the Lord. Only God possesses the freedom to do all He wishes.

CONSIDER the following truths regarding the freedom of God and fill in the blanks from the corresponding passages.

1. God is free to do all His pleasure without interference.

    Job 42:1-2
    Then Job answered the LORD and said,
    "I know that You can do all things,
    And that _____."

2. Unlike false gods, the Most High is a great king who is free to do all His pleasure.

Psalm 115:2-7
Why should the nations say,
"Where, now, is their God?"
But our God is in the heavens;
He _____.
Their idols are silver and gold,
The work of man's hands.
They have mouths, but they cannot speak;
They have eyes, but they cannot see;
They have ears, but they cannot hear;
They have noses, but they cannot smell;
They have hands, but they cannot feel;
They have feet, but they cannot walk;
They cannot make a sound with their throat.

Psalm 135:5-6
For I know that the LORD is great
And that our Lord is above all gods.

_____.

In heaven and in earth, in the seas and in all deeps.

> *Since He is the only God, the Creator of heaven and earth, He cannot endure that any creature of His own hands, or fiction of a creature's imagination should be thrust into His throne, and be made to wear His crown.*
>
> — C. H. Spurgeon

In these passages God is contrasted with man's highest conceptions of deity— idols. We find that no idol has the ability or right to do as it pleases.

3. God is free to take away anything He has given.

Job 9:12
"Were He to snatch away, who could restrain Him? Who could say to Him, '_____?'"

Job, given much, lost nearly everything. It is clear in the book of Job that this was allowed by God. Job's response is remarkable:

Now on the day when his sons and his daughters were eating and drinking wine in their oldest brother's house, a messenger came to Job and said, "The oxen were plowing and the donkeys feeding beside them, and the Sabeans attacked and took them. They also slew the servants with the edge of the sword, and I alone have escaped to tell you." While he was still speaking, another also came and said, "The fire of God fell from heaven and burned up the sheep and the servants and consumed them, and I alone have escaped to tell you." While he was still speaking, another also came and said, "The Chaldeans formed three bands and made a raid on the camels and took them and slew the servants with the edge of the sword, and I alone have escaped to tell you." While he was still speaking, another also came and said, "Your sons and your daughters were eating and drinking wine in their oldest brother's house, and behold, a great wind came from across the wilderness and struck the four corners of the house, and it fell on the young people and they died, and I alone have escaped to tell you." Then Job arose and tore his robe and shaved his head, and he fell to the ground and worshiped. He said,

"Naked I came from my mother's womb,
And naked I shall return there.
The LORD gave and the LORD has taken away.
Blessed be the name of the LORD." (Job 1:13-21)

4. God is free to choose when and toward whom He will exercise His vengeance.

    Isaiah 14:24-27
    The LORD of hosts has sworn saying, "Surely, just as I have intended so it has happened, and just as I have planned so it will stand, to break Assyria in My land, and I will trample him on My mountains. Then his yoke will be removed from them and his burden removed from their shoulder. This is the plan devised against the whole earth; and this is the hand that is stretched out against all the nations. _____

    _____
    _____
    _____*? And as for His stretched-out hand, who can turn it back?"*

God had long planned the downfall of the Assyrians. He alone has the right to cast down nations, as well as to raise them up.

5. God is free to raise up great men and nations.

God has the right to raise up Cyrus, an ungodly king, to bring about the rescue of the Jews from Babylon.

> Isaiah 45:5-7
> *I am the LORD, and there is no other;*
> *Besides Me there is no God.*
> *I will gird you, though you have not known Me;*
> *That men may know from the rising to the setting of the sun*
> *That there is no one besides Me.*
> *I am the LORD, and there is no other,*
> *The One forming light and creating darkness,*
>
> _____;
>
> *I am the LORD who does all these.*

God mentions His right to cast down or raise up nations in the prophecy of Jeremiah.

> Jeremiah 18:5-11
> *Then the word of the LORD came to me saying, "Can I not, O house of Israel, deal with you as this potter does?" declares the LORD. "Behold, like the clay in the potter's hand, so are you in My hand, O house of Israel. At one moment I might speak concerning a nation or concerning a kingdom to uproot, to pull down, or to destroy it; if that nation against which I have spoken turns from its evil, I will relent concerning the calamity I planned to bring on it. Or at another moment I might speak concerning a nation or concerning a kingdom to build up or to plant it; if it does evil in My sight by not obeying My voice, then I will think better of the good with which I had promised to bless it. So now then, speak to the men of Judah and against the inhabitants of Jerusalem saying, 'Thus says the LORD, "Behold, I am fashioning calamity against you and devising a plan against you. Oh turn back, each of you from his evil way, and reform your ways and your deeds."'"*

6. God is free to show mercy to whom He wishes.

In Paul's explanation of God's dealing with Israel, he reminds them of God's freedom.

> *Of all doctrines of the Bible none is so offensive to human nature as the doctrine of God's sovereignty. To be told that God is great, and just, and holy, and pure, man can bear. But to be told that "he hath mercy on whom he will have mercy," that he "giveth no account of his matters," – that it is "not of him that willeth, nor of him that runneth, but of God that showeth mercy," – these are truths that natural man cannot stand. They often call forth all his enmity against God, and fill him with wrath. Nothing, in short, will make him submit to them but the humbling teaching of the Holy Ghost.*
>
> —J. C. Ryle

Romans 9:13-15

Just as it is written, "Jacob I loved, but Esau I hated." What shall we say then? There is no injustice with God, is there? May it never be! For He says to Moses, "_____

_____

_____

_____. "

Wherever we look in Scripture, God is not only the Most High King, He also demonstrates that He acts with a perfect freedom, doing all that His holy person desires.

The author A. W. Pink summarizes these verses wonderfully:

Being infinitely elevated above the highest creature, He is the Most High, Lord of heaven and earth. Subject to none, influenced by none, absolutely independent; God does as He pleases, only as He pleases, always as He pleases. None can thwart Him; none can hinder Him . . . . God is unrivaled in majesty, unlimited in power, unaffected by anything outside himself. [32]

What thoughts do you have of God that are "too human"?

_____

_____

_____

_____

Which truth about God's sovereignty that you studied today was most helpful in elevating your thoughts of Him?

_____

_____

_____

_____

DAY 4: THE TERRORS AND HOPES CONNECTED TO OUR RESPONSE TO GOD'S SOVEREIGNTY

The Psalms often mention the rule of God. There are a great variety of responses that are appropriate when one realizes that someone who is eternal, self-existing, infinite, and all-wise is boss. Below are two very different, yet linked responses.

The LORD was my ALL; and that he overruled all, greatly delighted me.

— David Brainerd

Psalm 97:1
The LORD reigns, let the earth rejoice;
Let the many islands be glad.

Psalm 99:1
The LORD reigns, let the peoples tremble;
He is enthroned above the cherubim, let the earth shake!

Today you will be considering both realities: the terrors of rejecting the Most High, and the joy of submitting to His rule.

THE TERRORS OF REJECTING THE MOST HIGH KING

The psalmist in Psalm 99:1 calls for all people, in fact for the earth itself, to tremble and shake before the rule of this God. All of God's creation should possess a healthy fear, an awe-filled sense of living before the face of someone so infinitely greater than ourselves. This godly fear can be a very life-giving thing, flowing from a love for the king. On the other hand, there is also a terrible fear that comes when we reject His rule and prefer to place ourselves on the throne.

Rebellion against this king is a high crime. Because we have never personally encountered an earthly king like Him, it is hard for us to get the right measure of our crime each time we sin against God. Perhaps we might get closer to the truth of the matter if we consider the following things:

1. We can measure the greatness of a crime by considering who we are offending.

Sinning against God is not like sinning against an earthly monarch. After all, all our rulers are really just like everyone else, regardless of what family they have come from. But sin is an offense against the Creator.

CONSIDER the warning of the prophet Isaiah.

Woe to the one who quarrels with his Maker—
An earthenware vessel among the vessels of earth!
Will the clay say to the potter, "What are you doing?"
Or the thing you are making say, "He has no hands"? (Isaiah 45:9)

Maker! No ruler on earth has a right to that title. We have policemen, judges, governors, presidents, and kings; but we have no makers on earth. To sin against an elected official of high rank can carry a stiff penalty. To sin against the one who made and sustains your life is an altogether different matter. To sin against a human, no matter how powerful his rule, is not to be compared to sinning against Almighty God. No being can compare with your Maker in dignity: no crime can compare to your sin against Him.

2.   We can measure the greatness of a crime by its effects or consequences.

Some crimes might cost you a fine. Other crimes might cost you your freedom, and some jail time. What are the consequences of crimes against the Most High King?

Sin is the dare of God's justice, the rape of His mercy, the jeer of His patience, the slight of His power, and the contempt of His love.

— John Bunyan

SIN SEPARATES US FROM THE SOURCE OF HOPE IN THIS LIFE

Ephesians 2:12
. . . remember that you were at that time separate from Christ, excluded from the commonwealth of Israel, and strangers to the covenants of promise, having no hope and without God in the world.

SIN MAKES US SPIRITUALLY DEAD—
UNRESPONSIVE TO GOD, BUT ALIVE TO SIN'S TYRANNY

Ephesians 2:1-3
And you were dead in your trespasses and sins, in which you formerly walked according to the course of this world, according to the prince of the power of the air, of the spirit that is now working in the sons of disobedience. Among them we too all formerly lived in the lusts of our flesh, indulging the desires of the flesh and of the mind, and were by nature children of wrath, even as the rest.

SIN HAS MADE US BLIND AND DEAF TO GOD

Matthew 13:14-15

. . . You will keep on hearing, but will not understand;
You will keep on seeing, but will not perceive;
For the heart of this people has become dull,
With their ears they scarcely hear,
And they have closed their eyes,
Otherwise they would see with their eyes,
Hear with their ears,
And understand with their heart and return,
And I would heal them.

SIN MAKES EVEN OUR BEST RELIGION A THING THAT OFFENDS HIM

Isaiah 1:11-15

"What are your multiplied sacrifices to Me?"
Says the LORD.
"I have had enough of burnt offerings of rams
And the fat of fed cattle;
And I take no pleasure in the blood of bulls, lambs or goats.
When you come to appear before Me,
Who requires of you this trampling of My courts?
Bring your worthless offerings no longer,
Incense is an abomination to Me.
New moon and sabbath, the calling of assemblies—
I cannot endure iniquity and the solemn assembly.
I hate your new moon festivals and your appointed feasts,
They have become a burden to Me;
I am weary of bearing them.
So when you spread out your hands in prayer,
I will hide My eyes from you;
Yes, even though you multiply prayers,
I will not listen . . . ."

Everywhere you look, sin is a crime that brings consequences far deeper and more enduring than anything your earthly crimes might bring. The terror of rejecting this king is directly related to the measure of the crime and the majesty of the king.

Listen to the sober warning found in Nahum's first chapter:

> *A jealous and avenging God is the LORD;*
> *The LORD is avenging and wrathful.*
> *The LORD takes vengeance on His adversaries,*
> *And He reserves wrath for His enemies.*
> *The LORD is slow to anger and great in power,*
> *And the LORD will by no means leave the guilty unpunished . . . .*
> *Mountains quake because of Him*
> *And the hills dissolve;*
> *Indeed the earth is upheaved by His presence,*
> *The world and all the inhabitants in it.*
> *Who can stand before His indignation?*
> *Who can endure the burning of His anger?*
> *His wrath is poured out like fire*
> *And the rocks are broken up by Him . . . .*
> *But with an overflowing flood*
> *He will make a complete end of its site,*
> *And will pursue His enemies into darkness.* (Nahum 1:2-8)

The New Testament does not present any less terrifying a picture of rebellion against God.

> Hebrews 10:31
> *It is a terrifying thing to fall into the hands of the living God.*

The final book of our Bible gives a shocking scene of terror when Christ comes to judge humanity.

> Revelation 6:15-17
> *Then the kings of the earth and the great men and the commanders and the rich and the strong and every slave and free man hid themselves in the caves and among the rocks of the mountains; and they said to the mountains and to the rocks, "Fall on us and hide us from the presence of Him who sits on the throne, and from the wrath of the Lamb; for the great day of their wrath has come, and who is able to stand?"*

In summary, what are two things that will help us get a right measure of sin?

What are some of the consequences of sin?

_____

_____

_____

Rebellion, thankfully, is not the only possible response to His rule. By the amazing intervention of God, humanity is presented with another option: a willing surrender to the rightful king. Let's look at some of the motivations for such a surrender.

THE HOPE OF SUBMITTING TO THE MOST HIGH KING

This is God's universe, and He is doing things His way. You may think you have a better way, but you don't have a universe to rule. He makes the rules in His universe and you're going to have to come His way.

—J. Vernon McGee

If all of us were born with a sinful nature, born preferring to rule ourselves rather than submit to the king of heaven, what hope is there? Is there something more substantial than a vague idea that God is so sentimentally attached to mankind that He could never bring Himself to exercise His wrath against us? There is such a hope, and it is found in Psalm 99:1. This speaks of the place from which God rules: "He is enthroned above the cherubim." In that little statement is all of our hope. But of what is he speaking? It refers to a piece of furniture used in the worship of God in the Old Testament.

> Exodus 25:17-22
> *You shall make a mercy seat of pure gold, two and a half cubits long and one and a half cubits wide. You shall make two cherubim of gold, make them of hammered work at the two ends of the mercy seat. Make one cherub at one end and one cherub at the other end; you shall make the cherubim of one piece with the mercy seat at its two ends. The cherubim shall have their wings spread upward, covering the mercy seat with their wings and facing one another; the faces of the cherubim are to be turned toward the mercy seat. You shall put the mercy seat on top of the ark, and in the ark you shall put the testimony which I will give to you. There I will meet with you; and from above the mercy seat, from between the two cherubim which are upon the ark of the testimony, I will speak to you about all that I will give you in commandment for the sons of Israel.*

In the Old Covenant the dwelling of God's glory, whether in the tabernacle or the temple, was in the Holy of Holies. Within this sacred room the Ark of the Covenant was kept. On the top of the Ark there was a golden pan, with a golden angel on each side of it, both facing inward. These angels were called cherubim. Between the cherubim, on the golden pan, the blood of the sacrifice was sprinkled each year on the Day of Atonement. Here, between the cherubim, the glory of God was manifested, shining visibly. It is a beautiful object lesson for every believer: the place where God delights to manifest His glorious rule on planet earth is the very place where the sacrifice is offered, the righteous wrath of God is satisfied, and forgiveness provided—the mercy seat.

In the New Covenant the mercy seat finds its fulfillment in the work of Jesus that the Bible calls *propitiation*.[33]

> 1 John 2:1
> *My little children, I am writing these things to you so that you may not sin. And if anyone sins, we have an Advocate with the Father, Jesus Christ the righteous; and He Himself is the propitiation for our sins; and not for ours only, but also for those of the whole world.*

> 1 John 4:10
> *In this is love, not that we loved God, but that He loved us and sent His Son to be the propitiation for our sins.*

The Greek word for *propitiation* means "place of atonement," hence, the mercy seat. It is used in the New Testament to refer to the act of our Lord as He offered Himself on the cross to satisfy the righteous demands of God's justice and provide a full pardon for the sinner.

This is important because the benefits that the believer receives in the kingdom of God are based on the place of this throne: between the cherubim—where the atoning sacrifice is applied. If the Most High has gone to such great lengths to provide a place where we might find peace with Him, then we have a legitimate reason to rejoice in His rule.

Go back to an earlier Psalm and recall the advice given at its close:

> *Now therefore, O kings, show discernment;*
> *Take warning, O judges of the earth.*
> *Worship the LORD with reverence*
> *And rejoice with trembling.*
> *Do homage to the Son, that He not become angry, and you perish in the way,*
> *For His wrath may soon be kindled.*
> *How blessed are all who take refuge in Him!* (Psalm 2:10-12)

Here is the paradox created by God's gracious rule. In light of what you have studied this week, the only reasonable response is to worship God with fear

At the name of Jesus
Every knee shall bow,
Every tongue confess Him
King of glory now.
'Tis the Father's pleasure
We should call Him Lord
Who from the beginning
Was the mighty Word.

Name Him, brothers, name Him,
With Love as strong as death,
But with awe and wonder
And with bated breath;
He is God our Savior,
He is Christ the Lord,
Ever to be worshipped,
Trusted, and adored.

— Caroline Maria Noel

157

and rejoice with trembling. We must bow to the Son, that He not become angry and we perish when He comes with His anger kindled. For those who surrender to Him experience the happiness of finding refuge in the very king they once fought against.

WRITE > a prayer to God in response to these truths about Him.

_____

_____

_____

_____

_____

half-way

DAY 5: LIVING ON THESE TRUTHS

You have had an opportunity this week to be reintroduced the one person who has the right to rule over all. In fact, He is king by His very nature, and thus He was sovereign even before there were others to rule. He will be what He has always been—the Majesty on High (Hebrews 1:3-4).

While some have chosen to dispute the sovereign rights of God, others have given lip-service to the doctrine of God's rule while leaving it unapplied in their lives.

Today, once again, you will be using the metaphors taken from Colossians 2:6-7 to aid you in finding practical ways to apply this aspect of God's majesty in your life, your workplace, your home, and your church.

In the passage below, the five word pictures are in bold print:

> *Therefore as you have received Christ Jesus the Lord, so **walk** in Him, having been firmly **rooted** and now being **built up** in Him and **established** in your faith, just as you were instructed, and **overflowing with gratitude**.* (Colossians 2:6-7)

Let's consider how the truths we have studied this week can be lived upon by using these five pictures. [Please note that your answers to today's questions may overlap to some degree.]

HAVING RECEIVED CHRIST JESUS THE LORD . . .

1. Walk in Him

The word "walk" shows us two things about Christian living.

First, walking is an everyday activity that does not seem significant. We take thousands of steps in a day, and very few would be looked back upon as particularly noteworthy, much less spiritually meaningful. Our little, common choices each day may also seem insignificant, but like our steps, they do matter, because they add up to be the stuff of life. For this reason, truths about God must affect our common choices in everyday life.

Second, when a person in the ancient world walked, he or she almost certainly had a destination in mind. Today people often walk for exercise, and in that case the destination isn't important. You may walk on a treadmill or in circles around a track. That is not what Paul has in mind when he says "walk." Christians should be walking toward a definite destination: complete conformity to Christ's character. The little choices of each day, guided by the truths you are studying, should be aiming at that destination—Christlikeness. But why? Not for self-improvement, but for the pleasure and honor of our God.

With these in mind, go back and review this week's lessons. Below, write some of the ways in which you can apply these truths in everyday, apparently insignificant, ways that lead to the destination of Christlikeness.

Wicked men obey from fear; good men, from love.

— Augustine

_____

_____

_____

_____

_____

_____

2. Sink Your Roots in Him

Paul says that God has rooted every believer in Christ. Following Christ means daily sinking the roots of your life into the truths of God. Roots gain nutrients from the soil. Your soul may find temporary satisfaction in the junk food of our culture, or it will find lasting satisfaction in the feast of the immutable realities of God.

Go back and review this week's lessons. Below, write some of the truths that you feel are the most nourishing food for your soul. What must you feed upon if you are to live out the Christian life? Is there "junk food" that you should put away?

_____

_____

_____

_____

_____

_____

3. Build a Life on These Truths

Each truth you learn in this study can be seen as a brick. Combined with other truths, each brick will be an essential part of building a life with Christ as the foundation. Coming to Jesus in repentance and faith is the only place to begin, but good beginnings are not all there is to Christianity. Paul knew that the Colossian Christians needed more than a foundation built on Christ; they also needed a life built by His grace with His biblical truths. To leave the truths you are studying piled like bricks in a corner of your life would be a grave mistake. You don't want to look back after twelve weeks and see a dusty pile of bricks! You need a life that is a true dwelling place for God Himself.

Review this week's lessons and ask yourself, "In what ways can I build my life (my marriage, my family, my friendships, or my work) on the realities of the sovereign God?"

_____

_____

_____

_____

_____

4. **Become Established in Your Faith**

Paul used a word, translated in the NASB as "established," which conveys the idea of firming something up, making something stable, solid. In spiritual life, we might use the word *maturity*. You must grow to maturity in your faith (your grasp of the great realities of God), in part, so that you will not be easily swayed by false teaching or half-truths.

CONSIDER HEBREWS 5:12-14.

> *For though by this time you ought to be teachers, you have need again for someone to teach you the elementary principles of the oracles of God, and you have come to need milk and not solid food. For everyone who partakes only of milk is not accustomed to the word of righteousness, for he is an infant. But solid food is for the mature, who because of practice have their senses trained to discern good and evil.*

Here the writer is speaking to people who have heard the truth many times but have remained immature in their faith. He tells us that maturity comes from a life that applies and practices what it is learning. Through application, you are established, or matured, in the great realities of God.

Review this week's lessons. Below write some areas that the sovereignty of God needs to be applied to your faith so you will be established, solid, unwavering in your grasp of biblical truth.

_____

_____

_____

_____

_____

With these four pictures as guides, we never want to settle for new Bible-truths which are undigested, unapplied, unsettled, and sitting like a wasted pile of bricks.

There is one more picture we need to employ. Without this final metaphor our Christianity will not reflect God.

5. Do All of These with an Overflow of Gratitude to God

You can attempt to do 1-4 above, but without a grateful heart how can you honor God?

In the Old Testament Moses warned the people before they entered the Promised Land:

> *Because you did not serve the LORD your God with joy and a glad heart, for the abundance of all things; therefore you shall serve your enemies whom the LORD will send against you, in hunger, in thirst, in nakedness, and in the lack of all things; and He will put an iron yoke on your neck until He has destroyed you.* (Deuteronomy 28:47-48)

Surely that is a shocking word for us as well. If we go about our Christian lives, trying to walk, sink roots in, build upon, and be established in these truths, but we do so with ungrateful hearts, we can expect divine discipline.

Review this week's lessons. What reasons for gratitude toward God arise from the study of His sovereignty?

_____

_____

_____

_____

_____

May the God who possesses infinite authority grant you such a sight of His sovereignty that you can:

* walk (go about the normal things of life) in its atmosphere . . .

* sink roots for nourishment in it . . .

* build a life with it . . .

* grow firm and be established in your grasp of God's truth because of it . . .

* do all of this with an overflowing sense of gratitude to Him.

Rejoice, the Lord is King!
Your Lord and King adore;
Mortals, give thanks and sing
And triumph evermore.

— Charles Wesley

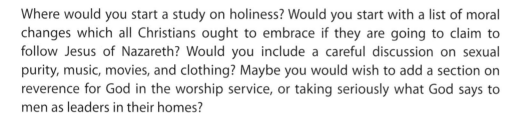

Behold your God

KNOWING THE HOLY AND RIGHTEOUS ONE

DAY 1: THE HOLY GOD

Where would you start a study on holiness? Would you start with a list of moral changes which all Christians ought to embrace if they are going to claim to follow Jesus of Nazareth? Would you include a careful discussion on sexual purity, music, movies, and clothing? Maybe you would wish to add a section on reverence for God in the worship service, or taking seriously what God says to men as leaders in their homes?

A true love of God must begin with a delight in His holiness.

—Jonathan Edwards

While all of these have their place in the Christian life, and all are impacted by the topic of holiness, none of them can be the starting place. They are too narrow to provide a foundation for a holy life. They need to be placed firmly on a foundation bigger than themselves. We are commanded to be imitators of God, but that is not where it all starts. We need to back up and look at the holiness of God. Once the mind and heart are captivated by the sight of the beauty of His holiness, the Christian will possess the foundation, motivation, guide, and goal for a life of holiness. After all, looking at God's holiness is meant to move us to know better how to love and follow Him. It cannot be an exercise that simply informs the mind with new facts. These realities must inform us, grip us, move us, and guide us through all the intricacies of a holy life. Your progress in holy living is directly related to your understanding and application of the biblical portrait of the Holy God.

GETTING A DEFINITION

Holiness is a word that essentially means "separated, marked off, placed apart, or withdrawn from common use."[34] In pagan religions the priest may be called holy, not because he is morally pure in his conduct but because he is separated from the common lot of humanity in order to serve his idol.

Many theologians consider holiness to be the primary attribute of God, the soil in which all other attributes grow. Paul Washer writes: "Holiness is the preeminent attribute of God . . . . Every divine attribute that can be studied is simply an expression of His holiness in that it *demonstrates* that He is distinct from His creation, absolutely separate, and a completely different being."[35]

God is essentially holy because He transcends all other things and people. In other words, He is separated in His essence from all that is not God. He is solitary. He is the only one in His category. God is also morally separate. He is clean, and no moral pollution, no sin in thought or deed, can ever dwell in Him. He is as infinitely separate from all that is morally impure and contaminating as He is from all that is created. He is *the* separate one, or *the* Holy One: not a part of creation, not touched with sin's contamination. Both aspects of His separation are important. Both are part of His glory. No one is like our God! As you begin to think of God's essential separation and moral separation, consider the truth of Stephen Charnock's statement:

> *Power is [God's] hand and arm, omniscience His eye; mercy his heart, eternity his duration, but holiness is His beauty . . . .* [36]

It is a simple but accurate description: "holiness is His beauty."

We often use the word *holiness* interchangeably with other words that are related to it, but not the same. One of these is *righteousness*. Righteousness is not holiness. Righteousness is a life that is morally straight, that conforms to a pattern of ethical behavior or law. Righteous choices flow from a holy life (a life separated unto a righteous God). We will consider righteousness later in the week.

Let's consider some fundamental truths about God's holiness:

1. God's holiness is self-existing.

As with all of God's personal perfections, holiness cannot come from nor rely upon any person outside of God. He is holiness. He is purity. He cannot exist in any other way.

> 1 John 1:5
> *This is the message we have heard from Him and announce to you, that God is Light, and in Him there is no darkness at all.*

God is Himself the Holy One. All other holiness comes from Him. He alone is essentially separate and pure. God's purity is portrayed in John's first letter through the metaphor of light. He is uncontaminated, like light. He is separate from darkness. There is no darkness in Him at all—none at all! He is the sum of all purity. He is unstainable in His moral perfection. Imagine light that penetrates a room. No matter what horrible thing is revealed by that light, the light remains uncontaminated.

Oh, but the holiness of God is a pure holiness, it is a holiness without mixture; there is not the least drop or the least dreg of unholiness in God!

— Thomas Brooks

2.   God's holiness is absolute.

It fills and influences all that God is and does. God hates sin. He cannot desire it, look on it with favor, or entice others with it.

Job 34:10
Therefore, listen to me, you men of understanding.
Far be it from God to do wickedness,
And from the Almighty to do wrong.

Habakkuk 1:13a
Your eyes are too pure to approve evil,
And You cannot look on wickedness with favor.

Psalm 5:4
For You are not a God who takes pleasure in wickedness;
No evil dwells with You.

James 1:13
Let no one say when he is tempted, "I am being tempted by God"; for
God cannot be tempted by evil, and He Himself does not tempt anyone.

3.   God's holiness is unique.

No one else is separate in the way that God is. All who are called holy in the Bible (e.g., angels, Israel, Christians) are holy because they are separated unto God. Holiness does not belong to them. It is attributed to them by virtue of their relationship to the one to whom holiness is essential.

No other "god" is holy like our God.

Exodus 15:11
Who is like You among the gods, O LORD?
Who is like You, majestic in holiness,
Awesome in praises, working wonders?

Our God is incomparable. No one is quite like Him.

Isaiah 40:25
"To whom then will you liken Me that I would be his equal?" says the
Holy One.

Even heaven and its inhabitants are not holy as He is holy, much less mankind.

Job 15:15-16
Behold, He puts no trust in His holy ones,
And the heavens are not pure in His sight;
How much less one who is detestable and corrupt,
Man, who drinks iniquity like water!

WHAT IS AN ADEQUATE RESPONSE TO A GOD WHO IS ESSENTIALLY AND MORALLY SEPARATE?

If we want to be eminently happy, we must strive to be eminently holy.

—J. C. Ryle

Do you begin to feel the wonder of it all? He is essentially separated from all else. He is solitary. He transcends all that is created, for He is the uncreated Creator. He also rises above every aspect of sin's pollution and influence. He is forever unstained and unstainable. Never has any people had such a beautiful king. Therefore, never has any people been obligated to respond in such a way as the Christian is to God. Below are passages that describe various responses that flow from an understanding of God's separateness.

SUMMARIZE the recorded response in each passage in the space provided.

1 Samuel 2:1-2
Then Hannah prayed and said,
"My heart exults in the LORD . . .
My mouth speaks boldly against my enemies,
Because I rejoice in Your salvation.
There is no one holy like the LORD,
Indeed, there is no one besides You,
Nor is there any rock like our God."

Psalm 99:3, 5, 9
Let them praise Your great and awesome name;
Holy is He . . . .
Exalt the LORD our God
And worship at His footstool;
Holy is He . . . .
Exalt the LORD our God
And worship at His holy hill,
For holy is the LORD our God.

Revelation 4:8

And the four living creatures, each one of them having six wings, are full of eyes around and within; and day and night they do not cease to say, "Holy, holy, holy is the LORD God, the Almighty, who was and who is and who is to come."

Revelation 15:4

Who will not fear, O Lord, and glorify Your name?
For You alone are holy;
For all the nations will come and worship before You,
For Your righteous acts have been revealed.

The deeper our views of His holiness grow, the deeper grows our love.

— Octavius Winslow

Psalm 97:12

Be glad in the LORD, you righteous ones,
And give thanks to His holy name.

1 Peter 1:14-17

As obedient children, do not be conformed to the former lusts which were yours in your ignorance, but like the Holy One who called you, be holy yourselves also in all your behavior; because it is written, "You shall be holy, for I am holy." If you address as Father the One who impartially judges according to each one's work, conduct yourselves in fear during the time of your stay on earth . . . .

DAY 2: THE ROLE OF FAITH IN THE LIFE OF HOLINESS, PART 1

God is holy. God has brought the Christian everlastingly near by the cross of His only begotten Son. What is the appropriate response from the believer? And how will the believer find the strength to give this response to God consistently and wholeheartedly?

As we read yesterday in Peter's first letter:

> *As obedient children, do not be conformed to the former lusts which were yours in your ignorance, but like the Holy One who called you, be holy yourselves also in all your behavior; because it is written, "You shall be holy, for I am holy."* (1 Peter 1:14-16)

Because your God is separate, live separated unto Him. Live a Godward life. Be holy.

Five hundred years ago, Martin Luther nailed his *Ninety-five Theses* to the door of All Saints' Church in Wittenberg. These ninety-five theological statements were intended for debate among concerned churchmen and academics. In spite of the danger of oversimplification, we can say that this document ignited the Protestant Reformation. People began to leave the Roman Catholic Church as they rediscovered the biblical truths being preached by Luther and other reformers, especially the doctrine of justification by faith. Protestants held the belief that man is saved by faith alone in Christ alone. The Roman Catholic response warned that such a view of God's forgiveness would never lead to a life of holiness. This has, in fact, been the criticism leveled at the evangelical doctrine of salvation by God's free grace through the ages. If we are freely pardoned, they say, what is the motivation for holy living? That is a very good question. It is a question the Bible answers.

Five hundred years later, we who are evangelicals must openly confess that when it comes to Godward living, the evangelical churches have little that would make the Roman Catholic Church envious. If you feel that this criticism is too harsh, simply look around a Christian bookstore, or examine the newest ideas churches are offering. We are flooded with material that promises to fix our broken lives and make us better (holier) people. On a positive note, the fact that this material exists indicates that some of us have a desire to live holy lives. But there is a deep problem with what we are being offered to make us holy. The systems that promise to transform us are not producing real and lasting change. They never have. Nearly two thousand years ago, Paul warned that there were schemes which seemed to be sure to produce holiness, but they were of no value in fighting against the sins of the heart.

Colossians 2:23
These are matters which have, to be sure, the appearance of wisdom in self-made religion and self-abasement and severe treatment of the body, but are of no value against fleshly indulgence.

Paul has something better to offer. In fact, Paul has *someone* better to offer.

> 1 Corinthians 1:30-31
> *But by His doing you are in Christ Jesus, who became to us wisdom from God, and righteousness and sanctification, and redemption, so that, just as it is written, "Let him who boasts, boast in the LORD."*

Christ is much more than the one who gives pardon and justification; Christ is the holiness of every believer. Much might be said about this verse, but at least we can affirm that Jesus is the source and guarantee of being separated unto God and living unto that God in holiness.

Here is the question every true follower of Jesus Christ faces: How do I get from 1 Corinthians 1:30-31 to 1 Peter 1:14-16? The answer is faith. The righteous man will live by faith (Romans 1:17).

What is faith? Faith is the choice to live upon what God reveals to be the truth. It is refusing to live upon the apparent and making our choices based upon the true. Faith is living as if God is telling us the truth about Himself, us, and life— and He is! We tend to think that faith is meant only for the entrance into the relationship with God through His Son. But faith is also the way we progress in holiness. One wise preacher says, "The way in is the way up."[37]

Paul's clearest explanation of how to progress in holiness is found in Romans 6. He spends a great deal of time explaining the labors of Christ as His people's representative, another "Adam." In chapter 6 he explains that a life devoted to sin is not merely unacceptable for a Christian; it is impossible. He gives a series of facts which flow from the realities of our relationship to Christ. He concludes this series with the first command to appear in the entire book of Romans.

Faith is deliberate confidence in the character of God.

— Oswald Chambers

> *Even so* consider *yourselves to be dead to sin, but alive to God in Christ Jesus.* (Romans 6:11)

Consider? What a strange command! It does not address outward actions. Considering is something the Christian does in his or her mind. Other translations use the word *reckon*. This is Paul's word for faith in Romans 6. The definition of *reckon* is to review the facts and recalculate based on those facts. Faith is exercised when the Christian weighs what has been said at the end of Romans 5 and the first half of Romans 6, and then recalculates life based on these facts.

A second set of commands follows:

> *Therefore do not let sin reign in your mortal body so that you obey its lusts, and do not go on presenting the members of your body to sin as*

instruments of unrighteousness; but present yourselves to God as those alive from the dead, and your members as instruments of righteousness to God. (Romans 6:12-13)

Here is the Godward life! Here is holiness. You recalculate your life based on the facts of Christ and then you refuse to let sin master you. You daily refuse to present your body (including your mind) to sin as its tool. Instead you daily present your whole person unto God as one that has been raised from the dead, and your body as a tool for His use.

Now, what exactly are the facts that facilitate this recalculation of life? What facts are so extraordinarily good that they have the magnitude and beauty to fuel a Godward life? Let's quickly glance at them today.

READ ROMANS 6:1-10. Below is a list of facts based on this passage. Fill in the blanks of the verses and consider the life-changing quality they possess for every Christian.

1. You must recalculate your life in relation to sin and God because you died to sin.

    May it never be! How shall _____

    _____

    _____ still live in it? (verse 2)

2. You must recalculate your life in relation to sin and God because the old you has been killed with Christ.

    Or do you not know that all of us who have been baptized _____ _____ have been baptized _____ _____? (verse 3)

3. You must recalculate your life in relation to sin and God because a new you has been raised to a new life!

    Therefore we have been buried with Him through baptism _____ _____, so that as Christ was raised from the dead through the glory of the Father, so we too might walk _____ _____. (verse 4)

4. You must recalculate your life in relation to sin and God because union with Christ (by faith, when the Spirit "baptized," or placed, you in Him) is the heart of this death to the old you and life for a new you. It is not something you have done or need to do.

For _____
_____, *certainly* _____
_____ *resurrection . . . .* (verse 5)

5. You must recalculate your life in relation to sin and God because you have shared in Christ's crucifixion and the old you (which is characterized by a body that is susceptible to sin) will not again be a slave of sin. Have you ever seen a corpse get up and obey the voice of sin? You are never again able to be under sin's dominion because the old you (who lived in sin's realm) died at the cross.

. . . knowing this, that our old self was crucified with Him, in order that _____,
so that we would no longer be slaves to sin; for he who has died is freed from sin. (verses 6-7)

6. You must recalculate your life in relation to sin and God because a new you (raised in Jesus' realm) has a new life with Him as surely as Jesus was raised from the dead!

Now if we have died with Christ, we believe that _____
_____, *knowing that Christ, having been raised from the dead, is never to die again; death no longer is master over Him.* (verses 8-9)

7. You must recalculate your life in relation to sin and God because what you see physically happen to Christ at the cross (death, finished dealing with our sin) and at the tomb (alive again to live unto God once more) has spiritually happened to you when you were united to Him by faith.

For the death that He died, He died _____;
but the life that He lives, He lives to God. (verse 10)

Here are the facts that Paul has been laying before the believers. United to Christ, everything has changed for them. Old things are passed away because of the cross, even the old self. A new life, a new self, is raised because of Christ's resurrection. These facts must be studied. They must be understood in light of what he has said earlier (especially in chapters 3-5 of Romans). They must be chewed on, considered, and you must reckon yourself (recalculate your life) differently now! This is a lifelong duty. It is not one that will come easily to you. Your personal experience of sin's continued ability to tempt and threaten you may shake your confidence in these facts.

Feelings are always easier to believe than facts. But Paul has given us a companion for the life of faith, Abraham. Paul reminds us in chapter 4 that Abraham did two things regarding the amazing statements God made regarding him and his future offspring. First, Abraham did not let go of God's words, he did not "become weak in faith," even when God's words were all he had, and all around him (his circumstances) seemed to cry out that those words could not be true (Romans 4:18-19). Second, Abraham did not shrink the statements of God to make them easier to believe. He did not "stagger" (KJV) at the immensity of the promises. Not only was he promised a child when it was too late for Sarah and him to have children, but he was promised an entire nation from his lineage, a people that would bring a blessing (the Messiah) to all the nations. It would have been easy for Abraham to reduce that promise to a more believable size, but he did not (Romans 4:20).

Christian, follow Abraham this week. Believe what God has said in Romans 6, without any diminution or reduction.

DAY 3: THE ROLE OF FAITH IN THE LIFE OF HOLINESS, PART 2

"The way in is the way up!" Faith in the Lord Jesus Christ is the way we started the Christian life, and this same faith is the way we continue to grow in Christlikeness. We began to think about this truth yesterday in our study of Romans 6:1-11. Today we will step back and look at faith's embrace of Jesus Christ on a larger scale.

Faith is living on what God has revealed. This is the way we enter into a relationship with God. We believe the Son, and we respond in repentance and faith (dependence). What else could one do once he has had his eyes opened to the truth about his sin and his Savior?

Faith is also a part of the daily Christian life. We believe what God has said about Himself and make our choices based on those truths. God provides for His children in Christ what is needed for this daily obedience. Faith allows us to receive right now a share of this provision. Faith, like an empty hand, stretches toward the Father every hour of every day, taking what is laid up in Christ (Ephesians 1:3) and living on that supply in the present moment.

COMMON DESTRUCTIVE ERRORS

Before we say more of faith it would be beneficial for us to consider three common errors that can quietly destroy the vitality of a believer's response to what God reveals:

IGNORANCE OF SCRIPTURE

Paul tells us in ROMANS 10:17:

> *So faith comes from hearing, and hearing by the word of Christ.*

Faith, being a response to what God reveals to us, cannot exist on general impressions, vague religious clichés, or good intentions. If you are willfully ignorant of large portions of the Bible, you are fundamentally undermining all hope of living a holy life by faith.

ALLOWANCE OF AN IMPOSTER

One of the deadlier counterfeits of faith in modern evangelicalism is positive thinking. This imposter may travel under various names, but at heart it is the opposite of faith. It tells us that if we think positively about a situation, then we can create a certain degree of positive reality. In fact, faith does not make a bad situation good or better. Faith *looks* upon the real and *lives* upon it. Positive thinking *denies* the real and attempts to *create* an alternative reality by a kind of mental self-manipulation. Faith lives on truths which do in fact fill the believer with great hope, but in the final analysis biblical faith and positive thinking are very different.

THINKING OF FAITH AS A RESPONSE OF ONLY PART OF YOU

We need a bit of Christian psychology here. We need to think rightly about the way we function. When we believe something to be true, it never affects only our intellect. If we are gripped with the factuality of something it will first alter our thinking, but next it will also change our desires and our will. Faith might be defined as the response of the whole of our person to what God has revealed in the Bible. If we have a "faith" that simply reads the facts of the Bible just to inform the intellect, or merely to stir the emotions, or only to alter the outward form of our life instead of embracing them with the totality of faith, then we are in danger of having a faith in name only that will never lead to true holiness. A Godward life will include every faculty of our person (mind, heart, and will), and thus it will be moved by a faith that also involves the totality of our person.

FAITH AND HOLY LIVING

All of this talk about faith must not be mistaken as insinuating that faith is the hope. Faith can never be our hope because it is not the source of spiritual life. Faith is like a pipe that taps into a great reservoir and channels the water to our home. What good would a circular pipe be? What good would it be if the pipe simply turned a circle and connected to itself? The pipe is not the source. Faith is nothing for us to hope in. If we trust in our trust, hope in our hope, believe in our belief, we will soon find that it is a very shaky foundation. Faith's real value is that it connects us to a divine person and His provision. Faith is only a pipeline; it needs to be connected to something bigger and better than itself. But since faith is the only pipeline by which we receive daily what we need for holy living, it is a very important pipeline, and we need to understand how it works.

Today we will be considering the following six things about faith which connect it with holy living:

- Faith unites you to the sanctifier.

- Faith is a gift from God and cannot be separated from other aspects of the New Covenant.

- Faith embraces all of Christ.

- Faith views a reconciled God.

- Faith appreciates the loveliness of Christ.

- Faith looks away from self-confidence and receives fresh supplies from Christ's sufficiency.

Let's look at each of these.

1. Faith unites us to the sanctifier.

Union with Christ is the source of all the Christian needs for holy living. All spiritual blessings are in Christ for the believer (Ephesians 1:3), but it is by union with Christ that we are able to experience them. Paul uses the phrases "in Christ" and "in Him" over 160 times in his letters. This union with Christ results in our benefitting from all He did as His people's representative. We were crucified with Him (Galatians 2:20), buried with Him (Romans 6:4), made alive, raised, and seated with Him in the heavenly places (Ephesians 2:5-6), and we will be glorified together with Him (Romans 8:17). Faith is the response of the believer which unites him or her to Christ.

And all fancied sanctification, which does not arise wholly from the blood of the cross, is nothing better than Pharisaism; and if persisted in, will end in Pharisaism. For when sanctification is considered as a separate work from justification, and wholly independent of it, by and by it is considered as a justifying work itself; and men profess and preach they are first to be justified by the blood of Christ, and then by their own obedience.

— John Berridge

2. Faith is a gift from God and cannot be separated from other aspects of the New Covenant.

Paul told the Philippians that faith was a gift granted to them for Christ's sake:

> *For to you it has been granted for Christ's sake, not only to believe in Him, but also to suffer for His sake . . . .* (Philippians 1:29)

This gift, received when the Holy Spirit awakens and regenerates the sinner, is the beginning of the Christian life. Faith is one of many gifts that are interconnected. They are all part of the New Covenant. They are all animated in the Christian by the Holy Spirit. It is impossible therefore to separate faith (which occurs in conversion, that initial turning to God through faith and repentance), justification (the declaration of God that the believer is now pardoned and righteous before the Law), and sanctification (the progressive transformation of the life to bring every area under the rule of Jesus Christ). If you think that a person can be a "believer" yet never be interested in true holiness, you are mistaken. You cannot have part of the Covenant. God gives a new nature as well as a new standing (justification). The new nature will show itself in holy living. Because of this connection, we can say that every believer is forgiven and every forgiven person will begin to be transformed to live a Godward life. Faith is critical to holiness because it is inseparable from the other changes included in the New Covenant.

3. Faith embraces all of Christ.

As we cannot pick and choose which parts of the New Covenant we might prefer, so we cannot embrace part of Christ by faith. Faith embraces the whole of the Savior—prophet, priest, and king. So faith guarantees that the Christian will listen to Christ's teachings, trust in Christ's priestly labors for his or her peace with God, and surrender to His authority. Faith never takes only part of Jesus.

4. Faith views a reconciled God.

Until we see God reconciled toward us through His Son, all efforts at holiness will flow from a wrong source. We may try to bribe God with our religion, as the Pharisees did in the days of the New Testament. Our best religious efforts will be spoiled by our attempt to use holy living as a way of buying favor with God. Faith believes what God says about the depths of our sin, but it also believes what God says about the sufficiency of Christ's cross. Seeing what God has done for us we are humbled, made grateful, and filled with love for the Savior. Having been forgiven much, we love much (Luke 7:47), and loving Him, we obey Him (John 14:15).

[D]aily to live in the contemplation and admiration of the love of Christ, daily reaching after a sweeter knowledge of it. And then do we know something of the love of Christ, when we know by heart-felt experience that it passeth all knowledge; comprehending with thankful amazement so much of it as to find it wholly incomprehensible. In this ocean let me wade, till self, finding no ground to stand upon, is swallowed up, and Thou, O Jesus, precious Jesus, art my All in all.

— John Berridge

5.   Faith appreciates the loveliness of Christ.

True holiness begins with a change of the heart, the deepest desires. The Christian has a new heart, and this new heart sees the perfections of Jesus Christ in a way that distracts him from the lesser attractions of sin. A holy life results when we find something infinitely more interesting than living for ourselves—living for the altogether lovely Jesus. Hypocrisy occurs when a religious person sees nothing more attractive than "self" getting what it wants. He may see the benefits of keeping rules, of attending church, of being very diligent in all the right things. What he does not see is the great attraction of Jesus Christ Himself. As soon as the hypocrite is promised what he wants (heaven, restored marriage, happy children, sense of purpose, personal significance), he will stop pursuing a life that desires to walk progressively nearer to Christ. But faith sees Christ as the great treasure of Christianity, and thus will continue to motivate the believer to walk in holiness with this Savior. When it comes to faith in Christ, loving is believing.

6.   Faith looks away from self-confidence and receives fresh supplies from Christ's sufficiency.

Faith is continually looking away from self and to Christ. Essential to all true faith is the reality that there is no spiritual hope in what we are, what we have learned, or what we are resolved to do. Faith turns away from the disappointing weakness it finds in ourselves and reaches toward Christ daily for all that we need to live a Godward life. This is why the Christian reads the Bible, prays, worships, meets often with other believers—not because he is so spiritually strong, but because he realizes he is so needy, and faith uses all these means to receive what is needed from God.

So we see that faith is at the heart of all real holy living.

DAY 4: THE RIGHTEOUS GOD

The Lord is King! Child
of the dust,
The Judge of all the earth
is just;
Holy and true are all His
ways;
Let every creature speak
His praise.

— Josiah Conder

The Rock! His work is perfect,
For all His ways are just;
A God of faithfulness and without injustice,
Righteous and upright is He.

(Deuteronomy 32:4)

Today you will begin to look at one of the most soul-strengthening attributes: the moral goodness of God. Another word for this is righteousness. In the Bible righteousness and justice are virtually synonymous, the two English words being translations from the same words in the original Hebrew and Greek. It depends upon the context of the passage as to which word, righteousness or justice, the translators choose.

The moral perfection of God that we call righteousness or justice has to do with His equity. He is and always does what is right, what is equitable. He is morally correct, always and only. We might say that His character and thus His actions are always ethically straight, without any twist or crookedness. Sin is called in-equity because it represents the absence of moral equality or rightness from human thoughts and actions.[38] So righteousness is that quality in God's person which guarantees that all He desires, thinks, says, and chooses is morally perfect, equitable, and right. When we apply this rightness of God to a moral situation, we call it justice.

We know something of righteousness and unrighteousness in our experience. We know of justice and injustice. But what does the Bible say about the righteousness and justice of God?

GOD'S RIGHTEOUSNESS IS ESSENTIAL TO HIS BEING

As with all His attributes, righteousness and justice are expressions of who God is, not something He maintains by anything He does. Being right and just are effortless for Him. His actions are right because He is right. His decisions are just because He is just.

GOD IS THE SOURCE OF RIGHTEOUSNESS

We must be clear if we are to avoid wrong views of God's moral perfection. God is not right because He keeps every rule perfectly. God is right and just because it is who He is. His righteousness and justice do not come from anything outside of Himself. They do not come from any law or influence. They come from who He is. He is the source of all righteousness and all justice. Yet we never need fear that God, not being under some higher code of right and wrong, will fail to act in perfect equity because His unchanging character is righteous. He cannot act in a way that is contrary to who He is.

GOD'S RIGHTEOUSNESS IS CONNECTED WITH HIS OTHER ATTRIBUTES

God is not made up of various qualities that operate harmoniously. God is a perfect unity. He possesses one gloriously undivided essence. Thus, every attribute is really a part of every other attribute. We discuss them separately to help our child-like grasp, but they can never exist separately. This ought to thrill the heart of every created being. Below are a few of God's attributes.

Imagine each attribute as if it were not interwoven with God's righteousness and in the blanks provided describe what that attribute would become. The first one is given as an example.

- All authority: _oppressive tyranny_
- All power: _____
- Love: _____
- Patience: _____
- Mercy: _____
- Wrath: _____

To be dependent upon a God who is all that the God of the Bible is, yet without this one quality of perfect righteousness, would be a terrible existence.

GOD DELIGHTS IN RIGHTEOUSNESS AND JUSTICE

There are different things which reveal the true character of a person.

- *Words* reveal something of a person's heart, but they are also easiest to fake.

- *Actions* are a more trustworthy revelation of a person's character. Yet a person may do things which he secretly wishes he did not have to do. So, even actions can mislead.

- *Delight* is one of the clearest revelations of the character of a person. Find out what a person delights in and you will know a great deal about that person's character.

READ the following passages.

UNDERLINE what delights your God.

Psalm 11:7
For the LORD is righteous, He loves righteousness;
The upright will behold His face.

Jeremiah 9:23-24
Thus says the LORD, "Let not a wise man boast of his wisdom, and let not the mighty man boast of his might, let not a rich man boast of his riches; but let him who boasts boast of this, that he understands and knows Me, that I am the LORD who exercises lovingkindness, justice and righteousness on earth; for I delight in these things," declares the LORD.

This same delight is found in the Son of God. In the following passage we find a prophecy of what type of king the Lord Jesus would be.

> Psalm 45:6-7
> *Your throne, O God, is forever and ever;*
> *A scepter of uprightness is the scepter of Your kingdom.*
> *You have loved righteousness and hated wickedness,*
> *Therefore God, Your God, has anointed You*
> *With the oil of joy above Your fellows.*

GOD'S RIGHTEOUSNESS IS UNIQUE TO HIMSELF

No angel in heaven and no person on earth has a righteousness like God's righteousness. He is unique, solitary, in this perfection.

> Job 4:17-19
> *Can mankind be just before God?*
> *Can a man be pure before his Maker?*
> *He puts no trust even in His servants;*
> *And against His angels He charges error.*
> *How much more those who dwell in houses of clay,*
> *Whose foundation is in the dust,*
> *Who are crushed before the moth!*

GOD'S RIGHTEOUSNESS IS INFINITE AND INCOMPREHENSIBLE

> Psalm 36:6
> *Your righteousness is like the mountains of God;*
> *Your judgments are like a great deep.*

The perfection of God's equity rises like mountains, high above humanity. It also reaches deep into the depths of ocean. It is beyond our measure, understanding, or accurate definition.

GOD'S RIGHTEOUSNESS IS TIMELESS, ETERNAL, ENDURING

COPY PSALM 119:142.

_____

_____

. . . a kind, equitable person may turn bitter and crotchety; a person of good will may grow cynical and callous. But nothing of this sort happens to the Creator. He never becomes less truthful, or merciful, or just, or good than He used to be.

—J. I. Packer

Can you pick a date in human history that marked the end of God's justice? Can you choose a date in the future that will be the last day God is righteous? It is an everlasting righteousness that you study for a few moments today.

GOD'S RIGHTEOUSNESS IS A SOVEREIGN RIGHTEOUSNESS, POSSESSING ALL RIGHTS TO DO AS HE DESIRES

COPY PSALM 89:14.

_____

_____

_____

God's authority is not only built upon perfect justice; His justice is empowered by an unlimited authority.

GOD'S RIGHTEOUSNESS IS UNCHANGING AND UNCHANGEABLE

God's love of what is right and His hatred of what is wrong will not change. He has not changed between the Old and New Testaments. He is not devoted to justice when He deals with the unbeliever but willing to bend the rules when He deals with His own children. He shows no partiality.

COPY PSALM 7:11-12.

_____

_____

_____

_____

God does not overlook judges that show partiality and take bribes because God is a righteous judge who has never, and will never, act in this manner.

> 2 Chronicles 19:7
> *Now then let the fear of the LORD be upon you; be very careful what you do, for the LORD our God will have no part in unrighteousness or partiality or the taking of a bribe.*

A MYSTERY ANSWERED!

With these things in mind, let us turn our attention to one of the greatest mysteries of all—the salvation of those who are unjust by the one judge who is perfectly just, or, put another way, the rescue of the unrighteous by the only judge who is perfectly righteous.

God has made it clear that sin is an activity that always, without exception, earns the paycheck of death.

> Romans 6:23
> *For the wages of sin is death, but the free gift of God is eternal life in Christ Jesus our Lord.*

How can God give eternal life to those who rightly deserve death? Does He bend His own rules to do so? Does He lower His standard of justice in order to let mercy rise above all?

Before we allow ourselves to think, "I do not care how He did it, I am just glad He saved me!" we need to seriously consider the implications of such a thought. In our everyday life, do we admire a judge who bends the rules to rescue his son or daughter from a prison sentence that he or she deserves? Do we not despise the judge who shows partiality and bends the rules? How can we truly worship and trust God if our very salvation was accomplished by the same means that an unjust earthly judge skirts the laws to free his criminal child?

How can the holiest judge declare the guiltiest people to be guiltless? Paul deals with this great dilemma in Romans 3. As you read the following passage, ask yourself: "Is this a passage all about me getting out of trouble with God, or is this a passage that vindicates God's choices which have led to my rescue while upholding His own righteous standard?"

READD▷ ROMANS 3:21-26.

Notice how often the issue of righteousness is mentioned.

- VERSE 21 — God has made obvious a righteousness that does not come from rule keeping. This is a righteousness about which the Old Testament speaks.

- VERSE 22 — This righteousness is God's righteousness that is received through faith by all who believe the claims of Christ, regardless of what kind of people they are.

- VERSE 24 — All humanity, having sinned, needs justification (to be declared right with the Law) as a gift from God, through Jesus' redemptive labors.

- VERSES 25-26 — In order to give this kind of gift to those who have earned death (Romans 6:23), God did not violate His justice. In fact, the crucifixion of Christ satisfied (propitiated) God's justice and thereby publicly demonstrated to all that God is righteous in the way He has offered mercy to those in the Old Covenant and in the New Testament churches. God is the just judge, and at the same time He is the one who justifies (declares guiltless) the guilty who have entrusted themselves to Jesus Christ alone.

It is the great mystery at the heart of our rescue: how can God declare me not guilty? How can He be "a righteous God and a Savior" (Isaiah 45:21) at the same moment? The answer is found at the cross.

Christ has fully endured the exact punishment that the Law demanded of His sinful people. The Law is satisfied, so to speak. Justice is upheld. It asks no more.

This wonderful reality is expressed in the following verse of John Newton's hymn:

> *Let us wonder; grace and justice*
> *Join, and point to mercy's store;*
> *When through grace in Christ our trust is,*
> *Justice smiles, and asks no more.*
> *He who washed us with His blood*
> *Has secured our way to God.*[39]

DAY 5: HOW WILL WE LIVE UNTO THE RIGHTEOUS GOD?

O worship the Lord in the
beauty of holiness;
Bow down before Him, His
glory proclaim;
With gold of obedience and
incense of lowliness,
Kneel and adore Him, the
Lord is His name.

— John Monsell

Each time we learn about our God we are required to give a corresponding and adequate response. Our response ought to correspond to, or match, the things we are learning. Our response should be adequate in light of the new truths we are learning. We do not want to give God a partial response. We do not want to merely have an intellectual response, adding new concepts to our minds. We do not want to give God a merely emotional response in which the stirring of our heart is the end of the matter. We do not want to give God a merely mechanical response in which we add new rules to our life. The only adequate response as we learn of God from the Bible is one that includes our understanding, our heart, and our volition.

Below are a number of verses that help us understand the responses given to the righteous and just God by believers through the centuries. Read the passages and consider how you can respond to our great God.

1. We worship the righteous and just God.

Stephen Charnock defined worship:

> *Worship is an act of the understanding, applying itself to the knowledge of the excellency of God, and actual thoughts of His majesty . . . . It is also an act of the will, whereby the soul adores and reverences His majesty, is ravished with His amiableness, embraces His goodness, enters itself into an intimate communion with this most lovely object, and pitches all his affections upon Him.* [40]

We want to take Charnock's definition and worship God for more than *doing right*—we want to adore and reverence God's majesty as the one who *is* righteousness and justice.

In Revelation we find a heavenly scene of worship, following the outpouring of God's righteous wrath.

> Revelation 15:3-4
> *And they sang the song of Moses, the bond-servant of God, and the song of the Lamb, saying,*
> *"Great and marvelous are Your works,*
> *O Lord God, the Almighty;*
> *Righteous and true are Your ways,*
> *King of the nations!*
> *Who will not fear, O Lord, and glorify Your name?*
> *For You alone are holy;*
> *For all the nations will come and worship before You,*
> *For Your righteous acts have been revealed."*

Here heaven erupts in worship, in that adoring reverence for God, as they see His righteousness expressed as He judges His enemies. It is a difficult scene to grasp, yet it is true. Even the great display of righteousness in judging the enemies of God is something that calls for adoration because it is a display of perfect righteousness.

> *Mark you, this is the very hell of hell—that men will know that they are justly suffering.*
>
> — C. H. Spurgeon

This response to God's righteous judgment fills the Psalms with songs of praise. Consider what the psalmist says below.

Psalm 96:11-13
Let the heavens be glad, and let the earth rejoice;
Let the sea roar, and all it contains;
Let the field exult, and all that is in it.
Then all the trees of the forest will sing for joy
Before the LORD, for He is coming,
For He is coming to judge the earth.
He will judge the world in righteousness.
And the peoples in His faithfulness.

2.   We plead for God to act based upon His perfect justice.

Consider the account of Abraham's interceding for the city of Sodom, based upon the justice of God.

Genesis 18:23-25
Abraham came near and said, "Will You indeed sweep away the righteous with the wicked? Suppose there are fifty righteous within the city; will You indeed sweep it away and not spare the place for the sake of the fifty righteous who are in it? Far be it from You to do such a thing, to slay the righteous with the wicked, so that the righteous and the wicked are treated alike. Far be it from You! Shall not the Judge of all the earth deal justly?"

Have you ever interceded with God on behalf of a spiritually mixed group, like a church, based upon His justice?

Applying this to the individual believer, we should consider the following most amazing statement:

1 John 1:9
If we confess our sins, He is faithful and righteous to forgive us our sins and to cleanse us from all unrighteousness.

Have you so fully understood the work of Jesus on the cross that you confess your own sins before God and then plead for the strictest justice?

3.   We confess God's perfect justice even when He judges us.

After seven years of being struck by God with a mental illness, the repentant king Nebuchadnezzar makes this statement about God's justice:

> *"Now I, Nebuchadnezzar, praise, exalt and honor the King of heaven, for all His works are true and His ways just, and He is able to humble those who walk in pride."* (Daniel 4:37)

Daniel pleads with God on behalf of a drifting Jewish people, and in his great prayer of confession He recognizes God's perfect justice in the ways He has judged His people.

READ DANIEL 9:3-19 and write below the times Daniel mentions God's righteousness in His actions against His rebellious people.

_____

_____

_____

4.   We delight to have all our manner of life conformed to the righteous pattern of Jesus Christ.

COPY EPHESIANS 4:22-24.

_____

_____

_____

_____

The Christian does not merely have a new list of rules; he or she has a new self. This new self (the new you in Christ) is to be continually and deliberately put on and applied to your daily circumstances. This new you with its new lifestyle reflects the righteous God who is at work in you. Though a righteous lifestyle never gives anyone entrance into the kingdom of God (which can only be entered by a spiritual new-birth), the new birth always begins to demonstrate itself by a righteous lifestyle.

This connection between being a child of God and righteous behavior is so sure that John tells us we can accurately judge the spiritual condition of a person by the pattern of his or her behavior.

COPY the following verses.

1 John 2:29

_____

_____

_____

1 John 3:7-8

_____

_____

_____

_____

_____

_____

Because God cares for us, our desire should not be to keep the law, but to please the Father. There is nothing that promotes holiness as the realization that we are "heirs of God and joint-heirs with Christ," that our destiny is certain and secure, that nothing in all creation can prevent it.

— Martyn Lloyd-Jones

Have you come to the place where you look for the beginnings, no matter how small, of a habitual righteousness in people before you call them Christians?

5. We will delight to speak of God's righteous character and activity.

Psalm 92:15
To declare that the LORD is upright;
He is my rock, and there is no unrighteousness in Him.

Psalm 71:15-16
My mouth shall tell of Your righteousness
And of Your salvation all day long;
For I do not know the sum of them.
I will come with the mighty deeds of the Lord GOD;
I will make mention of Your righteousness, Yours alone.

Psalm 145: 6-7

Men shall speak of the power of Your awesome acts,
And I will tell of Your greatness.
They shall eagerly utter the memory of Your abundant goodness
And will shout joyfully of Your righteousness.

Psalm 40:10

I have not hidden Your righteousness within my heart;
I have spoken of Your faithfulness and Your salvation;
I have not concealed Your lovingkindness and Your truth from the great
congregation.

How can you apply these verses to evangelism? Are you guilty of only speaking of God's love and mercy when you speak of the cross of Christ, and hiding the righteousness of God by not explaining it carefully?

How can you begin to bring the story of the righteousness and justice of God into the heart of your personal evangelism?

_____

_____

_____

_____

How can you apply these verses to counseling? How can you begin to apply the reality of a God who is righteous and only does what is right when you speak to needy Christians who are heartbroken, confused, or drifting?

_____

_____

_____

_____

The righteous God who does what is right, always what is right, and only what is right, is the God with whom we must deal. The one person who is morally perfect and will never bend the rules for anyone, not even His only begotten Son, is the God that the Scripture reveals to us. He is the only God there is. Is that the best news you could hear, or does that produce a genuine sense of despair in you?

KNOWING THE GOD OF WRATH

DAY 1: THE GOD WHO POSSESSES JUSTICE AND WRATH

Every aspect of the perfect character that God has revealed in Scripture ought to fill us with awe, that holy fear that makes us tremble and rejoice at the same time. Remember, we are not studying God so that we can discover how He can be more useful to us. And keep in mind that we are not allowed to adjust what He reveals of Himself to fit our concepts of what He should be like. Rather, we are contemplating the weight of His majesty, or His splendor, that we might know and love Him better.

This week you will have an opportunity to be taught by God through His Word about His perfect displeasure at sin, which reveals itself in His wrath.

Your response to understanding His wrath, as with all the other attributes you have studied, ought to resemble the psalmist's response in PSALM 145:1-3:

> *I will extol You, my God, O King,*
> *And I will bless Your name forever and ever.*
> *Every day I will bless You,*
> *And I will praise Your name forever and ever.*
> *Great is the LORD, and highly to be praised,*
> *And His greatness is unsearchable.*

William Ames, the seventeenth-century Puritan, defined theology as the study of how to live unto God. Learning about the wrath of God ought to fill the believer with wonder, praise, and a clearer understanding of how to live a Godward life.

If you embrace a view of God that leaves out any of His revealed attributes, you will only have an idol of your own making. This tendency might look different in each generation, but it is certainly visible when we start to talk of God's righteous displeasure at sin and His holy wrath.

A.W. Pink warned against this trend in the mid-twentieth century. He wrote:

> *It is sad indeed to find so many professing Christians who appear to regard the wrath of God as something for which they need to make an apology, or we at least wish there were no such thing. While some do not go so far as to openly admit that they consider it a blemish on the Divine character, yet they are far from regarding it with delight; they like not to think about it . . . . They don't consider it a theme for profitable contemplation.*[41]

But what does the Bible say? It never attempts to hide the reality of God's anger. It makes no effort to hide the fact that vengeance and fury belong to God, and that this is part of His majesty. If we are able to get a biblical understanding of this doctrine, we too will see the beauty, rightness, and perfection of God's wrath.

Listen to the Song of Moses, in which God reveals something of His holy anger against sin.

> *See now that I, I am He,*
> *And there is no god besides Me;*
> *It is I who put to death and give life.*
> *I have wounded and it is I who heal,*
> *And there is no one who can deliver from My hand.*
> *Indeed, I lift up My hand to heaven,*
> *And say, as I live forever,*
> *If I sharpen My flashing sword,*
> *And My hand takes hold on justice,*
> *I will render vengeance on My adversaries,*
> *And I will repay those who hate Me.* (Deuteronomy 32:39-41)

His wrath, anger, fury, and vengeance are as much a part of His majesty as His mercy, power, patience, faithfulness, and holiness. For God to exist as a holy and loving God, He must also be wrathful. He is holy; therefore, He is opposed to all that is polluted. He loves what is right and clean, and actively sets Himself against all that is sinful.

God hates sin. God is filled with a fiery displeasure and enduring rage, opposing sin with all His being in every person, place, and time in which He finds it. He hates it in Satan, Pharaoh, Jezebel, and Judas. He also hates it in Moses, David, and Peter. He hates sin in all its forms—respectable sins and heinously shocking sins. It is part of God's perfection that He is essentially opposed to sin.

A DESCRIPTION OF GOD'S WRATH

God's wrath is His unalterable abhorrence of all unrighteousness. It is the displeasure and indignation of God against every form of evil. God's wrath is not passive emotion. Rather it is linked with His determination to be the enemy of sin until it is fully vanquished. God is the avenger of all wrong, the implacable enemy of all that pollutes. This is one aspect of the weight of His majesty.

A WIDER PICTURE OF GOD'S WRATH

1.   God's wrath is essential to His person.

Wrath is not something that He can choose to possess or not to possess. He may not always exercise His wrath in the same manner, but He is essentially the one person who hates sin with an infinite hatred.

As in Isaiah's experience (6:3-5), it is not an exercise of power that humbles humankind but simply that the Lord displays himself as he always has been.

—J. A. Motyer

2.   God's wrath is unique.

He is solitary in His perfect hatred of all that is morally wrong. Others may hate sin to a limited degree, may hate some sins but not all sins, or may hate sins more one day than another. God's hatred of sin is unique; no one has ever hated sin like Him.

3.   God's wrath is immutable.

Malachi's statement, "I am the LORD, I do not change," applies to His wrath too. His opposition to sin cannot be altered by anything inside or outside of Him. We must be clear about this. God in the New Testament hates sin as much as He did in the Old Testament. He has not changed. The cross of Christ has not altered God's wrath. His righteous anger against sin has not grown less. Grace does not remove the fundamental quality of wrath in God. The only way the Christian can escape the wrath of God is by being in Christ, because Jesus Christ endured the wrath as our substitute, our representative.

4.   God's wrath is infinite.

There are no measurements for His hatred of sin. He often chooses to restrain it in mercy, but as an attribute it exists within the being of God without limit. If you look at God's wrath as it was poured out in the flood, upon Sodom and Gomorrah, or at the cross, or if you wait and see hell revealed at the end of time, even at these points God's anger against sin is hidden more than revealed.

5.   God's wrath is therefore incomprehensible.

If God's greatness (His magnitude) is "unsearchable" (Psalm 145:3), so are all of His attributes.

COPY   PSALM 90:11.

_____

_____

No human and no angel can fully comprehend the wrath of God toward a single sin.

6.   God's wrath is all-present and eternal.

As God exists in all places at once and at all times simultaneously, so does His wrath. That is, His hatred of sin exists everywhere God exists and in every moment that God inhabits. His aggressive opposition to sin cannot be excluded from any place or time. He hates sin in Muslim countries and in Christian countries. He hates sin today as much as He did in the days of Moses or Isaiah.

7.   God's wrath is all-knowing.

As God is effortlessly aware of all facts, His wrath is based upon a complete and flawless understanding of each person's sins. He judges righteously, testing the mind and the heart of each person (Jeremiah 11:20).

8.   God's wrath is all-powerful.

There are times when a righteous anger grips the Christian. Yet no Christian has ever possessed the infinite power of God with which to deal with sin. If God were to unleash His righteous anger against the sinner, who could restrain His hand? His wrath will one day roll over the unrepentant sinner like a tsunami. There will be no words to describe the union of all wrath and all power on that day.

COPY   JEREMIAH 10:10.

_____

_____

The god which the vast majority of professing Christians "love" is looked upon very much like an indulgent old man, who Himself has no relish for folly, but leniently winks at sin. Yet for one sin . . . the fallen angels were thrown out of Heaven, our first parents were banished from Eden, Moses was excluded from Canaan, Elisha's servant smitten with leprosy, and Ananias and Sapphira were cut off from the land of the living.

— A. W. Pink

9. God's anger is a holy anger.

Perfect purity of motive and manner, separated in all respects from any influence of sin, always attend the expression of His wrath. He is holy in all His ways, even in the display of His wrath.

10. God's wrath is patient.

Do not mistake the delay of judgment as proof that God no longer hates sin. We tend to act immediately when we are truly enraged. But God is slow to anger.

COPY NAHUM 1:3.

_____

_____

_____

As God's mercies are new every morning toward His people, so His anger is new every morning against the wicked.

— Matthew Henry

The word that the New Testament uses for wrath indicates a slow building, like the pressure of water against a dam. God is continually provoked, provoked by every sin of every person in every place and time. And yet He is never a hot-head. Wrath will come, but the one who hates sin most is also the slowest to anger. But when He does act in His holy anger, who will be able to stand before Him?

DAY 2: THE WRATH OF GOD TOWARD NINEVEH IN THE DAYS OF NAHUM

You have taken a glance at the bigger picture of God's wrath. Today you will have an opportunity to see what that looks like when it is exercised against the people of Nineveh.

Nineveh does not understand the living God, and in her ignorance she has made Him her enemy. The capital of the great Assyrian empire, Nineveh, was raised up by God to punish the idolatrous Israelites in the northern ten tribes; however, she became proud and desired to greedily take Judah as well. God cast Nineveh down in His wrath in the year 612 B.C. by the hands of the Babylonians.

Jonah, God's reluctant prophet, is sent to preach a message of impending judgment on the people of Nineveh. The prophet records an extraordinary example of national repentance, and God's wrath is restrained.

God's holy wrath is poured out on what He hates because it damages and destroys what He loves.

— Sinclair Ferguson

READD JONAH 3:4-10.

It is a sad evidence of human nature that 140 years later the people of Nineveh had once again become proud, merciless, idol-worshipping enemies of God. The Ninevites had become confident, hoping in their renowned city's defenses. A wall surrounded the capital that was 100 feet high, and wide enough for three chariots to ride side by side on its top. It had 1,200 defensive towers built throughout its seven and a half miles. The wall was surrounded by a moat that was 140 feet wide. They felt secure against the threat of any neighboring nation, but Nineveh had entered a conflict with the living God, and it was one she could not hope to survive.

Another prophet, Nahum, is given a message to deliver. In three chapters we read of the effects of God's wrath. There are two audiences for these words, as is often the case: the enemies of God, who are determined to continue in a course of rebellion; and the children of God, who are weak and despairing, but who have reason to hope that the activity of God will result in their purification and ultimate rescue.

NAHUM'S DESCRIPTION OF GOD

READD NAHUM 1:1-3a.

1. He is jealous.

Here we see the tender root of God's terrible wrath, jealousy. While there is a sinful jealousy, holy jealousy is linked with love and rightful possession. A husband is jealous for his wife's love; a king is jealous for his subjects' loyalty. God will not allow any rival when it comes to the honor He is due in creation. His burning jealousy for humanity's loyalty and love is greatly offended. Jealous wrath is at the heart of what we are reading about in Nahum's book. In holy jealousy God raised up the Assyrian empire in the first place, when dealing with idolatrous Israel. Jealousy for His people's safety cast proud Assyria down.

2. He is avenging and wrathful (possessing wrath).

He will avenge all wrong. It is who He is. His wrath is mentioned three times in these verses. He possesses an internal hatred of sin that is expressed in fury. It is never an out-of-control anger, but to those who are the objects of its focus, it will feel out-of-control.

His holy wrath is described in several different ways.

SLOW TO ANGER

Nineveh had lived against God many years and yet had not been destroyed. Perhaps they thought there was no wrath for them? But God tells them that He has wrath reserved for them. The delay is not due to God's indifference toward their sin, but His patience. They had experienced His patience for 140 years, dating to the period when Jonah preached to them.

GREAT IN POWER

He is not easily provoked, but once He has chosen to pour out His wrath, none can possibly stand before it. Even the delay of wrath is linked with power. His omnipotence is restraining an infinite wrath that is held in reserve until the right moment.

JUST AND RIGHTEOUS

God delights in moral purity and hates all law-breaking. God also delights in justice, and when His wrath is poured out it will not be extinguished until every guilty person receives a just sentence.

THE MEASURE OF GOD'S POWER

READD NAHUM 1:3b-8.

We mentioned that God's wrath was great in power—but how great? Nahum turns to nature to help us understand the infinity of this divinely powerful fury.

- Look up at the sky; see the storms. These terrify us, but they simply mark the way of the LORD, and the great thunder clouds are the dust about His feet.

- Look at the seas. They appear endlessly wide and deep, stretching everywhere. To God they are nothing; He merely rebukes them (as He did the Red Sea and the Jordan), and they are dried up.

- Look at the earth, with its fertile plains and forests (Bashan, Carmel, Lebanon). They appear to be an endless supplier of all humanity needs for food and shelter, yet if God turns His wrath against them for one moment, they wither.

- Look to the towering mountains and rolling hills. They feel unmovable and eternal to people like us, but God will shake them in His anger. The earth itself will heave and toss before the strength of His anger.

Some there be who sit in judgment upon the great Judge, and condemn the punishment which he afflicts as too severe. As for myself, I cannot measure the power of God's anger; but let it burn as it may, I am sure that it will be just.

— C. H. Spurgeon

195

- Look at the all-consuming power of fire. God's wrath will come like the eruption of the volcano, pouring out over a land, consuming all, even the stones—a sea of fire rolling over the land and its inhabitants.

The prophet then asks:

Who can stand before His indignation?
Who can endure the burning of His anger? (Nahum 1:6)

GOD'S MESSAGE TO NINEVEH

Now, the God of infinite wrath brings a message to Nineveh, capital of the Assyrian empire.

The first part of the message is spoken directly to Nineveh and Assyria.

READ NAHUM 1:9-11.

This nation has plotted against the God who raised them up for His use. Now God will make them like a pile of dried thorns. What can be done with the wood of thorns? Can you make a home with it? Can you build tools with it? It is worthless, and it will be burned. God will make the nation to act like a drunken man, stumbling about and unaware of his danger. Nineveh will fall and never rise again.

The second part of the message is directed toward Judah, God's people.

READ NAHUM 1:12-15.

God seeks what we should seek—his glory, in and through men—and it is for the securing of this end, ultimately, that he is Jealous.

—J. I. Packer

God had indeed used Assyria in earlier days to discipline Israel; however, they will not again afflict His people. God will break Assyria's power over His people. In fact, He has already sent out the royal command; it is as good as done. God's wrath will see to it that Assyria is forgotten, her idols destroyed, and her temple defiled. God Himself will dig her grave!

Stop and ask yourself: when you read words like these do you mistake them for poetic passion? Has the prophet become so caught up in his words that he has overstated the case? We are not always allowed to see the completion of prophecies, but in this case we know the outcome. Three centuries after this prophecy, Alexander the Great passed by the ruins of Nineveh and never even noticed it. So complete was its destruction that it was not discovered until 1842 by two archeologists, Layard and Botta.

It is no small thing to provoke the God of infinite wrath.

HOPE IN THE FACE OF GOD'S WRATH

There is one more thing in this passage that we must see about God's wrath—the hope!

COPY NAHUM 1:7-8.

_____

_____

_____

_____

COPY NAHUM 1:15.

_____

_____

_____

_____

Do you see it? The wrath of God, as terrible as it is to His enemies, is a source of hope to His people. God is good, and as such He is a stronghold and refuge for His people. His wrath will pour over the enemies of His church like a flood, pursuing them even into darkness. But the wrath of God against sin and sinners is good news for those who have run to Christ for refuge. And so the good news goes out: Peace! Pay your vows to God again! The enemy is cast down before the holy wrath of your God!

Nineveh must ask, as must all who reject Christ as the only refuge, "If God is against us, what does it matter who is for us?"

But every enemy of Christ that comes to Him repenting and believing, laying aside all argument and embracing the complete rights of the Savior-King, may say with the apostle Paul, "If God is _for_ us, who is _against_ us?"

DAY 3: THE WRATH OF GOD POURED OUT UPON HIS SON

We saw yesterday that just as God's wrath is a terrible reality for those who live against His rule, it is a source of unexpected hope for those who run to Him for refuge. Today you will find out how that can be. How can God's wrath being poured out on our sin be anything other than terror for us? How can a refuge be provided for the sinner by the living God who hates sin with a perfect hatred?

Today you will be looking at the clearest and most disarming display of God's wrath: the cross of Jesus Christ. It is the highest and clearest view we have of God's weighty majesty: His zeal, justice, mercy, wisdom, immutability, holiness, and wrath. Here is the great unveiling of divine glory. It is the place where the unrepentant sinner's hopes are dashed to pieces and the Christian's fears are alleviated.

Is it not amazing to you that the moment in which God so fully displays His wrath is the same moment that the most wretched sinner may look and find hope through Jesus Christ?

Our limited time today will be devoted to studying the cross, as the display of God's wrath, from three viewpoints:

- ABOVE THE CROSS – The view of the Lawmaker.

- UPON THE CROSS – The view of the sin-bearer.

- BELOW THE CROSS – The view of sinners.

THE GLORY OF GOD'S WRATH WAS SEEN FROM ABOVE THE CROSS

How does God view the outpouring of His wrath upon His only begotten Son?

We read in ACTS 2:22-23:

> *Men of Israel, listen to these words: Jesus the Nazarene, a man attested to you by God with miracles and wonders and signs which God performed through Him in your midst, just as you yourselves know—this Man, delivered over by the predetermined plan and foreknowledge of God, you nailed to a cross by the hands of godless men and put Him to death.*

Justice is as much vindicated by the redemption of Christ as if it had poured all its vials of wrath upon the sinner.

— C. H. Spurgeon

God's plan was accomplished at the cross, not the plans of the Jewish and Roman leaders. We can go further and say that it was the "good pleasure" of the Father to crush the Son under His wrath.

COPY ISAIAH 53:10.

_____

_____

_____

How can that be true? Isaiah 53 cannot be saying that God is displeased with the Son. The self-sacrifice of Jesus was the greatest display of His love for the Father (John 14:31). On the contrary, He has always been the delight of the Father.

We know this by prophecy.

> Isaiah 42:1a
> *Behold, My Servant, whom I uphold;*
> *My chosen one in whom My soul delights.*

We hear this from the Father at the beginning of Christ's ministry.

> Matthew 3:16-17
> *After being baptized, Jesus came up immediately from the water; and behold, the heavens were opened, and he saw the Spirit of God descending as a dove and lighting on Him, and behold, a voice out of the heavens said, "This is My beloved Son, in whom I am well-pleased."*

We hear this from the Father as Christ nears the cross.

> Matthew 17:5
> *While he was still speaking, a bright cloud overshadowed them, and behold, a voice out of the cloud said, "This is My beloved Son, with whom I am well-pleased; listen to Him!"*

The reason goes deep into the eternal good pleasure of the triune God. The Father chose the Son to be the mediator of a people. He would stand in their place as their representative, as Adam stood in the place of humanity in the garden. As Adam's failure was imputed to those whom he represented (the human race), so Christ's obedience would be imputed to His followers and their sin would be imputed to Him.

This is what Paul was referring to in ROMANS 5:15, 17, 19:

But the free gift is not like the transgression. For if by the transgression of the one the many died, much more did the grace of God and the gift by the grace of the one Man, Jesus Christ, abound to the many . . . . For if by the transgression of the one, death reigned through the one, much more those who receive the abundance of grace and of the gift of righteousness will reign in life through the One, Jesus Christ . . . . For as through the one man's disobedience the many were made sinners, even so through the obedience of the One the many will be made righteous.

It is put most clearly by Paul in 2 CORINTHIANS 5:21:

He made Him who knew no sin to be sin on our behalf, so that we might become the righteousness of God in Him.

Paul was not the only one to glory in this great substitution. Listen to Peter:

. . . and He Himself bore our sins in His body on the cross, so that we might die to sin and live to righteousness; for by His wounds you were healed. (1 Peter 2:24)

It was that transaction that made it fair for the Holy God to turn His face from the Son and to pour out His wrath upon Him. It was that transaction that made it true for Isaiah to say:

But the LORD was pleased
To crush Him, putting Him to grief;
If He would render Himself as a guilt offering,
He will see His offspring,
He will prolong His days,
And the good pleasure of the LORD will prosper in His hand. (Isaiah 53:10)

That plan, that "good pleasure" of the LORD, did in fact prosper in the hands of Jesus Christ as He offered Himself as the guilt offering on behalf of His people. As their representative, He not only lived a life of perfect obedience, but bore their guilt and suffered the full wrath of God that was due to them. When God views His wrath poured out on His Son, He sees the Christians' representative saving them by one great act of propitiation (Romans 3:21-26), and at the same time the Father sees His honor being vindicated as the just judge who justifies believers. Thus the cross is much more than a display of God's pity for sinners. It

Dear Lord, what heavenly wonders dwell
In Thy atoning blood!
By this are sinners snatched from hell,
And rebels brought to God.

— Anne Steele

is the legal transaction in which the Christian's sin is transferred to the sin-bearer, and the sin-bearer's righteousness is transferred to the Christian.

One glorious fact which we must not overlook is that the cross is the only place where God's wrath is fully satisfied. No act of judgment, not the flood, or the destruction of Sodom and Gomorrah, or the Babylonian exile, ever fully satisfied God's wrath. Even hell will never fully satisfy the legal requirements for punishment. Sin is an infinite offense. Hell can never end and must always be "the judgment to come" because hell is not payment for the infinite offense—it is punishment for crimes against God. The only place where we see the wrath of God toward sin fully satisfied is when the sinless Lamb of God bore the sins of His people on the cross and died. His infinite worth as the God-Man brought an infinite payment and satisfied God's wrath.

This brings us to our second point.

THE GLORY OF GOD'S WRATH WAS SEEN FROM UPON THE CROSS

What did Jesus think of the wrath of God as He bore it on the cross? He knew that the cross would vindicate the Father's expression of mercy to those who did not deserve it. Surely this vindication of the Father is part of what the writer of Hebrews is talking about.

> . . . *fixing our eyes on Jesus, the author and perfecter of faith, who for the joy set before Him endured the cross, despising the shame, and has sat down at the right hand of the throne of God.* (Hebrews 12:2)

Have you ever considered that the Son of God was the only man who has ever understood the wrath of God? The rest of us have woefully inadequate views of this perfection in God. The Lord Jesus understood the full measure of this holy anger, and yet He gave Himself freely to its crushing power on the cross.

By His own testimony, two reasons must have been in the mind of our Lord.

First, embracing the wrath of God on the cross was an act of obedience by the Son to the Father. By submitting Himself to the Father's wrath, He demonstrated that He loved His Father unreservedly.

John 14:30-31
I will not speak much more with you, for the ruler of the world is coming, and he has nothing in Me; but so that the world may know that I love the Father, I do exactly as the Father commanded Me. Get up, let us go from here.

Never forget that this is the most fundamental thing to Jesus—doing the good pleasure of His Father. He came to do the will of the Father who sent Him. He drank the "cup" the Father placed in His hands, the cup of wrath. This made the cross glorious to the Son.

Second, embracing the wrath of God on the cross was an act of astonishing love for His bride, the church.

> John 10:11-13, 17-18
> *I am the good shepherd; the good shepherd lays down His life for the sheep. He who is a hired hand, and not a shepherd, who is not the owner of the sheep, sees the wolf coming, and leaves the sheep and flees, and the wolf snatches them and scatters them. He flees because he is a hired hand and is not concerned about the sheep . . . . For this reason the Father loves Me, because I lay down My life so that I may take it again. No one has taken it away from Me, but I lay it down on My own initiative. I have authority to lay it down, and I have authority to take it up again. This commandment I received from My Father.*

The wounds of Christ were the greatest outlets of His glory that ever were. The divine glory shone more out of His wounds than out of all His life before.

— Robert Murray M'Cheyne

Later Paul stated the same thing to the Ephesian believers:

> *Husbands, love your wives, just as Christ also loved the church and gave Himself up for her, so that He might sanctify her, having cleansed her by the washing of water with the word, that He might present to Himself the church in all her glory, having no spot or wrinkle or any such thing; but that she would be holy and blameless.* (Ephesians 5:25-27)

Both of these realities would have made the cross a thing of dreadful glory to the Son.

THE GLORY OF GOD'S WRATH WAS SEEN FROM BENEATH THE CROSS

This is where we usually begin. We think of the benefit to the sinner. But having started with the pleasure of the Father and the motivation of the Son, we are now ready to better grasp the truly amazing grace of the cross as we view it from our perspective.

The cross proves forever that humanity cannot fix itself by any other means.

COPY GALATIANS 2:21.

_____

_____

If mankind could fix itself by rule-keeping, education, religious ceremony, or any other means, then Christ died in vain.

What is so glorious about the wrath of God being poured out on His Son for the sinner?

1. It removes the offense between God and the rebel, providing reconciliation.

UNDERLINE what Christ accomplished for the believer, as described in each of the following verses.

Ephesians 2:12-13
. . . remember that you were at that time separate from Christ, excluded from the commonwealth of Israel, and strangers to the covenants of promise, having no hope and without God in the world. But now in Christ Jesus you who formerly were far off have been brought near by the blood of Christ.

Colossians 2:13-14
When you were dead in your transgressions and the uncircumcision of your flesh, He made you alive together with Him, having forgiven us all our transgressions, having canceled out the certificate of debt consisting of decrees against us, which was hostile to us; and He has taken it out of the way, having nailed it to the cross.

2. It provides a means for a full pardon to be given by the High King to the lowest sinner.

Hebrews 10:11-14
Every priest stands daily ministering and offering time after time the same sacrifices, which can never take away sins; but He, having offered one sacrifice for sins for all time, sat down at the right hand of GOD, waiting from that time onward until His enemies be made a footstool for His feet. For by one offering He has perfected for all time those who are sanctified.

How can God forgive and still remain God? —that is the question. The Cross is the vindication of God. The Cross is the vindication of the character of God. The Cross not only shows the love of God more gloriously than anything else, it show His righteousness, His justice, His holiness, and all the glory of His eternal attributes. They are all to be seen shining together there. If you do not see them all you have not seen the Cross.

— Martyn Lloyd-Jones

Romans 8:1-3

Therefore there is now no condemnation for those who are in Christ Jesus. For the law of the Spirit of life in Christ Jesus has set you free from the law of sin and of death. For what the Law could not do, weak as it was through the flesh, God did: sending His own Son in the likeness of sinful flesh and as an offering for sin, He condemned sin in the flesh . . . .

3. It alters us so deeply when we come to Christ that we are forever distracted from the world and charmed by Jesus Christ.

COPY GALATIANS 6:14.

_____

_____

_____

The wrath of God, viewed in its fiercest and fullest expression at the cross, is a thing of terrible beauty. It is the weight of His majesty.

DAY 4: WHAT AROUSES THE INFINITE WRATH OF GOD

Not all the vials of judgment that have or shall be poured out upon the wicked world, nor the flaming furnace of a sinner's conscience, nor the irreversible sentence pronounced against the rebellious demons, nor the groans of the damned creatures—give such a demonstration of God's hatred of sin—as the wrath of God let loose upon His Son!

—Stephen Charnock

For every true follower of Jesus Christ a refuge has been provided through His cross. The greatest display of divine wrath, poured out on the sin-bearer, is also the greatest display of mercy and hope for those who deserve wrath. But Christianity is not merely being declared "not guilty" by the king. It is much more than that. Full royal pardon is only the beginning. Now the Christian desires, from gratitude, to live a life that is free from all that offends the Majesty on High. Perhaps we need reminding today of some of the things that arouse the wrath of God. They may surprise you.

1. God's wrath is aroused when you suppress His truth in unrighteousness.

COPY ROMANS 1:18.

_____

_____

While listening to a sermon or reading the Bible, have you ever held the truth at a distance? Have you ever prevented it from getting too close? It is easy to do. It also provokes God to wrath.

2.   God's wrath is aroused when you refuse to be satisfied with Him and His provisions; instead, you turn away from God in your heart to unjust gain.

COPY ISAIAH 57:17.

_____

_____

_____

_____

Have you ever felt empty in religion and allowed your heart to drift back to the old fillers? It is surprisingly easy to do. It provokes God to wrath.

3.   God's wrath is aroused when there is a hard-hearted, calloused, attitude toward sin.

COPY JEREMIAH 4:3-4.

_____

_____

_____

_____

_____

A hardened heart toward God while living in sin is an easy thing to allow. You probably would not notice its existence. Yet it provokes God to wrath.

4. God's wrath is aroused when spiritual privileges are taken for granted and you become careless with the things of God.

COPY AMOS 3:1-2.

_____

_____

_____

_____

It is easy to forget that from those to whom much is given, much is required. To be careless with the things of God in the midst of His many mercies (as in a church) is a thing so easy to do that we rarely recognize it. Yet it is something that provokes God to wrath.

5. God's wrath is aroused when people refuse the royal invitation from God to repent, believe, and follow His Son.

READ MATTHEW 22:1-14.

COPY verse 7.

_____

_____

It only takes a dull spiritual ear, a distracted life, to refuse the command of Christ, "Come to Me." You may neglect other invitations and suffer no consequences. The rejection of this invitation, however, brings everlasting exposure to God's wrath.

6. God's wrath is aroused when you give your heart secretly to something other than God.

READ JEREMIAH 2:1-13.

COPY verse 13.

_____

_____

_____

This is a very short list. You might avoid all of these things and still become the object of God's immutable anger. The Bible contains many other things that offend God. Have you considered that every sin arouses the wrath of a holy God? In the nineteenth century, Archbishop Trench gave an insightful list of biblical synonyms for sin. Below is Trench's eight-fold description of sin, each aspect of which arouses God's wrath.

- MISSING THE MARK – That is, a faulty aim. God has placed a target and our lives are to hit the bullseye. We miss the target. It is sin whether you shoot long or short.

- TRANSGRESSION – God has given us a line saying, "This far and no farther." When we cross the line, we sin.

- DISOBEDIENCE TO HIS VOICE – That is, a willful refusal to hear and obey. God has spoken. He has told us what is required of us. Any act of disobedience to the voice of God that we hear in the pages of Holy Scripture is sin. This can include failure to listen when God speaks and refusal to hear.

- FAILURE TO STAND WHEN ONE SHOULD STAND – When a grievous sin is being committed we ought to stand against it.

- IGNORANCE OF WHAT ONE SHOULD HAVE KNOWN – God has given us His word. If we neglect this word, and thereby are unaware of all we owe Him, our ignorance is a sin.

- DIMINISHING WHAT SHOULD HAVE BEEN GIVEN IN FULL MEASURE – That is, giving God in part what you owe Him in whole. Reducing the measure of your required response to what God has given is sin. Drawing lines with God and not giving Him all He is due is sin. Giving God some things in your life so that you may keep others is sin.

- INIQUITY OR LAWLESSNESS – That is, the non-observance of law. Our consciences could speak of many occasions where we said "no" to God. God's laws touch every area of life at all times. He deserves our obedience. We are not saved by keeping rules, even God's rules; however, the cross of Christ and His work in our hearts enable us to obey from a new spirit (Romans 7:4-16), they are not a cover for rebellion.

- DISCORD IN THE HARMONIES OF NATURE – That is, the upheaval of the rightful ordering of all things in God's creation. This discord may occur between spouses, between children and parents, between employees and employers, or between friends. Ultimately all disorder is between humanity and God, and it is a result of sin.

FOR CONSIDERATION

Consider how often one or more of these manifestations of sin are allowed in your life. Which of the above descriptions by Trench, or the biblical examples, do you find most often appearing in your life?

Consider how all of these have been laid upon the Savior so that as sin-bearer He might become your sin so that you might be given the righteousness which comes from God.

Consider how detestable all eight of these ought to be to every believer, having been delivered from slavery to these things which offend our king.

DAY 5: LIVING ON THESE TRUTHS

During the twelve weeks of this study, nothing will prove a deadlier enemy than a religion made only of new concepts. You can work hard at gathering truths about God in your mind, intellectually understanding them, and even being emotionally moved by them, yet never live on them. If you desire to live unto God, having simple aids for applying truth to your life will be of great benefit.

In several previous weeks, the five metaphors in Colossians 2:6-7 were used to aid us. Today, you will have an opportunity, using those five simple pictures, to contemplate how to apply your studies regarding God's wrath.

He that would be happy in Christ's service must not only know, but do.

—J. C. Ryle

In the passage below, the five word pictures are in bold print:

> *Therefore as you have received Christ Jesus the Lord, so **walk** in Him, having been firmly **rooted** and now being **built up** in Him and **established** in your faith, just as you were instructed, and **overflowing with gratitude**.* (Colossians 2:6-7)

Let's consider how the truths we have studied this week can be lived upon by using these five pictures. [Please note that your answers to today's questions may overlap to a degree.]

HAVING RECEIVED CHRIST JESUS THE LORD . . .

1. Walk in Him

The word "walk" shows us two things about Christian living.

First, walking is an everyday activity that does not seem significant. We take thousands of steps in a day, and very few steps would be looked back upon as particularly noteworthy, much less spiritually meaningful. Our little, common choices each day may also seem insignificant, but like our steps, they do matter—because they add up to be the stuff of life. For this reason, truths about God must affect our common choices in everyday life.

Second, when a person in the ancient world walked, he or she almost certainly had a destination in mind. Today people often walk for exercise, and in that case the destination isn't important. You may walk on a treadmill or in circles around a track. That is not what Paul has in mind when he says "walk." Christians should be walking toward a definite destination: complete conformity to Christ's character. The little choices of each day, guided by the truths you are studying, should be aiming at that destination—Christlikeness. But why? Not for self-improvement, but for the pleasure and honor of our God.

With these things in mind, go back and review this week's lessons. Below, write some of the ways you can apply these truths about God's wrath in even seemingly insignificant ways that lead to the destination of Christlikeness.

_____

_____

_____

_____

_____

_____

2. Sink Your Roots in Him

Paul says that God has rooted every believer in Christ. Following Christ means daily sinking the roots of your life into the truths of God. Roots gain nutrients from the soil. Your soul may find temporary satisfaction in the junk food of our culture, or it will find lasting satisfaction in the feast of the immutable realities of God.

Go back and review this week's lessons. Below, write some of the truths that you feel are the most nourishing food for your soul. What must you feed upon if you are to live out the Christian life? Is there "junk food" that you should put away?

_____

_____

_____

_____

_____

_____

3. **Build a Life on Truth**

Each truth you learn in this study can be seen as a brick. Combined with other truths, each brick will be an essential part of building a life with Christ as the foundation. Coming to Jesus in repentance and faith is the only place to begin, but good beginnings are not all there is to Christianity. Paul knew that the Colossian Christians needed more than a foundation built on Christ; they also needed a life built by His grace with His biblical truths. To leave the truths you are studying piled like bricks in a corner of your life would be a grave mistake. You don't want to look back after twelve weeks and see a dusty pile of bricks! You need a life that is a true dwelling place for God Himself.

Review this week's lessons and ask yourself, "In what ways can I build my life (my marriage, my family, my friendships, or my work) on the realities of the just wrath of God?"

_____

_____

_____

_____

_____

4. **Become Established in Your Faith**

Paul used a word, translated in the NASB as "established," which conveys the idea of firming something up, making something stable, solid. In spiritual life, we might use the word *maturity*. You must grow to maturity in your faith (your grasp of the great realities of God), in part, so that you will not be easily shifted by false teaching or half-truths.

CONSIDER HEBREWS 5:12-14.

For though by this time you ought to be teachers, you have need again for someone to teach you the elementary principles of the oracles of God, and you have come to need milk and not solid food. For everyone who partakes only of milk is not accustomed to the word of righteousness, for he is an infant. But solid food is for the mature, who because of practice have their senses trained to discern good and evil.

Here the writer is speaking to people who have heard the truth many times but have remained immature in their faith. He tells us that maturity comes from a life that applies and practices what it is learning. Through application, you are established, or matured, in the great realities of God.

Review this week's lessons. How does understanding God's wrath help your faith to be established, solid, and unwavering? In what ways have you failed to put the truths of His wrath to practical use?

_____

_____

_____

_____

_____

With these four pictures as guides, we never want to settle for new Bible-truths which are undigested, unapplied, unsettled, and sitting like a wasted pile of bricks.

There is one more picture we need to employ. Without this final metaphor our Christianity will not reflect God.

Few believers attend as strictly as they should to Christ's practical sayings and words. There is far too much loose and careless obedience to Christ's commandments.

—J. C. Ryle

211

5. Do All of These with an Overflow of Gratitude to God

You can attempt to apply 1-4, but without a grateful heart, how can you honor God?

In the Old Testament Moses warned the people before they entered the Promised Land:

> *Because you did not serve the LORD your God with joy and a glad heart, for the abundance of all things; therefore you shall serve your enemies whom the LORD will send against you, in hunger, in thirst, in nakedness, and in the lack of all things; and He will put an iron yoke on your neck until He has destroyed you.* (Deuteronomy 28:47-48)

Surely that is a shocking message for us as well. If we go about our Christian lives trying to walk in truth, sink roots in truth, build upon truth, and be established in truth, but we do so with ungrateful hearts, we can expect divine discipline.

Review this week's lessons. What reasons for gratitude toward God arise from the study of His wrath?

_____

_____

_____

_____

_____

_____

May the God who cannot be altered in His perfect character and purposes grant you such a sight of His wrath that you can live out your faith with joy and holy awe, giving thanks for His reconciling love and provision.

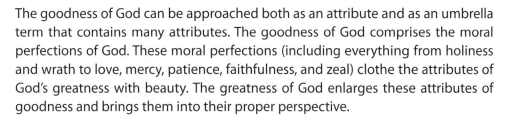

Behold your God

KNOWING THE GOD WHO IS GOOD

DAY 1: THE GOODNESS OF GOD

The goodness of God can be approached both as an attribute and as an umbrella term that contains many attributes. The goodness of God comprises the moral perfections of God. These moral perfections (including everything from holiness and wrath to love, mercy, patience, faithfulness, and zeal) clothe the attributes of God's greatness with beauty. The greatness of God enlarges these attributes of goodness and brings them into their proper perspective.

Go back and look at the key attributes of the earlier chapters in this book which describe God's greatness. Because of the attributes of greatness, God's goodness can never:

- be dependent on another person's actions or any particular circumstances

- be fully comprehended

- be lessened, made greater, or measured

- be limited with regard to action

- be limited with regard to place

- be limited with regard to time

- be mistaken or surprised

- be outmaneuvered, manipulated, or thwarted

- be tainted with any form of sin or compromise

God's goodness can only be seen correctly when it is filled with every aspect of God's greatness.

This invaluable truth explains why we began this study with the attributes of God's greatness and end with the attributes of His goodness. We are too prone to start with God's goodness because those qualities in God appear more directly "practical" and beneficial for us than the attributes of His greatness. But if we start with the goodness of God, we tend to reduce it to a man-sized goodness. In other words, we tend to reduce it to the kind of love, holiness, justice, zeal,

How good is the God we adore,
Our faithful, unchangeable Friend!
His love is as great as His power,
And knows neither measure nor end.

—Joseph Hart

patience, humility, mercy, and faithfulness that we see in humanity every day. Yet the goodness of God, in every description of it, is solitary. He alone is good in the way that we will be describing goodness. He is the source and standard of all the imperfect expressions of goodness we see around us. We must determine not to humanize God's attributes of goodness, and to prevent that we started our study with His greatness.

But there is another temptation that we may fall prey to if we are not careful. We may attempt to correct the humanized descriptions of God that are all too common in our religious culture by focusing on the transcendent greatness of God to the neglect of His goodness. We may feel, due to the abuse of these doctrines around us, that to spend significant time on the doctrines of God's love, mercy, grace, patience, and faithfulness might lead us into a self-centered and self-indulgent religion. We may think that focusing only on the infinite bigness of God will surely produce in us a determination to live holy lives.

These truths are foundational to walking with God, but when the Christian sees the transcendent majesty of God and then follows it with a serious look at God's goodness, it is the most pride-shattering, temptation-dimming thing he or she can do. It is the goodness of God that makes us love Him. It is the goodness of God that holds us to the course of consecration. It is the goodness of God that makes us repent when we stray. The goodness of God is a terrible and beautiful truth that crushes all forms of sin in the life of any believer that studies it in its biblical context. So, let's get to it!

GETTING A WORKING DEFINITION OF GOD'S GOODNESS

God is a pure and simple good; he is a light in whom there is no darkness, a good in whom there is no evil. The goodness of the creature is mixed, yes, that little goodness that is in the creature is mixed with much evil; but God is an unmixed good; he is good, he is pure good, he is all over good, he is nothing but good. God is an all-sufficient good.

— Thomas Brooks

Goodness is a term that is used so vaguely that it no longer carries any real meaning. In the Bible there are three uses of the word, and you must look at the context of the passage in which it appears to know which of the three fits that situation best.

First, goodness can refer to moral rightness. This is the type of goodness we are referring to when we speak of God's purity, justice, righteousness, and holiness. God's character is good. It contains no imperfections or pollution and it is always as it should be.

Second, goodness can refer to a beneficial quality of something. We might say a thing is good if it is suited to its intended use. Farm land is good if it is productive. A worker is good if he is qualified and fit for the tasks you give him. This sense of the word leads us to think of something as desirable. It can be used of things that are not necessarily moral or immoral.

Third, goodness can refer to benevolence, generosity, kindness, and good-will in a person. Paul speaks of the good pleasure, or kind intentions, of the Lord in our salvation (Ephesians 1:9). Our God is astonishingly kind-intentioned and benevolent toward us. He is kind to His enemies as well as His children.

> Matthew 5:43-45
> *You have heard that it was said, "You shall love your neighbor and hate your enemy." But I say to you, love your enemies and pray for those who persecute you, so that you may be sons of your Father who is in heaven; for He causes His sun to rise on the evil and the good, and sends rain on the righteous and the unrighteous.*

David writes in PSALM 34:8:

> *O taste and see that the LORD is good;*
> *How blessed is the man who takes refuge in Him!*

In that psalm we find a common occurrence: sometimes these three categories of goodness can overlap. God is morally perfect; that is true. All who take refuge in Him find that He is righteous and just. But surely David is speaking of more. God is perfectly suited as a refuge. He is beneficial to all that trust in Him. Yet there is more. God is good to us in that His good (kind) pleasure is to save all who repent and come to Him through faith in His Son. When referring to our God, *goodness* is a word infinitely full of meaning.

Goodness is known by other names when it is expressed in different situations:

- When God gives happiness that is not deserved, it is called *grace.*

- When God delights to take the lowest position to raise up the fallen, it is called *humility.*

- When God chooses to restrain righteous anger, it is called *patience.*

- When God delights to perform every aspect of His kind promises, it is called *faithfulness.*

- When God gives aid to the helpless, it is called *pity.*

- When God feels the hurt of those who hurt, it is called *sympathy.*

- When God becomes intensely earnest about the good of His people, it is called *zeal.*

He is good by nature and in all His actions. He is essentially, perpetually, superlatively, infinitely good. This week you will be looking at some of these expressions of God's goodness.

The Psalms are full of praise and gratitude for the goodness of God. It should not surprise us. The goodness of God, when we realize we do not deserve any expression of it, overwhelms us and fills our hearts with song. The Psalms present us with a union of doctrine and heart. They give the mind solid food for thought and then ignite the heart with such sights of God's goodness that a song seems the best response.

Let's look at one of these now, Psalm 107.

Psalm 107 is a song for the exiles returning home from seventy years in Babylon. It is a song that deals with more than an external rescue. As with many Old Testament songs, Psalm 107 finds its ultimate fulfillment in the coming of the Messiah and the accomplishing of all that the New Covenant will offer to God's children.

It opens with a command and a reason for the command:

> *Oh give thanks to the LORD, for He is good,*
> *For His lovingkindness is everlasting.*

Thanks is all we can give to the God who possesses all; and it is the least we can give. Yet it is not enough to be personally thankful; the psalmist calls on all those who have experienced the redemption of God to spread the news of His goodness to others. The kindness of God in our redemption is painted for us using four pictures of humanity's need:

- travelers who are lost in the desert (verses 4-9)

- prisoners in irons (verses 10-16)

- a sick man (verses 17-22)

- merchants tossed upon the waves of the sea (verses 23-32)

TRAVELERS WHO ARE LOST IN THE DESERT

READ PSALM 107:4-9.

Sinners, when God stoops, will you not stoop? When from the highest heaven he seeks you, will you not seek him?

— C. H. Spurgeon

Sin's power is in its false advertisement. It promises us a paradise, but in the end its temptations lead only to a mirage. Those who chase after sin are like people who wander through a desert, aimless and confused. They are lost in a hostile environment that cannot provide what they so desperately need. They are spiritually dying of hunger and thirst. They pursue every false hope and end up tired, but sin's wilderness can never provide a place of real rest.

Then, in their despair they cry out to the LORD, and in His goodness He rescues them. He pities them and leads them by a level path to a city they can inhabit. There He quenches their thirsty souls and satisfies their spiritual hunger with what is good.

Have you ever found yourself in the same place spiritually? Chasing after every false hope, you end up empty and thirsty, tired and having no place to rest your soul. Have you then cried to the LORD until He came in His goodness and rescued you?

Verse 8 gives us the appropriate response:

> *Let them give thanks to the LORD for His lovingkindness,*
> *And for His wonders to the sons of men!*

PRISONERS IN IRONS

READ PSALM 107:10-16.

The scene changes. We now see a prisoner in a dungeon, chained in the dark, weeping. The gloom of death hangs over his head and every day that passes only adds to the despair, as he is one day closer to execution. This misery is not unjust. The jail sentence was earned by a life that rebelled against God and spurned His counsel.

Then the prisoner turns his face toward the God he has rejected and pleads for mercy. His request is heard, and the God of all compassion turns to redeem him. God cuts the iron chains and shatters the prison doors. The shadow of death no longer hangs over this man. He is freed by the very God whom He spurned.

Have you ever been this man? Have you ignored the word of the true king and rebelled against His claims? Have you spurned His words by preferring to listen to your own feelings and opinions, or the opinions of your friends and family? Have you spent years pretending that you were the ruler of your own life, and so found yourself justly imprisoned in the guilt and power of your sin? Did you cry out to God and were you amazed that He delighted to show goodness to you in your prison? Did He free you from the guilt and tyranny of your self-centeredness?

If so, then the appropriate response is given in verse 15:

> *Let them give thanks to the LORD for His lovingkindness,*
> *And for His wonders to the sons of men!*

Long my imprisoned spirit lay
Fast bound in sin and nature's night;
Thine eye diffused a quickening ray,
I woke, the dungeon flamed with light;
My chains fell off, my heart was free,
I rose went forth and followed Thee.

— Charles Wesley

217

A SICK MAN

READ PSALM 107:17-22.

Imagine a man dying of an incurable disease that he contracted through a life of rebellion against God's authority. Now the disease affects all his life with a terrible and steady progress. He lies on a bed surrounded by food that he needs but for which he has no appetite. He is close to death. In this condition he turns his cries toward the true God, and God shows His goodness by healing him.

Have you ever been on a spiritual sick bed, or in a spiritual intensive care unit? Have you been surrounded by well-meaning family and friends who tried to help by bringing you religious things? Surrounded by the things of God, you did not take advantage of the opportunity because you had no real appetite for them. As you came up to the edge of death, did you cry out to God, and did He heal your soul from its diseases?

If so, verses 21-22 give you the appropriate response to the God who is good to fools:

> Let them give thanks to the LORD for His lovingkindness,
> And for His wonders to the sons of men!
> Let them also offer sacrifices of thanksgiving,
> And tell of His works with joyful singing.

MERCHANTS TOSSED UPON THE WAVES OF THE SEA

God has in Himself all power to defend you, all wisdom to direct you, all mercy to pardon you, all grace to enrich you, all righteousness to clothe you, all goodness to supply you, all happiness to crown you. God is a satisfying good, a good that fills the heart and quiets the soul.

— Thomas Brooks

READ PSALM 107:23-32.

Here we see a very different scene. We are no longer in the darkness of a dungeon, nor in the sick room. We are on the open sea with a merchant. While making an ordinary run, this merchant is caught in a storm. The waves rise up like mountains and cast the ship into the deep valleys of the sea. There is little reason to think he will survive this trip. Courage is gone. He cries to God. God shows compassion and stills the storm and guides the ship to a safe harbor.

Have you been in that boat, spiritually? Busy with life's normal tasks, you suddenly find yourself drowning in some sorrow or overwhelmed by some situation? You cry out to God and He stills the storm and brings you safely in?

If so, the appropriate response to the God of all goodness is found in verses 31-32:

> *Let them give thanks to the LORD for His lovingkindness,*
> *And for His wonders to the sons of men!*
> *Let them extol Him also in the congregation of the people,*
> *And praise Him at the seat of the elders.*

In four simple pictures the spiritual peril of humanity has been illustrated. So, too, has the kindness of God as He hears the cries of the distressed and rescues them out of all their troubles. As you end your lesson today, take time to re-read these four descriptions of your need and thank God for the rescue you have received, or, if you are lost, imprisoned, sin-sick, or storm-tossed, cry out to Him for help. He is your only hope!

DAY 2: THE HUMILITY OF GOD

One of the sweetest and deepest expressions of God's love is found in His humility. The proud person is like the side of a scale that has nothing in it—always raised high though empty. Love is weighty and moves us to humble ourselves for the good of those we love.

WHAT HUMILITY IS *NOT*

Humility is not rooted in, and maintained by, a continued flow of false statements:

- "I'm just a nobody."

- "I'm worse than everyone else."

- "I'm not good enough to be a part of this group."

- "My condition is so bad; I don't believe even God could fix it."

These statements are not true, and cannot form the foundation of a life of humility. Humility is quite different. It is the accurate understanding of who you really are before the living God.

WHAT HUMILITY *IS*

In his little book, *Humility*, Andrew Murray writes that this quality comes from three things.

> *It is condescension in Him to behold the things of heaven, to support the beings, direct the motions, and accept the praises and services of the angels themselves, for He needs them not, nor is benefited by them.*
>
> — Matthew Henry

First, as creatures we see that God is all, and before His immensity we are happy to take our proper place beneath Him. We are His creation, and we come to feel that "nothing is more natural and beautiful and blessed than to be nothing, that God may be all." This is where all true humility must find its foundation.

Second, as sinners we realize that we have many reasons to be humble before a holy God whose law we have repeatedly broken. Murray warns that this should not be the primary motivation for humility. If it is, then our humility will be a joyless virtue. This leads to a third motivation.

Third, as recipients of undeserved favor, we gladly humble ourselves before the God who has loved us in spite of our moral deformity and willful rebellion. The awareness of God's grace, Murray argues, humbles us more than the awareness of our sinfulness.[42]

When these three perspectives are held in balance, then the believer finds that humility becomes a joy.

What is genuinely astonishing is that the Majesty on High, the Most High God who transcends all others, delights in humility and is Himself the most humble. Perhaps you have never considered this attribute as fittingly applied to God. Reflect on the following passages which show the humility of God, especially as it is demonstrated through the person and work of His Son.

Let's start with a psalm.

FILL IN THE BLANKS from PSALM 113.

> *Praise the LORD!*
> *Praise, O servants of the LORD,*
> *Praise the name of the LORD.*
> *Blessed be the name of the LORD*
> *From this time forth and forever.*
> *From the rising of the sun to its setting*
> *The name of the LORD is to be praised.*
> *The LORD is _____ above all nations;*
> *His glory is _____ the heavens.*
> *Who is like the LORD our God,*
> *Who is enthroned on _____,*
> *Who _____ to behold*
> *The things that are in heaven and in the earth?*
> *He raises the poor from the dust*

And lifts the needy from the ash heap,
To make them sit with princes,
With the princes of His people.
He makes the barren woman abide in the house
As a joyful mother of children.
Praise the LORD!

What a contrast we find in this song of worship. God is high and exalted. He sits high above every nation, reigning gloriously in the heavens. He possesses a name that is to be praised all day long and in every generation. Yet He is delighted (for no one compels Him to act in this way) to humble Himself and take notice of the things that are occurring in heaven and on earth. And what does this exalted yet self-humbling God do when He stoops to notice earth's affairs? He raises up those who are the lowest, the poor and the needy. He places them with princes. He takes the barren mother and fills her home with the joys of a family.

Stop and consider this seriously: you were created by a God who is so transcendently high that any notice of the activity of angels in heaven requires that He stoop. Your God must humble Himself every time He looks upon earth and takes notice of your life, every time He thinks of your family, every time He hears your prayers. Have you ever thought adequately of the distance between Him and all else? Have you ever gloried in His humility? No other god, even in the imagination of sinful humanity, ever boasted in its humility; yet humility is one of the sweetest aspects of our God's weighty majesty.

This is seen most clearly in the person and work of His Son.

The incarnation of the Son of God is one of the clearest proofs of God's humility. Listen to the apostle explain this aspect of Jesus' character.

Much more is it condescension in Him to behold the things that are in the earth, to visit the sons of men, and regard them, to order and overrule their affairs, and to take notice of what they say and do, that He may fill the earth with His goodness, and so set us an example of stooping to do good, of taking notice of, and concerning ourselves about our inferiors.

— Matthew Henry

> *Have this attitude in yourselves which was also in Christ Jesus, who, although He existed in the form of God, did not regard equality with God a thing to be grasped, but emptied Himself, taking the form of a bond-servant, and being made in the likeness of men. Being found in appearance as a man, He humbled Himself by becoming obedient to the point of death, even death on a cross. For this reason also, God highly exalted Him, and bestowed on Him the name which is above every name, so that at the name of Jesus every knee will bow, of those who are in heaven and on earth and under the earth, and that every tongue will confess that Jesus Christ is Lord, to the glory of God the Father.* (Philippians 2:5-11)

Jesus, as the eternal Son of God, existed always in perfect equality with His Father. Co-equal with God, yet He did not grasp that equality of glory. Instead He happily laid aside (emptied Himself of) this glory by clothing Himself with a true human soul and body, in order to do the work of a servant, the Servant. As the Servant, He continued to humble Himself by taking the most undesirable role of sin-bearer on the cross. It was for this reason that as God and Man in one, Jesus of Nazareth was raised and exalted to the throne of heaven, at His Father's right hand. From there He will rule until all creation is brought into harmony with His throne. Those who reject His claims will one day fall before Him and confess that He is indeed Lord of all. And this ultimate triumph of the humble Son will bring everlasting honor to the humble Father who planned such a way of rescue.

Another expression of God's humility is found in the way He has designed the salvation of His enemies. Let's consider one more passage, in which Jesus Himself speaks autobiographically about humility.

> Matthew 11:28-30
> *Come to Me, all who are weary and heavy-laden, and I will give you rest. Take My yoke upon you and learn from Me, for I am gentle and humble in heart, and you will find rest for your souls. For My yoke is easy and My burden is light.*

The Lord of glory is offering rest to those who have been weighed down with shame and failure, who have not been able to find rest in anything this world offers, not even in the rules and rituals of Judaism. He offers His yoke, to be united in a relationship with Him in which He is Lord and He is the one who pulls the weight. How can He make such offers? Why does He care for the pitiful people? He explains that He is gentle and humble in heart. Only a humble God would be gentle with those who are pitiful because they have disobeyed Him. Only a humble God would give rest by bringing weary people into a union with Himself through His Son.

How are we to respond? Three things are apparent in these passages.

First, we stand in awe of the king described in Psalm 113. Write a prayer of praise to the king who humbles Himself to behold heaven and earth.

_____

_____

_____

_____

I have read in Plato and Cicero sayings that are very wise and very beautiful; but I never read in either of them, "Come unto me, all ye that labor and are heavy laden."

— Augustine

Second, we embrace the rest that only the humble God-Man could provide. We bring ourselves under His gracious rule, or re-consecrate ourselves to His care, and rest ourselves intentionally in His gentle humility. Write a prayer of consecration to the God who gives rest to those who come to Him.

_____

_____

_____

Humility is nothing but the disappearance of self in the vision that God is all.

— Andrew Murray

Third, we imitate our king; we follow Him today. Paul directed us in Philippians as to how that could be done.

> *Do nothing from selfishness or empty conceit, but with humility of mind regard one another as more important than yourselves; do not merely look out for your own personal interests, but also for the interests of others. Have this attitude in yourselves which was also in Christ Jesus . . . .* (Philippians 2:3-5)

Write some practical areas that you are aware of in which you need to quit looking out merely for your own personal interests and, like Christ, humbly consider others.

_____

_____

_____

DAY 3: THE GOODNESS OF GOD AS SEEN IN HIS FAITHFULNESS

Today and tomorrow you will be considering the aspect of God's goodness that forms the foundation for the believer's hope and the unbeliever's despair: the faithfulness of God. That God is always true to Himself and His word is not surprising to us. The immutable God cannot be altered. That He would be faithful to those who are or have once been opposed to His rule is an astonishing fact.

Faithfulness is certainly a quality that fallen humanity finds hard to cultivate. We tend to be faithful only so far as it benefits us, directly or indirectly. Breaking faith with others, failing to be what we say we are and do what we say we will do, is so

Infinite love prescribes, infinite wisdom shapes, infinite faithfulness and power execute all His purposes, thoughts, and doings concerning His people.

— Octavius Winslow

common that it is expected behavior. Sin has made us focused primarily on self. Sin might be described as self against God, and self against others. It is exceedingly rare to find a person whose "word is his bond" instead of a mask over his true condition.

The Christian is not free from unfaithfulness. If you truly love the Lord Jesus, then you understand your sin is an act of unfaithfulness toward Him. It is a source of grief to all Christians that they are still capable of such treachery against the God who is presently saving them.

READ the following biblical descriptions of mankind's unfaithfulness.

UNDERLINE the way it is expressed.

Psalm 5:9
There is nothing reliable in what they say;
Their inward part is destruction itself.
Their throat is an open grave;
They flatter with their tongue.

Psalm 78:8
. . . A stubborn and rebellious generation,
A generation that did not prepare its heart
And whose spirit was not faithful to God.

Psalm 78:37
For their heart was not steadfast toward Him,
Nor were they faithful in His covenant.

Proverbs 20:6
Many a man proclaims his own loyalty,
But who can find a trustworthy [faithful] man?

Isaiah 1:21
How the faithful city [Jerusalem] has become a harlot,
She who was full of justice!
Righteousness once lodged in her,
But now murderers.

Hosea 6:4
What shall I do with you, O Ephraim?
What shall I do with you, O Judah?
For your loyalty is like a morning cloud
And like the dew which goes away early.

Treachery in marriage, among friends or colleagues, and in churches, is a heart-breaking matter. How refreshing it is to be able to lift your eyes above the unfaithfulness of sinful humanity and to see the one who is faithfulness itself, steady and unalterably trustworthy at all times.

DEFINING GOD'S FAITHFULNESS

How faithful is God? It would be helpful to get a definition of faithfulness.

One of the Hebrew words most often used for "faithfulness" (*'emuwnah*) is used in at least ten different ways in the Bible. Its earliest occurrence in the Scripture, Exodus 17:12, describes the steadiness of Moses' hands as he was helped by Aaron and Hur. Steadiness and firmness, then, are the basic ideas behind faithfulness. After this the word's usage shifts toward the idea of honesty, steadfastness, moral trustworthiness, and stability. The word is used almost entirely in connection with God or those in whom God is working.

Now, let's think of this steadiness, this firmness and stability, in our God.

1.   It is a self-existing faithfulness.

God does not have to work to maintain His faithfulness. It comes effortlessly to Him because it is part of what and who He is. It is essential to who God is.

> Psalm 89:8
> *O LORD God of hosts, who is like You, O mighty LORD?*
> *Your faithfulness also surrounds You.*

It is a beautiful picture: the Lord ruling before a great army. He bears incomprehensible might in Himself. But all around Him is the splendor of His faithfulness, His steadfastness.

Part of His faithfulness is that He always acts consistently with His character. He is sure. He is stable. He cannot be other than what He is, ever. He cannot act out of character. His character is always true to itself. Therefore, He cannot but be faithful and true to His words. God's faithfulness in His actions flows from what He is.

2.   It is an immutable faithfulness.

Our best efforts to be faithful are subject to change because we change. A nation may shift in its alliances and fail to keep its agreements because a

Great is Thy faithfulness,
O God my Father,
There is no shadow of
turning with Thee;
Thou changest not, Thy
compassions, they fail not
As Thou hast been Thou
forever wilt be.

— Thomas Chisholm

new government has taken power. But the immutable God can never act inconsistently with Himself. His faithfulness is rooted in the fact that He will always be true to Himself in His works and His words, and this spills over into His dealings with creation.

God cannot be tempted to be unfaithful to His character or word. Men often change due to the pressure of strong desires, fears, weakness, the loss of interest, or because of some interference or influence from without. Can you even imagine a person big enough to shift God? Can you imagine an event that would make Him alter His promises? Not one of these can in the least influence the uncreated I AM. He does not change.

3.   It is an eternal faithfulness.

> Psalm 119:90
> *Your faithfulness continues throughout all generations;*
> *You established the earth, and it stands.*

4.   It is an incomprehensible faithfulness.

His steadfastness is beyond the grasp of our minds or the description of our pens. The psalmist uses the metaphor of distance and height to express this.

> *Your lovingkindness, O LORD, extends to the heavens,*
> *Your faithfulness reaches to the skies.* (Psalm 36:5)

IMPLICATIONS OF GOD'S FAITHFULNESS

Have you ever considered just how often the biblical writers mention the implications of belonging to the God who alone is faithful? Tozer wrote: "You can live on froth and bubbles and little wisps of badly understood theology—until the pressure is on. And when the pressure is on, you'll want to know what kind of God you're serving."[43] Let's consider some of the ways that the faithfulness of God affects the life of the Christian.

The oath infallible
Is now my spirit's trust;
I know that He who spoke
the word
Is faithful, true and just.

— William Williams

- It is the fabric of our relationship with God through His saving work.

> Hosea 2:20
> *And I will betroth you to Me in faithfulness.*
> *Then you will know the Lord.*

- It is a faithfulness that is expressed in the form of the covenant God makes with His people.

  Deuteronomy 7:9
  Know therefore that the LORD your God, He is God, the faithful God, who keeps His covenant and His lovingkindness to a thousandth generation with those who love Him and keep His commandments . . . .

- It is a faithfulness that the believer can lean upon when the storms of temptation blow hard.

  1 Corinthians 10:13
  No temptation has overtaken you but such as is common to man; and God is faithful, who will not allow you to be tempted beyond what you are able, but with the temptation will provide the way of escape also, so that you will be able to endure it.

- It is His faithfulness that moves Him to discipline His drifting people.

  Psalm 119:75
  *I know, O LORD, that Your judgments are righteous,
  And that in faithfulness You have afflicted me.*

- It is His steadfastness, His faithfulness, that is so comforting when the repentant person seeks forgiveness.

  1 John 1:9
  If we confess our sins, He is faithful and righteous to forgive us our sins and to cleanse us from all unrighteousness.

- It is His faithfulness that forms a foundation for our boasts in Him.

  Hebrews 10:23
  Let us hold fast the confession of our hope without wavering, for He who promised is faithful . . . .

- God is not only the restorer of His people, but in His faithfulness He is their keeper.

  1 Thessalonians 5:23-24
  Now may the God of peace Himself sanctify you entirely; and may your spirit and soul and body be preserved complete, without blame at

the coming of our Lord Jesus Christ. Faithful is He who calls you, and He also will bring it to pass.

Below, write a list of the areas of the Christian's life that are affected by God's faithfulness, based on the verses above.

_____

_____

_____

_____

Before we end this day, please consider that the faithfulness of God is also the source of hopelessness to those who hope to escape His wrath while living for themselves. Listen to John's description of the final judgment and notice his mention of God's faithfulness.

COPY REVELATION 19:11.

_____

_____

_____

_____

If the faithful God is for you, who can be against you? But if the faithful God is against you, what does it matter who is for you?

DAY 4: THE FAITHFULNESS OF GOD AS SEEN IN THE LABORS OF HIS SON

The New Covenant labors of Jesus Christ demonstrate the faithfulness of God to keep His word to humanity. But the foundation of the New Covenant is laid deeper than God's steadfastness as He keeps His word to believers. The labors of Jesus are first and foremost a manifestation of His faithfulness to His Father who entrusted Him with the task of redemption.

It is often profitable to step back from our own salvation and see the bigger picture of the Son's faithfulness to His Father as the foundation of our confidence that this covenant of grace will not fail. To see the Son's faithfulness, we will look at an Old Testament song which contrasts the unfaithfulness of Judah, the failed servant of God, with the steadfastness of the Messiah, the faithful Servant. Isaiah speaks of this in chapter 50 of his prophecy.

JUDAH, THE UNFAITHFUL SERVANT OF GOD

READ the passage below.

UNDERLINE the various expressions of Judah's unfaithfulness.

> Isaiah 50:1-3
> *Thus says the LORD,*
> *"Where is the certificate of divorce*
> *By which I have sent your mother away?*
> *Or to whom of My creditors did I sell you?*
> *Behold, you were sold for your iniquities,*
> *And for your transgressions your mother was sent away.*
> *Why was there no man when I came?*
> *When I called, why was there none to answer?*
> *Is My hand so short that it cannot ransom?*
> *Or have I no power to deliver?*
> *Behold, I dry up the sea with My rebuke,*
> *I make the rivers a wilderness;*
> *Their fish stink for lack of water*
> *And die of thirst.*
> *I clothe the heavens with blackness*
> *And make sackcloth their covering."*

Look at the unfaithfulness of God's people.

- They act as if God had divorced them. They are living as if they are free to find another spouse or god.

- They act as if God had sold them. They are living as if they are free to find another master or lord.

- They are unresponsive when God calls them to return.

- They seem to have forgotten that God is powerful and could restore them. He reminds them of the displays of His power in the past when He rescued them.

If Jesus undertook to bring me to glory, and if the Father promised that he would give me to the Son to be a part of the infinite reward of the travail of his soul; then, my soul, till God himself shall be unfaithful, till Jesus shall cease to be the truth, thou art safe.

— C. H. Spurgeon

229

Do you see yourself in this description? Do you see your church in this passage?

- Do we act as if we have been divorced and are free to search about for another husband?

- Would people who attend our churches describe us as a people living as if we were free to find another master, to live by another's rules?

- Are you personally unresponsive to God, hearing sermons and reading the Bible but never really giving God the response required?

- Has your church chosen to look for clever new ways to make the gospel work, having forgotten that her God has sufficient power to restore her?

JESUS, THE FAITHFUL SERVANT OF GOD

Now let's look at the faithfulness of the Messiah, the Servant of God.

READ the passage below.

UNDERLINE the descriptions of the Messiah's faithfulness to His Father.

My dear Redeemer and my Lord,
I read my duty in Thy Word;
But in Thy life the law appears
Drawn out in living characters.

Such was Thy truth and such Thy zeal,
Such deference to Thy Father's will,
Such love, and meekness so divine,
I would transcribe and make them mine.

— Isaac Watts

Isaiah 50:4-6
The Lord GOD has given Me the tongue of disciples,
That I may know how to sustain the weary one with a word.
He awakens Me morning by morning,
He awakens My ear to listen as a disciple.
The Lord GOD has opened My ear;
And I was not disobedient
Nor did I turn back.
I gave My back to those who strike Me,
And My cheeks to those who pluck out the beard;
I did not cover My face from humiliation and spitting.

Strangely, the description of the Son's faithfulness starts with the results.

- The Son has the words He needs to sustain the weary soul.

- The Son has the hearing of one who is a perfect pupil.

Now we come to the root of these qualities.

- The Son was never disobedient to what the Father taught Him in the Scriptures.

- The Son was obedient even when it meant the cross.

A listening ear, a fully responsive heart—these were the marks of the Son's faithfulness to the Father. Never, not even once, did He wake up and read the Bible and pray and refuse to give His Father His whole-hearted obedience to what He heard that day from Him. Two words are used in the Hebrew to describe ways He theoretically might have been unfaithful, one meaning "disobedient," and one meaning "turn back" (verse 5). The first one has the idea of open rebellion. Christ never told His Father "No." But the second is subtler. It carries the idea of simply stepping back from the edge, or side-stepping someone and letting him run past you. Jesus never side-stepped the commands of God and let them quietly pass by, as if He had never heard them.

We have all proven unfaithful servants in both of these ways. There are things you have read or heard from God's word and you have quietly but determinedly told God, "No!" Yet there are other things that you have heard and read which pricked your conscience and instead of arguing with God or outright rebelling against Him, you quietly stepped aside and let the command pass you by and pretended it was not for you. This is something Jesus never did.

The faithfulness of the Son to the Father becomes all the more amazing when you consider the foreshadowing of the cross in this passage. Listen again to verse 6:

> *I gave My back to those who strike Me,*
> *And My cheeks to those who pluck out the beard;*
> *I did not cover My face from humiliation and spitting.*

Does the prophecy remind you of the scene on the night of Jesus' crucifixion?

MARK 14:65 records the end of that Jewish trial:

> *Some began to spit at Him, and to blindfold Him, and to beat Him with their fists, and to say to Him, "Prophesy!" And the officers received Him with slaps in the face.*

Think carefully on the faithfulness of the Son. Day after day, for approximately thirty-three years, His joy in life was to express His love to the Father through a perfect faithfulness. As He grew up, He met with His Father each morning, learning that day all that the Father wished to teach Him. A perfect pupil! No sin in His heart or mind to cloud the lessons. Each day He responded with faithfulness to all that the Father showed Him. But one day He awakened and sat at His Father's feet and He understood that that would be the day He would become the sin-bearer, the day He would be crucified according to the Father's plan from eternity past. Did He alter His response when He realized that the cross was next? No. He set His face "like flint" (Isaiah 50:7) and faithfully went forward like He did every

It was a lonely path He trod,
From every human soul apart;
Known only to Himself and
   God
Was all the grief that filled
   His heart,
Yet from the track
He turned not back,
Till where I lay in want and
   shame,
He found me—Blessed be
   His name!

— C. A. Tyderman

other day. He did not rebel at that moment. He did not avoid obedience quietly, as if He had not heard the Father's words. He is the perfectly faithful Servant of God.

This of course does not surprise the believer. Read the passages below that mention Jesus' faithfulness.

COPY ISAIAH 11:5.

_____

_____

_____

_____

COPY HEBREWS 2:17; 3:2.

_____

_____

_____

_____

_____

_____

COPY REVELATION 1:5.

_____

_____

_____

Christ is alone, solitary, in this quality. God has called many to serve Him. He has gifted them and entrusted them with extraordinary tasks that touched on God's honor and the good of His kingdom. Many have, by God's aid, accomplished the task the Father gave them. Yet not one has given God flawless faithfulness, except Jesus Christ.

Consider some sad proofs of the unfaithfulness of even the best of believers:

- Noah, after a century of faithful obedience, got drunk and made opportunity for his son's sin.

- Abraham, though a man of unusual faith, tried to help God, fathering a son (Ishmael) by his wife's female servant.

- Moses, known for his meekness, was provoked by the constant complaint of the Jews, dishonored God before them after years of faithful service, and lost his right to lead the people into the Promised Land.

- Gideon, after destroying the idols of his village and driving off the enemies of Israel, later made an ephod of gold that was worshipped.

- David, a man after God's own heart, abused his position of power, stole Uriah's wife, and then had her husband put to death.

- Solomon, for all his wisdom, married foreign wives who loved idols. Toward the end of his reign he used the royal treasury to fund the beginning of idolatry in the nation of Israel.

- Peter, so often bold, denied Jesus Christ three times on the night of His betrayal.

We could list more, but that is enough to make it clear that God's adopted children still are capable of unfaithfulness. God is essentially, infinitely, immutably faithful. He is steadfast and trustworthy. It is who He is. Paul tells us that Jesus Christ is the union of true humanity with all the fullness of deity. As God and man, Jesus too is essentially, infinitely, immutably faithful. It is who He is.

Day 5: Living on These Truths

You have had an opportunity this week to begin to consider the goodness, humility, and faithfulness of God. Today you will again be taking the metaphors of Christian growth found in Colossians 2:6-7 and applying them to these truths.

In the passage below, the five word pictures are in bold print:

> *Therefore as you have received Christ Jesus the Lord, so **walk** in Him, having been firmly **rooted** and now being **built up** in Him and **established** in your faith, just as you were instructed, and **overflowing with gratitude**.* (Colossians 2:6-7)

God is God. Because He is God, He is worthy of my trust and obedience.

— Elisabeth Elliot

Let's consider how the truths we have studied this week can be lived upon by using these five pictures. [Please note that your answers to today's questions may overlap to a degree.]

HAVING RECEIVED CHRIST JESUS THE LORD . . .

1. Walk in Him

The word "walk" shows us two things about Christian living.

First, walking is an everyday activity that does not seem significant. We take thousands of steps in a day, and very few steps would be looked back upon as particularly noteworthy, much less spiritually meaningful. Our little, common choices each day may also seem insignificant, but like our steps, they do matter—because they add up to be the stuff of life. For this reason, truths about God must affect our common choices in everyday life.

Second, when a person in the ancient world walked, he or she almost certainly had a destination in mind. Today people often walk for exercise, and in that case the destination isn't important. You may walk on a treadmill or in circles around a track. That is not what Paul has in mind when he says "walk." Christians should be walking toward a definite destination: complete conformity to Christ's character. The little choices of each day, guided by the truths you are studying, should be aiming at that destination—Christlikeness. But why? Not for self-improvement, but for the pleasure and honor of our God.

With these in mind, go back and review this week's lesson on God's humility. Below, write some of the ways in which you can apply these truths in everyday, apparently insignificant, ways that lead to the destination of Christlikeness.

_____

_____

_____

_____

_____

_____

2. Sink Your Roots in Him

Paul says that God has rooted every believer in Christ. Following Christ means daily sinking the roots of your life into the truths of God. Roots gain nutrients from the soil. Your soul may find temporary satisfaction in the junk food of our culture, or it will find lasting satisfaction in the feast of the immutable realities of God.

Go back and review this week's lessons on God's goodness from Day 1. Below, write some of the truths that you feel are the most significant food for your soul. What things did you learn this week about God that you realize you must feed upon if you are to live out the Christian life?

_____

_____

_____

_____

_____

_____

3. Build a Life on These Truths

Each truth you learn in this study can be seen as a brick. Combined with other truths, each brick will be an essential part of building a life with Christ as the foundation. Coming to Jesus in repentance and faith is the only place to begin, but good beginnings are not all there is to Christianity. Paul knew that the Colossian Christians needed more than a foundation built on Christ; they also needed a life built by His grace with His biblical truths. To leave the truths you are studying piled like bricks in a corner of your life would be a grave mistake. You don't want to look back after twelve weeks and see a pile of bricks! You need a life that is a true dwelling place for God Himself.

Review this week's lessons on God's faithfulness and ask yourself, "In what ways can I build my life (my marriage, my family, my friendships, or my work) on the realities of the faithful God?"

_____

_____

_____

_____

_____

4. Become Established in Your Faith

Paul used a word, translated in the NASB as "established," which conveys the idea of firming something up, making something stable, solid. In spiritual life, we might use the word *maturity*. You must grow to maturity in your faith (your grasp of the great realities of God), in part, so that you will not be easily shifted by false teaching or half-truths.

CONSIDER HEBREWS 5:12-14.

> *For though by this time you ought to be teachers, you have need again for someone to teach you the elementary principles of the oracles of God, and you have come to need milk and not solid food. For everyone who partakes only of milk is not accustomed to the word of righteousness, for he is an infant. But solid food is for the mature, who because of practice have their senses trained to discern good and evil.*

Here the writer is speaking to people who have heard the truth many times but have remained immature in their faith. He tells us that maturity comes from a life that applies and practices what it is learning. Through application, you are established, or matured, in the great realities of God.

Review this week's lessons on faithfulness. Below write some areas that the faithfulness of God needs to be applied to your life so you will be established, solid, unwavering in your grasp of biblical truth.

_____

_____

_____

_____

_____

_____

Be still, my soul: the Lord is on thy side;
Bear patiently the cross of grief or pain;
Leave to thy God to order and provide;
In every change He faithful will remain.
Be still my soul: thy best, thy heavenly Friend
Through thorny ways leads to a joyful end.

— Katharina von Schlegel

With these four pictures as guides, we never want to settle for new Bible-truths which are undigested, unapplied, unsettled, and sitting like a wasted pile of bricks.

There is one more picture we need to bring to mind. Without this final metaphor our Christianity will not reflect God.

5. Do All of These with an Overflow of Gratitude to God

You can attempt to apply 1-4, but without a grateful heart, how can you honor God?

In the Old Testament Moses warned the people before they entered the Promised Land:

> *Because you did not serve the LORD your God with joy and a glad heart, for the abundance of all things; therefore you shall serve your enemies whom the LORD will send against you, in hunger, in thirst, in nakedness, and in the lack of all things; and He will put an iron yoke on your neck until He has destroyed you.* (Deuteronomy 28:47-48)

Surely that is a shocking message for us as well. If we go about our Christian lives trying to walk in truth, sink roots in truth, build upon truth, and be established in truth, but we do so with ungrateful hearts, we can expect divine discipline.

Review this week's lessons. What reasons for gratitude toward God arise from the study of each of the attributes you studied this week?

GOODNESS

_____

_____

_____

HUMILITY

_____

_____

_____

FAITHFULNESS

_____

_____

_____

May the God who possesses amazing goodness, humility, and faithfulness grant you such a sight of these perfections that you can:

- walk (go about the normal things of life) in its atmosphere . . .

- sink roots for nourishment in it . . .

- build a life with it . . .

- grow firm and be established in your grasp of God's truth because of it . . .

- do all of this with an overflowing sense of gratitude to Him.

KNOWING THE GOD OF LOVE

DAY 1: THE LOVE OF GOD

God's incomprehensible and infinite love would deserve our study and adoration even if we were never allowed to receive it. But thank God, we are recipients of it! Yet it is not all about us; it is about God and the weight of His majesty. The love of God visibly displays the unique splendor of the One who made us for Himself, and that is the chief reason we are studying it this week.

In his letter to the Ephesians, Paul prays that the young believers would be able to get a better understanding of this divine love.

> *For this reason I bow my knees before the Father from whom every family in heaven and on earth derives its name, that He would grant you, according to the riches of His glory, to be strengthened with power through His Spirit in the inner man, so that Christ may dwell in your hearts through faith; and that you, being rooted and grounded in love, may be able to comprehend with all the saints what is the breadth and length and height and depth, and to know the love of Christ which surpasses knowledge, that you may be filled up to all the fullness of God.* (Ephesians 3:14-19)

The attributes of [God's] love are identical with Himself. Necessarily so, for "God is love." In making that postulate it is but another way to say God's love is like Himself, from everlasting to everlasting, immutable.

— A. W. Pink

Paul's prayer is necessary because in some ways the love of God is much more difficult to comprehend than His eternity or infinity. It appears to be a simple concept to grasp, showing up on church signs and bumper-stickers. Everyone seems ready to accept the fact that God is love. But when we are able to see ourselves as we truly are, the reality that God loves any of us is one of the most difficult biblical truths to understand and believe. It shocks our moral sense of fairness for a God like Him to delight in people like us. This love, beyond all telling or comprehending, is one of the sweetest objects of study for every Christian as well as one of the most misunderstood and abused. This week we will sit at the feet of the Most High and listen to what He says to us about His love.

But a warning first! You must determine by God's help not to simply acquire abstract concepts regarding God's love. This reality must be brought down into your life in practical ways. You must not be satisfied to merely understand how it fits theologically with other aspects of God's character (His righteous anger, for example). Ask God to help you understand His love, believe His love, experience His love, and abide in His love in ways that produce the most God-glorifying lifestyle possible. No attribute has more potential, when rightly understood, to alter your life.

GOD IS!

In 1 JOHN 4:8 we read these well-known words:

> *The one who does not love does not know God, for God is love.*

When John says that God is love, he is not saying that this is all there is to God. He expects that you are reading this sentence in the context of the whole Bible. It is a precious truth about our God, but it is not the only truth. We must not allow ourselves to reason in the following manner: "God is love, so we can rightly say, Love is God." This statement about God must be kept in close connection with other statements about God. For example, John uses this formula two other times.

In his Gospel he records Jesus' conversation with a Samaritan woman who is focused on the externals of religion. Jesus responds to her misguided questions with:

> *God is spirit, and those who worship Him must worship in spirit and truth.* (John 4:24)

Again in the opening chapter of John's first letter we read about the perfect moral nature of God and how it affects those who want to walk in fellowship with Him.

> *This is the message we have heard from Him and announce to you, that God is Light, and in Him there is no darkness at all.* (1 John 1:5)

Now John is not saying that all there is to God is "light" or "spirit." Nor can we say that all we need to know about God's actions is that they are moved by love, for "God is love." It is an observable trend that when people misunderstand and misapply the truths of the Bible, those truths tend to be downgraded to mere weightless phrases. This is nowhere more obvious than in the statement, "God is love."

A path back to a biblical understanding and experience of divine love can be discovered! We must get a clear definition of divine love, and then view it as united to the other attributes of God.

DEFINING DIVINE LOVE AND CONNECTING IT TO GOD'S OTHER ATTRIBUTES

Let's get a clear view of the love that belongs essentially to God. God's love springs from His moral perfection, His goodness. It is that perfection in God that moves Him to deal benevolently and kindly with all His creation. That general love for His creation we might call *common grace*. Yet there is a higher love. There is the love that God displays toward some of those who live against Him. This special and distinguishing grace is seen in the choosing and sending of the Son of God as our Savior. Having identified Himself with the welfare of His lost and wandering people, all three persons of the Godhead are engaged in bringing the children of God to Him in a relationship of peace and love through the New Covenant.

The ground of God's love is only and wholly in Himself . . . . There is no love nor loveliness in us that should cause a beam of His love to shine upon us.

— Thomas Brooks

Love is an umbrella term; it contains many different expressions. These expressions differ according to different circumstances that divine love encounters. For example:

- *Mercy* is God's love reaching out to the guilty.

- *Grace* is God's love poured out on the undeserving.

- *Pity* is God's love embracing the helpless and hopeless.

- *Delight* is God's love resting satisfied upon those who are "in Christ."

Now we can put weight to a word that has become weightless by connecting it to the other attributes of God. God's character, free from the fragmenting imperfections of sin, is a perfect unity. Harmony between all of His attributes is the only possibility for Him. He has never known, and never will know, any degree of internal conflict. Let's consider God's love in connection with His other perfections that you have recently studied.

1. God's love is independent and self-existing.

God owes His existence to no one, and likewise, His love is independent of anything in us. That is, it is self-originating love. Nothing in you could have called it forth. A common way to say this is to say that He drew all of His reasons for loving us from within Himself.

COPY DEUTERONOMY 7:7-8.

_____

_____

_____

_____

_____

_____

*O love of God, how strong
and true
Eternal, and yet ever new;
Uncomprehended and
unbought,
Beyond all knowledge and
all thought.
Self-fed, self-kindled, like
the light,
Changeless, eternal, infinite.*

— Horatius Bonar

2.   God's love is incomprehensible and immeasurable.

If we were to study God's love for a lifetime, asking for help from the greatest theologians and combining all we find with all that the angelic host knows, we would only be at the edge of the endless realm, only knowing as much of His love as a person knows of an entire conversation when he hears a single, whispered word. No matter where you look, even at the cross, more of this infinite love is hidden than revealed.

Paul points to the incomprehensible quality of God's love in EPHESIANS 3:17-19, praying:

> *. . . that you, being rooted and grounded in love, may be able to comprehend with all the saints what is the breadth and length and height and depth, and to know the love of Christ which surpasses knowledge . . . .*

3.   God's love is eternal and timeless.

Some days seem to be more notably filled with the experience of God's love than others. There are epochs in human history when the love of God appears more visibly active. And yet, His love exists in infinite supply in every moment of time. It exists above time.

COPY JEREMIAH 31:3.

_____

_____

4. God's love is present everywhere.

Some places may seem to be filled with the love of God and others seem to lack it. As with time, place is no limitation with regard to God and His love.

Paul preached at Athens, reminding them that when speaking of God:

> . . . *He is not far from each one of us; for in Him we live and move and exist . . . .* (Acts 17:27-28)

What is true of God is true of each of His attributes. The love of God is not essentially far from anyone.

5. God's love is all-knowing.

As you considered in previous weeks, God is all-knowing. Remember the following statements?

In 1 SAMUEL 2:3 Hannah prayed:

> *Boast no more so very proudly,*
> *Do not let arrogance come out of your mouth;*
> *For the LORD is a God of knowledge,*
> *And with Him actions are weighed.*

We read in JOB 34:21-22:

> *For His eyes are upon the ways of a man,*
> *And He sees all his steps.*
> *There is no darkness or deep shadow*
> *Where the workers of iniquity may hide themselves.*

These are terrifying realities that no one can escape, but there is a refuge in the reality that God's gracious love is linked with His all-knowing. Christians can find a sure rest for a troubled mind when they realize that the one person who knows them perfectly also loves them perfectly.

6. God's love is the love of the Most High King—Sovereign.

God's love has all the power, and He has the right to act as He sees fit. He is free to love without interference.

O Sovereign Love, to thee I cry,
Give me thyself, or else I die.

— Charles Wesley

Job 42:2
I know that You can do all things, and that no purpose of Yours can be thwarted.

As none of us deserves to be loved by this God, He is free to give His extraordinary love to whom He wishes, or to withhold it from whom He wishes.

COPY ROMANS 9:15-16.

_____

_____

_____

_____

_____

7. God's love is a righteous and just love.

It is never moved to a bad decision by sentimentalism. God always exercises His love in a way that is perfectly pure and right. God always withholds love in a way that is perfectly fair and just. We may not always understand God's choices, but we can hold to the fact that His love is always guided by His righteousness.

In the second chapter of Hosea, God speaks of the loving way He will reconstruct His relationship to His idolatrous people. He uses the metaphor of a repaired marriage. Note in the following verse that even in this gracious act He does not abandon His righteousness or justice.

> *I will betroth you to Me forever;*
> *Yes, I will betroth you to Me in righteousness and in justice,*
> *In lovingkindness and in compassion,*
> *And I will betroth you to Me in faithfulness.*
> *Then you will know the LORD.* (Hosea 2:19-20)

8. God's love is faithful.

God will not fail in His love for His people, regardless of how often they seem to forget Him.

Isaiah 49:15-16

Can a woman forget her nursing child
And have no compassion on the son of her womb?
Even these may forget, but I will not forget you.
Behold, I have inscribed you on the palms of My hands . . . .

Never have we known a love quite like the love of God. These are only a few examples of how you can gain a clearer and weightier understanding of an attribute that has been almost taken for granted, even by people who care little for God. In the coming days, you will be looking at some specific expressions of God's love, with the goal of living in that reality.

LIST the truths that you recall from today's lesson about God's love. God's love is:

_____

_____

_____

_____

_____

_____

Take some time to think about these truths and thank God for His perfect love.

Can a woman's tender care
Cease toward the child she
  bare?
Yes, she may forgetful be,
Yet will I remember thee.
Mine is an unchanging love,
Higher than the heights above,
Deeper than the depths beneath,
Free and faithful, strong as
  death.

— William Cowper

DAY 2: THE LOVE OF CHRIST FOR HIS CHURCH

God's love can be seen in two distinct ways: His general kindness toward all creation, and His distinguishing love toward His church. The general kindness, or common grace, is spoken of when the Bible says that "He causes His sun to rise on the evil and the good, and sends rain on the righteous and the unrighteous" (Matthew 5:45). This is a comforting truth for humanity, since we have all been born into the camp of His enemies (Romans 5:10).

Today you will be studying something far more wonderful, the truly amazing grace of God. Here is a love that is specific, a love that belongs only to the people of God. It is a love that rises far above the common grace shown to all creation.

I am a son of love, an object of love, a monument of love, of free love, of distinguishing love, of peculiar love, and of love that passeth knowledge, and why should I not walk in love?

— John Bunyan

Paul speaks of this love in EPHESIANS 5:25-27:

> *Husbands, love your wives, just as Christ also loved the church and gave Himself up for her, so that He might sanctify her, having cleansed her by the washing of water with the word, that He might present to Himself the church in all her glory, having no spot or wrinkle or any such thing; but that she would be holy and blameless.*

Paul's letter to the Ephesians is classified as a cyclical letter. This means that Bible scholars believe that it was written in a way that would state the general truths of Christianity, and that it was meant to be passed from Ephesus to other cities in the region. In this letter Paul does not address any specific problems in a local church. He writes about the great truths of Christianity that apply to all believers in all circumstances.

Ephesians may be summarized as a letter that unfolds both the benefits believers receive from being united to the risen Lord and the life that is to flow from these privileges. After three chapters of doctrine, Paul deals with areas of practical obedience in chapters 4 through 6. These include how believers are to maintain unity in the church, submit to each other in humility, rethink family and work, and engage in battle with spiritual enemies.

Paul speaks to the issue of marriage in verses 22-33 of chapter 5. There are other passages on marriage, but none compares to what we read in Ephesians. Here Paul moves from the love of a husband for his wife to the greater mystery of Christ's love for His church.

The love described is a love that is for His church, only for His church. We can say a couple of things about this before we examine the passage.

IT IS A DISTINGUISHING LOVE

That is, it is not experienced by all creation, and therefore those who receive it are distinguished by it. What do you think the most distinguishing mark of a Christian is? Do you think it is his or her religious activities or moral decisions? Do you think it is the way he or she dresses or talks? Many things set Christians apart from the culture, but nothing distinguishes them so much as the reality that they have been loved by God.

IT IS AN EXCLUSIVE LOVE

It is a love for the church alone. In fact, it is not appropriate that it be given to all without discrimination. This may sound strange to our ears, believing as we often do that all humanity deserves the fullest love of its Creator. In human relationships we understand exclusive love. A husband loves his wife in a way that he does not love his neighbor's wife. It would be wrong for him to love another woman with the same love that he gives his own wife. Or think of a mother: she loves her children. She loves other children also, but not in the same way that she loves her children. Even a king may care for his subjects. He is not uncaring with regard to the subjects of other nations, but he does not give them the same care that he gives to his own subjects.

Paul's message is clear in this passage, and it is a truth seen throughout the Bible. Christ's love for His church is the root of His saving actions that set the Christian apart from the world.

In Ephesians 5:25-27, we find three great truths:

1. Christ's love leads Him to give Himself for His church.

2. Christ's gift of Himself for the church has the immediate aim of setting His people apart and cleansing them.

3. Christ's gift of Himself for His church guarantees an ultimate presentation of His people, perfected before the Father.

CHRIST'S LOVE LEADS HIM TO GIVE HIMSELF FOR HIS CHURCH

This gift must include all that He did for the rescue of His people. It started in eternity past, as He dedicated Himself to the task of being our Redeemer. Then, nearly 2,000 years ago, He came from heaven and entered our world as a true human born of the virgin, Mary. He perfectly carried the Law, fulfilling all that the Father asked. He showed us the Father in all He said and did. He died on the cross as our substitute, was raised for our justification, and now rules in heaven, interceding for each Christian.

Why did He do all of this?

Love to the Father, love to his people, and that love sustained at its most intense level throughout his suffering and offering, fills [Christ's] atoning achievement with fragrance for the Father and comfort for us.

— Douglas MacMillan

_____

_____

_____

_____

It is true that He did all of this for love to His church, but something else must be considered. He did it primarily for the Father who chose Him and sent Him for this task. Listen carefully to Jesus' words on the night of His betrayal.

FILL IN THE BLANKS from the passages below.

> John 14:30-31
> *I will not speak much more with you, for the ruler of the world is coming, and he has nothing in Me; but so that the world may know*
>
> _____
>
> _____.
>
> *Get up, let us go from here.*

We must start here—Jesus loved the Father and delighted to do His will, so Jesus went to the cross for love of the Father. But there is a second object of love in the substitutionary death of Jesus: the church.

> John 10:17-18
> *For this reason the Father loves Me, because I lay down My life so that I may take it again. No one has taken it away from Me,* _____
>
> _____
>
> _____. *I have authority to lay it down, and I have authority to take it up again. This commandment I received from My Father.*

Jesus never did anything on His own initiative—except here. The Father does not take Christ's life from Him, nor do the Romans or the Jewish leaders. The cross is Jesus' highest expression of love for His church, and the Father allows His Son to give Himself of His own initiative.

Later, in EPHESIANS 5:1-2, we read that this gift of Himself for His church was a sweet smelling, pleasing sacrifice in the sight of the Father:

> *Therefore, be imitators of God, as beloved children; and walk in love, just as Christ also loved you and gave Himself up for us, an offering and a sacrifice to God as a fragrant aroma.*

CHRIST'S LOVE HAS AN IMMEDIATE AIM

Go back to Ephesians 5:26. His love effectively results in the sanctifying (setting apart) and cleansing of His church. His death not only rescued us from the penalty of sin, through it He bought us for Himself. Because of His death, we are forever His property, His subjects.

Titus 2:14

. . . [Christ Jesus], who gave Himself for us to redeem us from every lawless deed, and to purify for Himself a people for His own possession, zealous for good deeds.

But Christ's love does more than make us His own people; it also cleanses us. He takes a people whose nature has been polluted by sin and cleanses them. How is this done? If we compare Ephesians 5:26 with other Scriptures, we see that the Lord sent His Spirit with the gospel to wash the repentant sinner. The result is that the Christian is given a new nature, a new birth. The word of God alone cannot cleanse the soul, cannot bring us from spiritual death to life, but in the hands of the Almighty Spirit it can and does!

Paul speaks of this washing and the agency of the Holy Spirit in his epistle to Titus:

> *He saved us, not on the basis of deeds which we have done in righteousness, but according to His mercy, by the washing of regeneration and renewing by the Holy Spirit.* (Titus 3:5)

The result is that the once-polluted sinner is made alive and clean in the sight of God. Paul gives us the result in the first chapter of Ephesians:

> *. . . just as He chose us in Him before the foundation of the world, that we would be holy and blameless before Him . . . .* (Ephesians 1:4)

The Old Testament love poem, written by Solomon, gives the following statement from the husband to his wife. It is a fitting picture of Christ's statement to His church, made possible by His extraordinary labors on her behalf:

> *You are altogether beautiful, my darling,*
> *And there is no blemish in you.* (Song of Solomon 4:7)

CHRIST'S LOVE HAS AN ULTIMATE AIM

This distinguishing love guarantees not only present cleansing by the Spirit, but future completion and presentation to the Father by the Son.

READ EPHESIANS 5:27 again.

Did you see it? Christ will present the church (to His Father) complete. She will be all glorious, sharing the glory of her Lord!

Let us love the Lord who bought us,
Pitied us when enemies,
Called us by his grace and taught us,
Gave us ears and gave us eyes:
He has washed us with his blood,
He presents our souls to God.

—John Newton

Many passages speak of this great day. One of the most encouraging is found in JUDE 24-25.

COPY these verses.

_____

_____

_____

_____

_____

_____

Jesus will make you stand before His Father blameless—and it will be Jesus' joy to do so!

Another passage is 1 CORINTHIANS 15:24-28:

> . . . then comes the end, when He hands over the kingdom to the God and Father, when He has abolished all rule and all authority and power. For He must reign until He has put all His enemies under His feet. The last enemy that will be abolished is death. For He has put all things in subjection under His feet. But when He says, "All things are put in subjection," it is evident that He is excepted who put all things in subjection to Him. When all things are subjected to Him, then the Son Himself also will be subjected to the One who subjected all things to Him, so that God may be all in all.

Christ, upon presenting the church complete and seeing all enemies placed beneath His rule, will hand it all over to the Father, so that all might praise God the Father for the great work of His Son. It is an amazing sight: your rescue is one small part of the cosmic restoration of the rule of God over every aspect of the universe and the ultimate exaltation of God.

Further, it is astonishing to think that all the love that has been shown to the church, from before creation until today, will be outdone by what is yet to come. The coming expressions of divine love are the best ones!

No wonder the apostle Paul writes as he does to the Ephesian Christians.

FILL IN THE BLANKS from EPHESIANS 5:1-2.

> *Therefore be _____ of God, as*
> *_____ children; and walk in love,*
> *just as Christ also loved you and gave Himself up for us, an offering*
> *and a sacrifice to God as a fragrant aroma.*

Christian, ask the Lord to give you such a sight of the unique and exclusive love that He has for His people that you too would give yourself to imitating Him, walking in love, and being a fragrant and pleasing aroma to your God.

DAY 3: LOVE'S QUESTIONS AND ANSWERS FOR THE CHRISTIAN

The love of God is not just a general benevolence and kindness, but a distinguishing and gripping reality. He loved His church from eternity and will never fail to love her. This love is not merely divine feelings or good intentions, but a mighty force that takes the battlefield for us. What has His love accomplished? It has set Christians apart, washed them, and will one day present them complete in glory.

Now, all of that is very good, good beyond human explanation; but what about the plaguing questions that haunt our steps as we battle daily with sin, externally and internally? What about when the cry, "Wretched man that I am! Who will set me free from the body of this death?" (Romans 7:24) is much more common than the other cry, "Thanks be to God through Jesus Christ our Lord!" (Romans 7:25)? How can the doctrine of God's love lay hold of the Christian so that he or she is enabled to "run the race" with enduring joy?

The bedrock foundation that God has provided for every follower of Christ is clearly portrayed at the end of Romans 8. This passage might be described as a series of questions that the love of God asks and answers for the Christian. Let's look at this solid foundation today.

> Romans 8:31-39
> *What then shall we say to these things? If God is for us, who is against us? He who did not spare His own Son, but delivered Him over for us all, how will He not also with Him freely give us all things? Who will bring a charge against God's elect? God is the one*

who justifies; who is the one who condemns? Christ Jesus is He who died, yes, rather who was raised, who is at the right hand of God, who also intercedes for us. Who will separate us from the love of Christ? Will tribulation, or distress, or persecution, or famine, or nakedness, or peril, or sword? Just as it is written, "For Your sake we are being put to death all day long; we were considered as sheep to be slaughtered." But in all these things we overwhelmingly conquer through Him who loved us. For I am convinced that neither death, nor life, nor angels, nor principalities, nor things present, nor things to come, nor powers, nor height, nor depth, nor any other created thing, will be able to separate us from the love of God, which is in Christ Jesus our Lord.

These verses contain the questions that all Christians ask when they see how often they fail to live a Godward life, how often they revert back to selfishness, pride, and unbelief. God has asked these questions for you in Romans 8, and He has provided you with the answers, which are fundamentally tied to His love.

We may summarize the four questions here as follows:

- What about my enemies, will they overcome me?
- What about my daily needs, will they be supplied?
- What about the legitimate charges that can be brought against me?
- Will anything be able to separate me from God's love?

Remember, these questions can only be asked and answered correctly after Paul has given us eight chapters in which he explains the nature of mankind's sin and God's way of rescuing through the work of Jesus Christ. These statements of divine love are far from mere sentimental feelings; they are the conclusion of eight chapters of doctrine! Romans 8:31-39 is built on "these things" that Paul has talked about in the previous chapters. They have a root system that goes deep into the character and activity of God. You will never understand or appreciate the weight of God's love until you come to this section after working through Romans 1:1-8:30.

We do not have time to cover the first eight chapters, so let's just get the address on this letter correct. When you get a letter (and Romans is a letter), the first thing you look at is the address. Who is this meant for? Me, or someone in my home? Maybe it was meant for the previous owner. Or maybe it is an advertisement meant for anyone willing to read it. The Bible is very specific about addresses. God does not want you to open and read someone else's mail. You may be terribly mistaken by reading the Bible and not paying attention to the address and the recipient.

At the end of Romans 8:31-39 we have the exact address, the clue to the recipients of such wonderful news: "the love of God, *which is in Christ Jesus our Lord.*" In other words, this passage can only be for those who are in Christ (who have repented and run to Him in faith, and given all they know of themselves to Him and taken all they know of Him for themselves). These are the ones God unites to His Son by the Holy Spirit. They are Christ's people, and He is theirs—forever. And which Jesus are we speaking of? We are speaking of "our Lord." He is their master now, their owner. If this is not you, you may read Paul's letter to Christians, but you must understand that it is not talking about you—until you give yourself to this Lord, you are reading someone else's mail.

Here are the questions:

1.   What about my enemies, will they overcome me?

> *What then shall we say to these things? If God is for us, who is against us?* (Romans 8:31)

The person who is devoted to living for King Jesus must do so in a world that is hostile to His claims. There are enemies that attend every step of the Christian's path. We must ask: what about these enemies? Will they win in the end? Paul gives us a simple "if . . . then" kind of statement in verse 31. In this context, the "if" has the meaning of "since." We might translate this verse, "*Since* God is for us . . . ." Is God for the Christian? Yes. He has engaged Himself to be their rescuer by the New Covenant.

He will not allow any of His people to fall away and be lost (John 6:37-40). The simple logic is this: If God is for you, what does it matter who is against you? The Christian can bring every enemy to the throne of God in prayer and ask this question of God: "Since You are for Your children, please deal with this enemy in Your timing and in Your way." Every doubt can be brought to Him; every mocking person; every religious idea which raises itself up against the gospel of Jesus Christ; every adversary living in the world or having crept into the church. All the adversaries in the Christian's mind and heart, taken all together, are no threat to the true followers of Jesus because God is for them.

Blest be the Lord, my strength, my shield,
Amid the dangers of the field;
'Tis he instructs me for the fight,
And arms me with resistless might.
His constant love, his saving power,
Is my defense, my sacred tower.

— Anne Steele

The opposition of all enemies against the Christian is as useless as their opposition against the Christian's Savior.

READ PSALM 2:1-6 below.

> *Why are the nations in an uproar*
> *And the peoples devising a vain thing?*
> *The kings of the earth take their stand*
> *And the rulers take counsel together*
> *Against the LORD and against His Anointed, saying,*
> *"Let us tear their fetters apart*
> *And cast away their cords from us!"*
> *He who sits in the heavens laughs,*
> *The Lord scoffs at them.*
> *Then He will speak to them in His anger*
> *And terrify them in His fury, saying,*
> *"But as for Me, I have installed My King*
> *Upon Zion, My holy mountain."*

Rebellion is useless. God will reign through His Son, the chosen king. So, too, all attacks on the church will ultimately fail.

2. What about my daily needs, will they be supplied?

> *He who did not spare His own Son, but delivered Him over for us all, how will He not also with Him freely give us all things?* (Romans 8:32)

Have you ever asked: "Will God tire of my incessant asking and pleading? Will the supplies of His love run low?" The answer is, *never*. The logic is clear. Paul makes a comparison, starting with the larger gift and moving to the smaller. If God has given His Son, would He now withhold the smaller gifts that you need in daily life? Having given His most expensive gift, will He begrudge giving you daily pocket-change? If God were stingy, He would not have given His Son.

Paul explains God's greater gift in a negative statement: what He did *not* do. He did not spare Christ. He did not spare Him in the sense that He allowed all of our sin to be placed on Him. He did not cut corners with Jesus, and He will not cut corners in His giving us all Christ has earned for us. He also did not spare Christ in the sense that in giving His Son He gave to us lavishly without any hint of restraint. Now, if Christ was given fully, will the Father withhold any good thing from you?

CONSIDER the following contrasts.

God giving the eternal Son.	God giving daily supply to the believer.
God giving the Son for His enemies.	God giving to His adopted children.
God giving to those who did not want Christ.	God giving to those who ask in Jesus' name.

Paul's point is clear: to doubt the ongoing provision of all you need from God is the height of absurdity.

3. What about the legitimate charges that can be brought against me?

> *Who will bring a charge against God's elect? God is the one who justifies; who is the one who condemns? Christ Jesus is He who died, yes, rather who was raised, who is at the right hand of God, who also intercedes for us.* (Romans 8:33-34)

Paul does not argue that no charge could be found against you. There are charges that we feel *could* be, even *should* be, levelled against us. The Christian feels the weight of sin's sinfulness more after coming to Christ than before. Sin is no longer the protected darling of your heart; it has become your greatest grief. The conscience can be alarmingly accusative. The enemy of your soul may continually remind you of your shortcomings, using family, friends, and co-workers to do so. Paul is arguing that God's love has made such perfect provision for your justification that it is of no use for anyone to accuse you to God.

Paul's argument is that God Himself justifies the believer; that is, He places the believer in a totally different relationship to Him. Because Christ has lived perfectly and died sacrificially, all who are in Him receive the benefits of these two aspects of His righteousness. Or, as Paul says to the Corinthians:

> *He made Him who knew no sin to be sin on our behalf, so that we might become the righteousness of God in Him.* (2 Corinthians 5:21)

The believer's sin transferred to the Lamb of God, and His righteousness transferred to the repentant believer—these transactions result in justification. We stand before God as children before a father, not as criminals before a judge. We relate to God and He relates to us through His perfect Son. Christ's labors

Look upon the conversation [life] of any one saint, consider the frame of his heart, see the many stains and spots, the defilements and infirmities, wherewith his life is contaminate, and tell me whether the love that bears with all this, be not to be admired.

—John Owen

have brought every Christian into a new position, a new state before the law of God. We are declared guiltless. Now if God Himself has declared you guiltless, who can bring a charge that would stick?

No one can successfully bring a charge against any Christian in the eyes of God—not Satan, not the world, not even a person's own conscience. Let's admit it: no one on earth can have a longer list of our sins than we do! Even God Himself will not bring His offended law against you. He has purposely cast away your guilt and forgotten your offenses.

> Micah 7:18-19
> *Who is a God like You, who pardons iniquity*
> *And passes over the rebellious act of the remnant of His possession?*
> *He does not retain His anger forever,*
> *Because He delights in unchanging love.*
> *He will again have compassion on us;*
> *He will tread our iniquities under foot.*
> *Yes, You will cast all their sins*
> *Into the depths of the sea.*

CONSIDER the New Covenant promise repeated in HEBREWS 10:17:

> *"And their sins and their lawless deeds*
> *I will remember no more."*

Your great accuser may stand at your right hand to condemn you, but your great Advocate stands at the right hand of God to plead for you. And greater is he that is for you, than all that are against you.

— Octavius Winslow

How can anyone bring a charge against a Christian when the King-Judge who delights in unchanging love has cast his sins into the depths of the sea?

A second reason that no charge against a true Christian will stick is that Jesus Himself is seated beside His Father now, pleading our case as our defense attorney and mediator, standing for us alongside the Father, making all charges impossible. This is the eternal Son of God who became a man precisely so that He could fully save His followers. He is God. He is man. He stands between the Father and the broken-hearted Christian, pleading his or her case.

> Hebrews 7:24-25
> *. . . but Jesus, on the other hand, because He continues forever, holds His priesthood permanently. Therefore He is able also to save forever those who draw near to God through Him, since He always lives to make intercession for them.*

Amazingly, this is exactly what the Father asked Him to do. Can you imagine the all-wise Father raising His Son for our justification, and then allowing accusers to bring about our final condemnation? In light of this great salvation, who could possibly hope to turn God against you with accusations when they see both Father and Son "for you"?

4.   Will anything be able to separate me from God's love?

   Who will separate us from the love of Christ? Will tribulation, or distress, or persecution, or famine, or nakedness, or peril, or sword? . . . But in all these things we overwhelmingly conquer through Him who loved us. For I am convinced that neither death, nor life, nor angels, nor principalities, nor things present, nor things to come, nor powers, nor height, nor depth, nor any other created thing, will be able to separate us from the love of God, which is in Christ Jesus our Lord. (Romans 8:35-39)

As God's mercies are new every morning toward His people, so His anger is new every morning against the wicked.

— Matthew Henry

No Christian need fear any accusation, any person, any event, or any circumstance. The love of God is continually working to preserve His people. He will not let anything separate them from Himself. All who are in Christ Jesus the Lord are forever and immutably in the love of God.

Before we end our day, consider how terrifying it is for those who are not "in Christ Jesus our Lord." If you are holding Him at arm's length:

*   God Himself is "against" you, so what does it matter who is "for" you?

*   You must scratch about trying to find spiritual supplies to make it through another empty day.

*   All accusations brought against you regarding your sin will be effective.

*   You are now and will forever be separated from the love of God, unless you repent and come to the One who gives life.

It is a misery beyond description—to stand before this God, but to be outside of Christ and therefore without hope.

WRITE an answer to each of the four questions in your own words.

WHAT ABOUT *MY* ENEMIES? WILL THEY OVERCOME ME?

_____

_____

_____

WHAT ABOUT *MY* DAILY NEEDS? WILL THEY BE SUPPLIED?

_____

_____

_____

WHAT ABOUT THE LEGITIMATE CHARGES THAT CAN BE BROUGHT AGAINST *ME*?

_____

_____

_____

WILL ANYTHING BE ABLE TO SEPARATE *ME* FROM GOD'S LOVE?

_____

_____

_____

DAY 4: GOD'S CONSTRAINING LOVE

"The old has gone and is gone for good; the new has come and keeps on coming." These transformations, step by step, sometimes slow and painful, especially where they are working against patterns of long-ingrained sin, are the result of that sinner being carried out of the kingdom of darkness and translated into the kingdom of the Son of God's love.

— Jeremy Walker

Do you ever envy the life of a faithful follower of Christ, like the apostle Paul, and wonder how he found strength for such a life? Attracted to that level of consecration, that captivating awareness of God's real nearness, you set yourself to press forward. But what happens? You find the same old sins and stubborn resistance impeding your progress. Any real change in your life seems to require a dreadful conflict. Perhaps you then hear that devious whisper, "Such a life is not for you." And if it happens often enough, you believe it and settle for what has been called a "poor, dying rate of Christianity."

The young pastor Robert Murray M'Cheyne felt the same struggle and described it in the following quote:

> *Forgiven all trespasses that are past, the eye looks inwards with a clearness and an impartiality unknown before, and there it gazes upon its long-fostered affections for sin, which, like ancient rivers, have worn a deep channel into the heart; its periodic returns of passion, hitherto irresistible*

and overwhelming, like the tides of the ocean; its perversities of temper and of habit, crooked and unyielding, like the gnarled branches of a stunted oak. Ah, what a scene is here! What anticipations of the future! What forebodings of a vain struggle against the tyranny of lust, against old habits and ways of acting, and of speaking, and of thinking.[44]

So you are left with a clouded view of the gospel-provisions and an aching complaint: "I am a forgiven person, but I am not a sanctified person." While forgiveness without sanctification is all that the hypocrite desires, it is an unbearable place for those who love Jesus Christ. The good news is that the love of God that reaches us through the mighty labors of Jesus Christ has provided for more than forgiveness—it transforms the believer into the image of Christ.

Today we will consider both aspects of this sanctifying power: the objective and the subjective work of God's love.

THE OBJECTIVE ASPECTS OF GOD'S LOVE IN OUR RESCUE

Objective truths are truths that do not start with our experiences. They are realities that exist outside of us. They are not dependent upon our understanding, believing, or experiencing them. They are true regardless of us. Generally, they are accomplished *for* us, not *in* us.

We will follow Paul's teaching here. When Paul embraced Christ, he was immediately altered by what Christ had done on the cross. That is, there were certain realities that became his by virtue of being united to Christ. Below are passages in which Paul links the death of Christ to changes in his own life. In each, he emphasizes different reasons why the objective work of Christ on the cross makes living for sin impossible for the Christian.

UNDERLINE the verses or phrases in the following passages that show why the work of Christ makes living a life of sin impossible for the Christian.

Romans 6:1-11

What shall we say then? Are we to continue in sin so that grace may increase? May it never be! How shall we who died to sin still live in it? Or do you not know that all of us who have been baptized into Christ Jesus have been baptized into His death? Therefore we have been buried with Him through baptism into death, so that as Christ was raised from the dead through the glory of the Father, so we too might walk in newness of life. For if we have become united with Him in the likeness of His death, certainly we shall also be in the likeness of His resurrection, knowing this, that our old self was crucified with Him, in order that our body of sin might be done away with, so that we would no longer be slaves to sin; for he who has died is freed from sin. Now if we have died with Christ, we believe that we shall also live with Him, knowing that Christ, having been raised from the dead, is never to die again; death no longer is master over Him. For the death that He died, He died to sin once for all; but the life that He lives, He lives to God. Even so consider yourselves to be dead to sin, but alive to God in Christ Jesus.

Romans 14:7-9
For not one of us lives for himself, and not one dies for himself; for if we live, we live for the Lord, or if we die, we die for the Lord; therefore whether we live or die, we are the Lord's. For to this end Christ died and lived again, that He might be Lord both of the dead and of the living.

Galatians 2:20
I have been crucified with Christ; and it is no longer I who live, but Christ lives in me; and the life which I now live in the flesh I live by faith in the Son of God, who loved me and gave Himself up for me.

2 Corinthians 5:14-15
For the love of Christ controls us, having concluded this, that one died for all, therefore all died; and He died for all, so that they who live might no longer live for themselves, but for Him who died and rose again on their behalf.

Let's back up and take a quick look at what is contained in these passages.

First, in Romans 6:1-11, the point is that faith brings one into union with Christ. When this occurs, all that Christ has done *for* the sinner is applied *to* the sinner. The sinner is affected by what Christ has done for him or her. Christ died; the sinner died. That is, the old "you" or "self" has been crucified. A new "you" has been raised up to live a new life. Sin can no longer rule over you as it once did. You are not under its jurisdiction any longer. You died to that old realm of the tyranny of sin and were raised with a new life in the realm of Christ's rule. This is not something the Christian is commanded to do. It is done to him or her. But the Christian is commanded to reckon or calculate life based on these new realities. Now that there is a new you in a new realm with a new master, living as a slave of sin as you once did is not possible.

Second, in Romans 14:7-9, the point is that Christ's mighty victory—a perfect life and a sacrificial death—has guaranteed that all belong to Him. He is Lord of the dead and the living. We now live and die for Him; living for ourselves is no longer an option.

Third, the point in Galatians 2:20 is that this union with Christ that results in the old you dying with Christ and a new you being raised with Him puts you in a completely different relationship to Christ. Your union is so close that Christ lives in you and the very life you are now living is accomplished by a continual supply that you receive through faith from Christ, who loved you and gave Himself for you. Now you have all you need for holiness.

Finally, in 2 Corinthians 5:14-15, Paul explains that Christ's death on behalf of your sin guarantees that all united to Him died to sin's rule. His cross now mandates that all who have died with Him and been raised with Him live for Him, not for themselves.

The cross of Christ brings about an end to sin's rule over His people, solidifies His royal right to their allegiance, connects them to the source of a holy life (Jesus Himself), and binds them to Him with cords of gratitude. In short, it makes returning to the old life impossible and guarantees a new life of obedience (imperfect but genuine) will result.

THE SUBJECTIVE ASPECTS OF GOD'S LOVE IN OUR RESCUE

There are things that we experience because we believe in Christ, that affect how we live. Paul has hinted at this in 2 CORINTHIANS 5:14-15:

> *For the love of Christ controls us, having concluded this, that one died for all, therefore all died; and He died for all, so that they who live might no longer live for themselves, but for Him who died and rose again on their behalf.*

The love of Christ for Paul, understood and experienced by Paul, controlled Paul. It is important that we not attribute this powerful influence merely to Paul's love for Jesus. That is of course there. But in this verse Paul is emphasizing that his personal experience of Christ's love controlled his behavior.

The word translated "controls" here is full of meaning. It was used in various ways in the first century.

*O to grace how great a debtor
Daily I'm constrained to be!
Let that grace, Lord, like a
    fetter,
Bind my wandering heart
    to Thee.
Prone to wander, Lord, I feel it;
Prone to leave the God I love;
Take my heart, O take and
    seal it,
Seal it from Thy courts above!*

— Robert Robinson

- It meant *to constrain*. A horse was kept from distraction by putting blinders on its eyes. It was "controlled." The word thus shows that the love of

Christ holds Paul on a course, undistracted, capturing his focus with an irresistible object.

- It meant *to hold things together* by an outward pressure. Christ's love holds Paul's life together, regardless of other pressures.

- It meant *to influence or compel* one to move in a certain direction. Paul's life was kept from drifting, and more—kept moving forward in the right direction—by the continual experience of Christ's love.

- It meant *to be completely controlled, to be owned or claimed* by something. Paul was no longer "his own." He no longer existed for himself. He had been captured and was daily under the control of the mighty influence of an undeserved love from the very king he once mocked.

So, from Paul's pen we get a glimpse of the secret of his obedience. He was constrained and kept from distractions, held together when temptation would pull him in various directions, moved onward even when the path was difficult, and aware that he could never exist for himself again—all by the awareness that Christ loved him!

Now, how do we cultivate this kind of awareness of God's love? It involves faith on our part. Not positive thinking. Rather, the believer must lay hold of truths revealed in Scripture and live upon them. The bridge between the realities God has revealed in the Bible and your life is faith.

Imagine a ladder. The top rung is a life of obedience. But you cannot leap up to this rung. There are other things that lead to it. The first step is an awareness of what the Bible says about Christ's love to His people. John says we love [God] because He first loved us (1 John 4:19). It is therefore only as you get clearer views of the various aspects of Christ's love that you are able to be affected by this reality. Vague, cultural clichés about God's love will do little good here.

The second rung is faith. You must take what God says and risk everything to live upon it. You must live as if God always tells the truth (and He does). You must take biblical statements and find room for them to fit into your daily life. How exactly does Christ love His people? How does that change your life at home, work, school, or church? How does that alter the plans and deepest desires of your soul?

The third rung is where you take the great statements of the Bible and make them personal—God, infinitely exalted and incomprehensibly pure, has loved me in and through His Son. The shock of it, the amazingness of it, must crash against you as you realize that this is true of every believer. If you isolate yourself by unbelief and say that God cannot love you in this way, you will never find the love of Christ controlling your behavior.

Christ told His followers to abide in Him. We are to abide in His love and to respond to that love more and more by loving Him in return. Our love is then expressed in obedience, as was His love for the Father. "We love, because He first loved us" (1 John 4:19).

— Clyde Cranford

The final rung is obedience. We love Him because He loved us. We obey Him because we love Him (John 14:15). Love to Christ, produced by knowing His love for us, is the mighty engine that moves us forward daily in obedience.

Studying, understanding, embracing, applying, and delighting in the undeserved love of the Holy One will move the true Christian to obey. It will constrain, hold together, drive, and control the Christian.

This is the way forward in obedience. There is no shortcut. There is no book on holiness that can get you there faster. Paul knew of no other way. Obedience, true obedience from the heart, always flows from the life of the believer as that believer gains an ever clearer grasp of the love that Christ is pouring out on him or her.

As you study these passages about the God who loves, labor by His help to get such a sight of His love that faith can bring it down to everyday life, producing a cheerful consecration.

DAY 5: KEEPING OURSELVES IN THE LOVE OF GOD!

When we study the love of God and consider how it ought to compel us to obey and give ourselves wholly to Him, we are often pained by the great distance between what we are reading and how we are living. Certainly there is a sanctifying power in God's love; it expels all lesser loves from the heart. And just as certainly, in the New Covenant God promises to write His law within us, on renewed hearts. Hence the obedience we give God is no longer from outward coercing. It is now accomplished by an inward compelling. Salvation means that obedience to someone else is now part of our new nature. It is natural to obey our Savior.

Ye may yourself ebb and flow, rise and fall, wax and wane; but your Lord is this day as he was yesterday; and it is your comfort that your salvation is not rolled upon wheels of your own making, neither have ye to do with a Christ of your own shaping.

— Samuel Rutherford

Although obedience is now ingrained in our nature because of the new birth, and disobedience now feels very unnatural, it does not mean that living for God is effortless. Sadly, we know this by personal experience and observation. We also know it by the frequent commands in the Bible regarding loving God and its fruit of obedience. Today we will look at the love of God and how the experience of this love is to be cultivated as one part of remaining faithful to Him until the end.

Jude, the half-brother of Jesus, gives us help in his little epistle:

> *But you, beloved, building yourselves up on your most holy faith, praying in the Holy Spirit, keep yourselves in the love of God, waiting anxiously for the mercy of our Lord Jesus Christ to eternal life.* (Jude 20-21)

WHAT'S GOING ON WHEN JUDE WRITES?

Jude tells us that he was hoping to write a letter about the great realities of the Christian faith, but due to the deceptive entrance of false teachers into the church he had to write a letter of warning instead. These teachers were masked as Christians, but they taught lies that led to immoral lifestyles of self-indulgence. God would judge them, but Jude warns the believers to be on guard against their wrong doctrines. The church is told in verse 3 to contend earnestly for the faith. In verse 17 they are told to remember the warnings of the apostles about false teachers.

This is where we tend to stop in responding to false teaching. Theologians write their books to answer the lies, and pastors read them. Pastors preach against the lies, and the people try to remember the warnings. This, however, is an insufficient response to wrong teaching. Many who stop here find themselves later in life embracing the self-indulgent versions of "Christianity."

Jude gives further instructions:

> *But you, beloved, building yourselves up on your most holy faith, praying in the Holy Spirit, keep yourselves in the love of God, waiting anxiously for the mercy of our Lord Jesus Christ to eternal life. And have mercy on some, who are doubting; save others, snatching them out of the fire; and on some have mercy with fear, hating even the garment polluted by the flesh.* (Jude 20-23)

LIST the action words found in the passage above that Jude gives to those who are beloved of God and facing the deceit of religious lies.

1. _____

2. _____

3. _____

4. _____

5. _____

In this list, the first four can be applied to Christians as individuals; the fifth speaks clearly about the Christian as part of a body. The first four contain one main verb—"keep" yourselves in the love of God. This command is surrounded by three participles: "building," "praying," and "waiting." This helps us understand that at the heart of perseverance for the Christian is the duty of keeping oneself in God's love. The other three are connected to that duty. The duty does not exist on its own and the others will not occur in the life of a person who does not keep himself or herself in the love of God.

EXAMINING THESE PHRASES

Let's take these one at a time:

1. *Building yourselves up on this holy faith . . .*

The faith spoken of here is the body of facts that form the gospel. We are commanded to be busy building our lives on an ever clearer understanding of the facts of Christianity. We must not stop with vague ideas of the New Covenant. Quick glances at Christ and Sunday School generalities will not protect against the subtle lies of the false teachers.

2. *Praying in the Spirit . . .*

Clear understanding of biblical doctrines is necessary, but it is not enough. There must be a continuous drawing near to God with a real dependence. This kind of praying is motivated by the Holy Spirit. Paul mentions the work of the Spirit in conjunction with our praying:

> *In the same way the Spirit also helps our weakness; for we do not know how to pray as we should, but the Spirit Himself intercedes for us with groanings too deep for words; and He who searches the hearts knows what the mind of the Spirit is, because He intercedes for the saints according to the will of God.* (Romans 8:26-27)

It is a display of inexcusable pride for us to carefully study right doctrine without adding a life of child-like dependence as expressed in prayer.

3. *Keep yourselves in the love of God . . .*

We are to labor to keep ourselves firmly planted in the realities of God's love. The heart is to be kept warm toward our Savior and cold toward the world.

However matters go, it is our happiness to win new ground daily in Christ's love, and to purchase a new piece of it daily, and to add conquest to conquest, till our Lord Jesus and we be so near the other that Satan shall not draw a straw or a thread betwixt us.

— Samuel Rutherford

4. *Waiting eagerly . . .*

The best is yet to come for the Christian. There is a full inheritance ahead, of which we have only received the down-payment in this life. Consider the amazing passage written by Paul in Romans regarding the completion of the Christian when Christ returns.

> *For I consider that the sufferings of this present time are not worthy to be compared with the glory that is to be revealed to us. For the anxious longing of the creation waits eagerly for the revealing of the sons of God. For the creation was subjected to futility, not willingly, but because of Him who subjected it, in hope that the creation itself also will be set free from its slavery to corruption into the freedom of the glory of the children of God. For we know that the whole creation groans and suffers the pains of childbirth together until now. And not only this, but also we ourselves, having the first fruits of the Spirit, even we ourselves groan within ourselves, waiting eagerly for our adoption as sons, the redemption of our body. For in hope we have been saved, but hope that is seen is not hope; for who hopes for what he already sees? But if we hope for what we do not see, with perseverance we wait eagerly for it.* (Romans 8:18-25)

There is a completion coming for the Christian that will spill over and affect all creation; therefore, all creation is eagerly (on tip-toe) looking for our final glorification. Note that building, praying, and waiting are present and continuous activities.

Now, regarding others:

5. *Snatch from danger those who have been deceived, guarding against contagion.*

His love is in perpetual bloom. It is always in summertide. The roots are deeply buried in Himself; therefore, the branches cannot fade.

— Henry Law

No individual Christian is allowed to guard only himself or his family. We are obligated to consider those around us. They too are in danger of being deceived, and we must diligently walk alongside them, even snatching them from danger if necessary. The safety of the believer is not merely that he or she is "in Christ" but also that he or she is in Christ's church.

At the heart of all of this is the need to *keep oneself in the love of God*. What does this mean?

IT DOES *NOT* MEAN:

- Keep yourself loving God.

It is God's love for you that is the focal point here, *not* your love for God. Keep yourself in that reality. Maintaining your love for God is important, but it is *not* the starting point.

- Keep yourself as one of God's loved ones.

Paul is *not* saying that you have to live so as to maintain a place in God's family. This passage is speaking about your experience of His love, your fellowship with Him, not the foundation of your relationship with Him. It is an experiential statement, not a positional one. You are keeping in near fellowship with your heavenly Father, you are not keeping yourself adopted.

IT *DOES* MEAN:

- Keep yourself in continual awareness of the love of God for you in Christ.

Christian, like Paul's example yesterday, keep the reality that you are loved by God before your mind so regularly that you are compelled and constrained by it.

This duty is found in Jesus' command to His followers in John 15.

COPY JOHN 15:9-11.

_____

_____

_____

_____

_____

_____

_____

That fellowship was mentioned in the previous chapter.

FILL IN THE BLANKS from JOHN 14:21, 23.

He who has My commandments and _____
_____ is the one who loves Me; and he who
loves Me will be _____ by My Father, and I will
_____ him and will _____
Myself to him.

. . . If anyone loves Me, he will _____ My word; and My
Father will love him, and _____
_____
_____.

Notice that the pattern our Lord gives us for keeping in the awareness of His love involves living in a continual responsiveness to Him—obedience. In fact, this was His pattern on earth. He was loved by the Father, and He lived in the enjoyment of that love by walking in harmony (obedience) with the Father. Christians are loved by the Son in the same way, and if they walk in harmony with the Son (obedience), they will abide (set up tent) in the atmosphere of His love. In the 14th chapter of John, Jesus makes it clear that those who love Him demonstrate it by their obedience, and the result is an ongoing and increasing revelation of God to them and an intimacy with Him that is not available to those who walk in disobedience.

At the heart of perseverance in the Christian life, even when surrounded by false teaching, is the continual cultivation of the awareness of God's love for you in Christ. This cultivation will involve ongoing study and meditation on the many facets of this divine affection. Passages like these from Jeremiah must form a part of your spiritual diet:

> *The LORD appeared to him from afar, saying,*
> *"I have loved you with an everlasting love;*
> *Therefore I have drawn you with lovingkindness."* (Jeremiah 31:3)

> *I will make an everlasting covenant with them that I will not turn away from them, to do them good; and I will put the fear of Me in their hearts so that they will not turn away from Me. I will rejoice over them to do them good and will faithfully plant them in this land with all My heart and with all My soul.* (Jeremiah 32:40-41)

O! For a single eye to look unto Jesus, an humble heart to sit at His feet, and a simple soul to hear and believe every word, from His gracious lips, that we may know the love of Christ—constantly know it, by heart-felt sense of it. This, this is the one thing needful, to make poor sinners rich, vile sinners holy, and miserable sinners happy in time, and joyful to eternity.

— William Mason

But it will also include a life lived in harmony with the king's authority, walked on the king's paths. It is impossible to live in the warm sunshine of His covenanted love at the same time you walk in the shadows of sin.

We close this week on the theme of God's love with an extended quote from the nineteenth-century Baptist minister, J. C. Philpot:

> We are ever looking for something in self to make ourselves acceptable to God, and are often sadly cast down and discouraged when we cannot find that holiness, that obedience, that calm submission to the will of God, that serenity of soul, that spirituality and heavenly mindedness which we believe to be acceptable in his sight, and to make us acceptable too. Our crooked tempers, fretful, peevish minds, rebellious thoughts, coldness, barrenness and death, our alienation from good and headlong proneness to ill, with the daily feeling that we get no better but rather worse, make us think that God views us just as we view ourselves. And this brings on great darkness of mind and bondage of spirit, till we seem to lose sight of our acceptance in Christ, and get into the miserable dregs of self, almost ready to quarrel with God because we are so vile, and only get worse as we get older.
>
> Now the more we get into these dregs of self, and the more we keep looking at the dreadful scenes of wreck and ruin which our heart presents to daily view, the further do we get from the grace of the gospel, and the more do we lose sight of the only ground of our acceptance with God. It is "in the Beloved" that we are accepted, and not for any good words or good works, good thoughts, good hearts, or good intentions of our own. Not but that the fruits of godliness are acceptable in God's sight; not but that our continual sins are displeasing in his eyes. But we must draw a distinction between the acceptance of our persons and the acceptance of our works, between what we are as standing in Christ and what we are as still in the flesh.[45]

KNOWING THE GOD WHO IS PATIENT AND ZEALOUS

DAY 1: THE PATIENCE OF GOD

The LORD is gracious and merciful;
Slow to anger and great in lovingkindness.
(Psalm 145:8)

A bold person is rarely a gentle person, and a gentle person is not often bold. A merciful person usually finds justice difficult, and a person concerned with justice is often unmerciful. But in the perfection of our God, we see a flawless union and balance of seemingly opposite virtues. This week you will have an opportunity to consider attributes which would appear to be incompatible— patience and zeal.

God's patience is His willingness to bear with the offenses or provocations of His creatures, who deny His rights and rebel against His rule. God's patience is distinct from our patience.

Let's consider a few facts.

No earthly father loves like Thee;
No mother e'er so mild,
Bears and forbears as Thou hast done
With me, Thy sinful child.

— Frederick W. Faber

GOD'S PATIENCE IS ESSENTIAL TO HIS NATURE AND SELF-EXISTENCE

God does not need to remind Himself to be patient. God does not try to be patient. God does not find it easy to be patient one day and difficult the next. Patience is part of God's majesty and it comes naturally to Him. God's patience does not find its source in anything outside of Himself. No one has taught Him how to be patient. No circumstances have combined to promote patience in our God. God was infinitely patient before there was a creation toward which to show His patience.

The Bible uses a variety of descriptions for God's patience:

* God is slow to anger.

* God is long-suffering.

* God is not easily provoked.

God's patience might be thought of as the product of the union of other attributes: mercy, power, and wisdom. Let's look at some passages that demonstrate this.

MERCY

Patience must include mercy, for patience implies that God must be slow to anger with those who are provoking Him by sin.

COPY > PSALM 145:8.

_____

_____

FILL IN THE BLANKS > from 2 PETER 3:9.

The Lord is not slow about His promise, as some count slowness,

_____

_____, *not wishing for any to perish but for all to come to repentance.*

POWER

Patience might appear to demonstrate a lack of ability in God to do all His good pleasure, but in fact, patience is a great display of God's power. He is restraining His righteous anger.

Numbers 14:17-18
But now, I pray, let the power of the Lord be great, just as You have declared, "The LORD is slow to anger and abundant in lovingkindness, forgiving iniquity and transgression; but He will by no means clear the guilty, visiting the iniquity of the fathers on the children to the third and the fourth generations."

COPY > NAHUM 1:3.

_____

_____

_____

_____

READ ROMANS 9:22 below.

What if God, although willing to demonstrate His wrath and to make His power known, endured with much patience vessels of wrath prepared for destruction?

Each restraint of divine wrath by an almighty power, revealing an astonishing patience with the enemies of God, is a greater display of divine power than the creation of a thousand new worlds. On the contrary, man's hotheadedness reveals his weakness.

FILL IN THE BLANKS from PROVERBS 16:32.

He who is slow to anger is _____ _____, and he who rules his spirit, _____ _____.

WISDOM

God's patience does not continue to exist because He lacks a plan of action for those who are rebelling against Him. Rather, it is a perfect wisdom that guides the restraint of God's wrath. We may react rashly or delay too long. Yet God's long-suffering is always guided by an infallible wisdom. It is patience with divine purpose. We see this reflected when God describes the cause of patience in a wise man.

FILL IN THE BLANKS from PROVERBS 19:11.

A man's _____ makes him slow to anger, And it is his _____ to overlook a transgression.

HE IS NOT LIKE US

Do you see that the patience of God is an expression of various aspects of His majesty? How differently the world views God's refusal to be easily provoked by sin! Having described some of the aspects of God's character which combine in His exercise of patience, we need to clarify this portrait by considering what is *not* at the heart of God's long-suffering.

Consider the things that are often at the heart of our delayed responses.

Quite often people believe that God has not immediately responded to their rebellion because He is like them. "Maybe," they ask, "He is indifferent to the

He that can restrain His anger is greater than the Caesars and Alexanders of the world, that have filled the earth with their slain carcasses and ruined cities. By the same reason, God's slowness to anger is a greater argument of His power than the creation of a world or dissolving it with a word; in this He has a dominion over creatures, in the other over Himself.

— Stephen Charnock

whole matter of right and wrong?" The Lord warns people who think that way in PSALM 50:21:

> *These things you have done and I kept silence;*
> *You thought that I was just like you . . . .*

At times we may lack the integrity required to keep our word. We may become slack in performing our promises. God's patience may be mistaken as being motivated by that same kind of slackness.

> 2 Peter 3:9
> *The Lord is not slow about His promise, as some count slowness, but*
> *is patient toward you, not wishing for any to perish but for all to come*
> *to repentance.*

There are times when we are patient with those who have sinned against us because we realize that we are partly to blame. We too sinned in the situation, and therefore we find it easier not to be provoked. This is common in the home or workplace. Imagine a mother against whom a rebellious teenager has sinned. That mother is tempted to react quickly, but then she remembers how her own sinfulness in the situation may have made things worse. Feeling that she is partly to blame, she may be slow to respond.

Yet God has never found Himself partly to blame for any of the sins we have committed against Him. His patience is not like our guilty unresponsiveness.

Again, there are times when we appear patient, but really we are ignorant of the facts, unaware of the situation. An employer may appear very patient with you when you are failing to do your work. In reality he is not patient; he simply does not understand exactly how lazy you have been. If he knew, he would certainly respond.

God is never unaware. Every sin is committed in front of His eyes. He knows every detail of every sin. He has watched as you quietly desired what He has denied. He has listened to your thoughts as you secretly planned how you could get what He would not give. He was there when you rejected His authority and chose to live for yourself. He was aware of everything you did to cover your sin and to put the blame on others. His delayed response is not due to ignorance. It is rooted in the fact that He is slow to anger.

We may not respond to a situation because we simply cannot do anything about it. At the workplace we may lack the necessary authority to put things right. We may lack the wisdom to respond to a family member who is offending us. We may lack courage. So we simply decide to forget it happened and get on with life. Yet God possesses an infinite wisdom, so that He always knows exactly how and when to respond, and He alone possesses all power necessary to enable Him to do all that is required. Could the patience of such a being possibly be caused by His inability to do anything about our rebellion?

Again, we may not respond to an offense because the offender is useful to us and we do not want to jeopardize that beneficial relationship. Imagine a situation at church in which a fellow member often offends you. You fear that if you were to respond to him, he would become angry. Maybe he would quit his position, and you are convinced that you need his labor. Everyone at church may think of you as a patient person when in truth you are just being pragmatic. Yet God never needs any of us. The reason for God's patience is not that He fears that if He responds to our sin we will become angry and no longer help Him in His kingdom work.

Considering the truths studied today, write in the blanks below any misconceptions you have had regarding God's patience with sinners.

_____

_____

_____

What aspects of God's patience lead you to worship Him ?

_____

_____

_____

O the tenderness and graciousness of the Lord's patience with His people! How patiently He bears with their ungrateful repining, their secret rebellion, their cold love, their cruel unbelief, with their continual backslidings. Truly the patience of God after grace is greater than before grace. How this thought should subdue our rebellious spirits, break our hard hearts, and lead us, in every fresh remembrance, to the blood of Christ to wash in the fountain open for sin and uncleanness.

— Octavius Winslow

DAY 2: OUR RESPONSE TO THE GOD WHO IS SLOW TO ANGER

Today you will consider three questions. A correct understanding of the answer to the first two will help you to adequately respond to the third. Let's give these significant thought.

1. With whom is God patient?

Though God's common grace (*i.e.*, His delight in doing good) is extended to all His creation, the patience of God is a more specific expression of His majesty. God is good to all animal life. God is good to the holy angels. God is

There is no study of God that presents the infinity of His nature more impressively than the study of His perfections; and among those perfections nothing, perhaps, more strikingly illustrates that infinity than His patience.

— Octavius Winslow

not patient with animals and angels. Patience is an expression of God's moral perfection which is shown only to those who are provoking God by their sin. So God's patience is extended to sinful creatures. But we can be still more specific.

God's patience is not extended to the fallen angels. They rebelled once against His majesty and were immediately cast down. Those fallen angels are now awaiting judgment; however, nowhere in the Bible does God describe this period of waiting as an expression of His good patience. It is more akin to a king who holds prisoners guilty of high treason until the appropriate day for execution. They are not held in prison awaiting execution because of the king's patience, but because it serves the affairs of state for them to be executed at some future time rather than immediately. Peter tells us in his second letter that God did not spare the angels who sinned, but cast them down to hell and delivered them into chains of darkness (2 Peter 2:4). Isaac Watts wrote a hymn contrasting the manner in which God responded to the sin of angels and the sin of humanity.

> *From heaven the sinning angels fell,*
> *And wrath and darkness chained them down;*
> *But man, vile man, forsook his bliss—*
> *And mercy lifts him to a crown.*
>
> *Amazing work of sovereign grace,*
> *That could distinguish rebels so;*
> *Our guilty treason called aloud*
> *For everlasting fetters too.*[46]

Think of it! There is only one type of being that is shown patience by the offended Majesty on High. The only beings with whom God is slow to anger and not easily provoked are humans. You are the only type of being to whom God has ever shown patience. That leads us to the second question.

2.   How patient is He with us?

It is impossible to get an accurate measure of God's patience because it is an infinite quality in God. He does not always exercise His patience in the same way. He may choose to extend His patience beyond our reckoning, or He may choose to withdraw it. But in Himself, our God possesses infinite patience. Perhaps we might get a better understanding of the immensity of God's gift to us in His long-suffering if we think of how we measure a person's patience on earth.

- One's patience can be measured by how many people are offending him or her.

We might find our patience tested when one person at work or home is unkind to us. We rarely find ourselves in a situation in which every person offends us. Yet God is provoked by every person on the planet because every person sins. Here is God's assessment of humanity in the days of Noah:

> *Then the LORD saw that the wickedness of man was great in the earth, and that every intent of the thoughts of his heart was only evil continually.* (Genesis 6:5)

The Holy God is being provoked by a people whose thoughts and intentions are continually evil, and only evil.

- One's patience can be measured by the number of ways in which he or she is being offended.

The measure of our offense is directly related to the measure of our obligation which we fail to fulfill. In other words, the provocation is as wide and deep as God's rights which are being ignored. An employer may have to exercise patience with an employee during the work week. Yet God, whose rights touch every event and every minute of our lives, is being provoked by sin in every way. We may admire the employer who is patient forty hours each week. But we worship the living God whose majesty is seen in His refusal to be easily provoked when all humanity sins against Him in all circumstances, in all places, and at all times.

- One's patience can be measured by the depth of the offense that he or she endures.

We find ourselves more willing to be patient with minor, surface-level offenses. But our offenses against God are not so. They touch the very being of God. Every sin is an attack on His person, His attributes, and His rights. It is very personal. We deny Him, misrepresent Him, twist His words, and try to bribe Him with a pretense of religion. No human has ever been offended as deeply as every sin offends the Creator. No patience is like God's patience.

Now, understanding that you are the only kind of being to whom God has ever extended patience, and understanding something of the measure of that patience which you have been continually receiving, you should be better prepared to answer the third question.

3. How ought we to react to God's patience?

The response that God desires from us as we view His patience is clearly explained in Scripture.

FILL IN THE BLANKS from the verses below using the NASB translation.

All of the Christian's life is one of repentance.

— Martin Luther

Joel 2:13
And rend your heart and not your garments.
Now _____ to the LORD your God,
For He is gracious and compassionate,
_____, abounding in lovingkindness
And relenting of evil.

Romans 2:4
Or do you think lightly of the riches of His _____ and
_____ and _____, not knowing
that the kindness of God leads you to _____?

2 Peter 3:9
The Lord is not slow about His promise, as some count slowness, but is
patient toward you, not wishing for any to _____
but for all to come to _____.

It is unmistakably clear that the delayed wrath of God, His slowness to anger and refusal to be provoked, is meant to make us consider the sinfulness of sinning against such a God. God's patience is a great motivator for all of us to more fully and quickly turn back to Him. It is a devilish thing when we who experience divine patience use it as an excuse to continue living for ourselves.

DAY 3: THE ZEAL AND JEALOUSY OF GOD

We come now to another of God's perfections, another aspect of His incomparable majesty. It is an attribute that one might think could not exist alongside patience. God possesses infinite zeal. That is, there is a keenness in God, an intensity of earnestness, which goes beyond anything we have seen in our world.

We all know people who are passionate, even extreme, about something. They are single-minded, devoting their all to the pursuit of one thing. In humanity, this tends to be a quality more often seen in the young. Old age often erodes it, or corrects it with an appropriate balance.

Yet there is and always has been one God who has possessed immeasurable zeal. His zeal does not need to be balanced, and the passing of years will never quench it. His actions have always been united to an infinite intensity of purpose—guided flawlessly by perfect wisdom and justice, executed by unlimited power, and supported by an incontrovertible sovereignty. He cannot exist otherwise. This is who He is.

There is another English word used to express God's zeal in the Bible—jealousy. Jealousy and zeal are translated from the same root words in the original languages of the Bible. Like justice and righteousness, they are indistinguishable except in the way they are applied to a specific situation. Thus, the jealousy of God is His immeasurable intensity when applied to an object of His love. We understand His jealousy to express the strongest love and deepest devotion. It includes a rightful possession of what belongs to Him and Him alone. Because God has an indisputable right to all He has created, His jealousy (intense desire for it) is never a sinful or inappropriate jealousy. Because His intensity is united to His goodness, it is never an unholy zeal.

Let's consider the scriptural testimony regarding this aspect of God's weighty majesty.

*Zeal is that pure and heavenly flame,
The fire of love supplies . . . .*

—John Newton

UNDERLINE ▷ the words *jealous, jealousy, zeal,* and *zealous* in the passages found in this day's study. Consider the words in the context of the passage. What is being said about God's jealousy or zeal?

1. God's jealousy is an essential part of His character.

He could not be God without being a God of jealousy. He makes this clear by telling us that Jealous is His name, and that He is Himself a consuming fire.

Exodus 34:12-14
Watch yourself that you make no covenant with the inhabitants of the land into which you are going, or it will become a snare in your midst. But rather, you are to tear down their altars and smash their sacred pillars and cut down their Asherim—for you shall not worship any other god, for the LORD, whose name is Jealous, is a jealous God . . . .

Deuteronomy 4:23-24

So watch yourselves, that you do not forget the covenant of the LORD your God which He made with you, and make for yourselves a graven image in the form of anything against which the LORD your God has commanded you. For the LORD your God is a consuming fire, a jealous God.

2. God's jealousy and zeal are primarily expressed in regard to His name (reputation) and His people.

After generations of idolatry, Judah was judged by God. After seventy years in a Babylonian exile, Judah was rescued by God. But why did He bother? In part He did so because His name was attached to these people. His reputation as God was at stake before the world. He would rescue them and grant them a new, repentant heart so that the world would see what kind of a God He was. Listen to God's message through the prophet Ezekiel.

Jealousy is called the rage of a man, but it is God's holy and just displeasure. Those cannot worship God aright who do not worship him alone.

— Matthew Henry

Therefore say to the house of Israel, "Thus says the Lord GOD, It is not for your sake, O house of Israel, that I am about to act, but for My holy name, which you have profaned among the nations where you went. I will vindicate the holiness of My great name which has been profaned among the nations, which you have profaned in their midst. Then the nations will know that I am the LORD," declares the Lord GOD, "when I prove Myself holy among you in their sight. For I will take you from the nations, gather you from all the lands and bring you into your own land. Then I will sprinkle clean water on you, and you will be clean; I will cleanse you from all your filthiness and from all your idols. Moreover, I will give you a new heart and put a new spirit within you; and I will remove the heart of stone from your flesh and give you a heart of flesh. I will put My Spirit within you and cause you to walk in My statutes, and you will be careful to observe My ordinances . . . .

Then you will remember your evil ways and your deeds that were not good, and you will loathe yourselves in your own sight for your iniquities and your abominations. I am not doing this for your sake," declares the Lord GOD, "let it be known to you. Be ashamed and confounded for your ways, O house of Israel!" (Ezekiel 36:22-27, 31-32)

And later in the same book we read:

> *Therefore thus says the Lord GOD, "Now I will restore the fortunes of Jacob and have mercy on the whole house of Israel; and I will be jealous for My holy name."* (Ezekiel 39:25)

God is jealous also for His people, for they belong to Him. He bought them and called them out from the world. Therefore, they are not free to give themselves to the idols they once lived for. James writes to a church that was drifting. Some of its people wanted the friendship of the world again. Listen to these words:

> *You adulteresses, do you not know that friendship with the world is hostility toward God? Therefore whoever wishes to be a friend of the world makes himself an enemy of God. Or do you think that the Scripture speaks to no purpose: "He jealously desires the Spirit which He has made to dwell in us"?* (James 4:4-5)

Verse 5 is notoriously difficult to translate. Probably the best way of understanding it is, "The Spirit which He made to dwell in us yearns jealously." That is, the Holy Spirit, imparted to us by God at conversion, yearns enviously for our total loyalty and devotion to Him. He claims our undivided love. He will not tolerate any rival for our affection.[47] God the Spirit yearns jealously to have all the devotion of each and every Christian. It is His right.

3. God's jealousy is most often aroused by the introduction of idolatry into His people's hearts.

Exodus 20:3-6
You shall have no other gods before Me. You shall not make for yourself an idol, or any likeness of what is in heaven above or on the earth beneath or in the water under the earth. You shall not worship them or serve them; for I, the LORD your God, am a jealous God, visiting the iniquity of the fathers on the children, on the third and the fourth generations of those who hate Me, but showing lovingkindness to thousands, to those who love Me and keep My commandments.

Deuteronomy 32:16, 21
They made Him jealous with strange gods;
With abominations they provoked Him to anger . . . .
"They have made Me jealous with what is not God;
They have provoked Me to anger with their idols."

4. God's jealousy is wonderfully seen in the rescue of His people through His Son.

In Isaiah's day there was a prophecy given regarding a child, a son. This son would be God's chosen Savior for His people. The things said about His rule and His character baffle the mind. God assures the people that nothing Isaiah has told them is too good to be true—"the zeal of the LORD" will accomplish all of this through this son.

> *For a child will be born to us, a son will be given to us;*
> *And the government will rest on His shoulders;*
> *And His name will be called Wonderful Counselor,*
> *Mighty God, Eternal Father, Prince of Peace.*
> *There will be no end to the increase of His government or of peace,*
> *On the throne of David and over his kingdom,*
> *To establish it and to uphold it with justice and righteousness*
> *From then on and forevermore.*
> *The zeal of the LORD of hosts will accomplish this.* (Isaiah 9:6-7)

5. God restores His people from their drifting ways by His zeal.

Zechariah 8:2-3
> *Thus says the LORD of hosts, "I am exceedingly jealous for Zion, yes, with great wrath I am jealous for her." Thus says the LORD, "I will return to Zion and will dwell in the midst of Jerusalem. Then Jerusalem will be called the City of Truth, and the mountain of the LORD of hosts will be called the Holy Mountain."*

6. God protects His people from their enemies because of His zeal.

In Isaiah's day the hope of Jerusalem was not in armies but in the zeal of God that guaranteed that He would always preserve a remnant.

> *The surviving remnant of the house of Judah will again take root downward and bear fruit upward. For out of Jerusalem will go forth a remnant and out of Mount Zion survivors. The zeal of the LORD of hosts will perform this.* (Isaiah 37:31-32)

In Nahum's day God warns the enemies of His people (Assyria):

> *A jealous and avenging God is the LORD;*
> *The LORD is avenging and wrathful.*

They that love not have no hate, no jealousy, but where there is an intense, an infinite love, like that which glows in the bosom of God, there must be jealousy.

— C. H. Spurgeon

282

The LORD takes vengeance on His adversaries,
And He reserves wrath for His enemies. (Nahum 1:2)

7.   God's jealousy and zeal are perfectly displayed in His Son.

Nowhere is the zeal and jealousy of God more clearly seen in action than in the Father's sending of His Son and in that Son's labors.

ISAIAH 42:13 speaks of God going forth like a warrior who is roused to battle. Chapter 42 is speaking of the coming of God in the person of His Son, the Servant. Listen to Isaiah's description of Jesus:

The LORD will go forth like a warrior,
He will arouse His zeal like a man of war.
He will utter a shout, yes, He will raise a war cry.
He will prevail against His enemies.

The following statement from Psalm 69 was applied to Christ when He cleansed the temple of money-changers (John 2:17).

For zeal for Your house has consumed me . . . . (Psalm 69:9)

8.   It is a terrible expression of divine judgment when He withdraws that normal expression of His zeal for His people, allowing them to go on in their sin without interruption.

Isaiah grieved over the condition of Judah in his day. They were like sons who shocked their father by an inexplicable life of rebellion. They grieved the Spirit of God. They had entered into the remedial judgment of God. One sign of this judgment was that God's zeal appeared to be altered toward them.

The prophet lifts his voice to God in a heart-rending prayer:

Look down from heaven and see from Your holy and glorious habitation;
Where are Your zeal and Your mighty deeds?
The stirrings of Your heart and Your compassion are restrained toward me.
For You are our Father, though Abraham does not know us
And Israel does not recognize us.
You, O LORD, are our Father,
Our Redeemer from of old is Your name. (Isaiah 63:15-16)

Though God was their true Father, He no longer seemed to possess the normal zeal a dad does for his straying child. It is a terrible thing when sin causes God to appear as if He lacks zeal toward His people.

9. It is insane to provoke our own God to jealousy.

Paul warned the Corinthians that they were in danger of provoking God to jealousy by their sin. Then he asks them a very significant question. It is one we might ask ourselves when we take obedience lightly in the church.

> *Or do we provoke the Lord to jealousy? We are not stronger than He, are we?* (1 Corinthians 10:22)

10. God's jealousy and zeal provide a base upon which you may plead with Him.

God's jealousy and zeal have proven to be a powerful argument with God in Scripture. Take a look at how the wife pleads with her husband in Song of Solomon:

> *Put me like a seal over your heart,*
> *Like a seal on your arm.*
> *For love is as strong as death,*
> *Jealousy is as severe as Sheol [the grave];*
> *Its flashes are flashes of fire,*
> *The very flame of the LORD.*
> *Many waters cannot quench love,*
> *Nor will rivers overflow it;*
> *If a man were to give all the riches of his house for love,*
> *It would be utterly despised.* (Song of Solomon 8:6-7)

She is pleading for an enduring security. She wants to have her name written over his heart (love/jealousy) and his arm (strength). She wants to know that he will always exercise both jealous love and strength on her behalf. Love is stronger than death. Jealousy is as severe as the grave. They are like the flame of God. Nothing can quench them. Nothing can purchase them. When you see your heart becoming indifferent toward your Savior, when you feel temptation pulling strongly at your soul, plead with God based upon His jealousy to act on behalf of His rights. Plead that He would trample all His competitors in your life. Remind Him of His jealousy and zeal for those whom He has purchased.

Do not rest while God's fatherly zeal and loving jealousy seem lacking in your life or in the life of your church.

DAY 4: LIVING ON THESE TRUTHS

If you are a Christian, you belong to the one God who possesses a zeal and jealousy that are beyond description or calculation. If you are a Christian, you are fundamentally obligated to follow this God as you see Him in His Son. In fact, Paul says that you are to be an imitator of God, as His beloved child (Ephesians 5:1).

Zeal and jealousy come easily to some people, due to their temperament. However, we are talking today about a zeal and jealousy that are the fruit of the Spirit's work within His people. What would that look like? How can you reflect the jealousy of God? How can you express a zeal that would show the world something of the perfection of your Savior?

Today you will again be using the metaphors of Christian progress found in Colossians 2:6-7. At the end of the lesson you will be hearing more about the theme of God's zeal and how we must live in light of that truth. However, before you hear that sermon it would be beneficial if you were given an opportunity to really think through some of those applications for yourself. It is not an attribute we often consider and not one that we have adequately applied to the way we live.

Below is a list of passages including an inappropriate response as well as several appropriate responses to the God who possesses an infinite zeal and jealousy for His name and His people. Read the passages and combine them with the lessons on God's zeal and jealousy. Use them to think through the metaphors found in Colossians 2:6-7.

A believing man will be a zealous man. Faith makes a man zealous. Faith shows itself by zeal. Not by zeal for a party or a system or an opinion; but by zeal for Christ—zeal for His church —zeal for the carrying on of His work on earth.

— Horatius Bonar

COUNTERFEIT ZEAL—MISDIRECTED PASSION

Romans 10:2-3
For I testify about them that they have a zeal for God, but not in accordance with knowledge. For not knowing about God's righteousness and seeking to establish their own, they did not subject themselves to the righteousness of God.

Acts 22:3-4
I am a Jew, born in Tarsus of Cilicia, but brought up in this city, educated under Gamaliel, strictly according to the law of our fathers, being zealous for God just as you all are today. I persecuted this Way to the death, binding and putting both men and women into prisons.

Philippians 3:6
. . . as to zeal, a persecutor of the church . . . .

ZEAL FOR GOD'S HONOR SHOWN IN OUR OBEDIENCE

Titus 2:14

. . . [Christ Jesus] gave Himself for us to redeem us from every lawless deed, and to purify for Himself a people for His own possession, zealous for good deeds.

ZEAL FOR GOD'S HONOR SHOWN BY OUR PUTTING AWAY THE HALF-MEASURES IN OUR SERVICE TO HIM

Our walk counts far more than our talk, always!

— George Mueller

Ezra 7:23

Whatever is commanded by the God of heaven, let it be done with zeal for the house of the God of heaven, so that there will not be wrath against the kingdom of the king and his sons.

ZEAL FOR GOD'S HONOR SHOWN IN OUR REPENTANCE

2 Corinthians 7:10-11

For the sorrow that is according to the will of God produces a repentance without regret, leading to salvation, but the sorrow of the world produces death. For behold what earnestness this very thing, this godly sorrow, has produced in you: what vindication of yourselves, what indignation, what fear, what longing, what zeal, what avenging of wrong! In everything you demonstrated yourselves to be innocent in the matter.

Revelation 3:19

Those whom I love, I reprove and discipline; therefore be zealous and repent.

ZEAL FOR GOD'S HONOR SHOWN IN THE WAY WE HELP OTHER BELIEVERS

2 Corinthians 11:2-3

For I am jealous for you with a godly jealousy; for I betrothed you to one husband, so that to Christ I might present you as a pure virgin. But I am afraid that, as the serpent deceived Eve by his craftiness, your minds will be led astray from the simplicity and purity of devotion to Christ.

One more time, here is the passage in which Paul gives us five descriptive metaphors for Christian growth:

*Therefore as you have received Christ Jesus the Lord, so **walk** in Him, having been firmly **rooted** and now being **built up** in Him and **established** in your faith, just as you were instructed, and **overflowing with gratitude**.* (Colossians 2:6-7)

Let's consider how the truths of God's zeal and jealousy can be lived upon by using these five pictures. [Please note that your answers to today's questions may overlap to some degree.]

HAVING RECEIVED CHRIST JESUS THE LORD . . .

1. Walk in Him

The word "walk" shows us two things about Christian living.

First, walking is an everyday activity that does not seem significant. We take thousands of steps in a day, and very few steps would be looked back upon as particularly noteworthy, much less spiritually meaningful. Our little, common choices each day may also seem insignificant, but like our steps, they do matter—because they add up to be the stuff of life. For this reason, truths about God must affect our common choices in everyday life.

Second, when a person in the ancient world walked, he or she almost certainly had a destination in mind. Today people often walk for exercise, and in that case the destination isn't important. You may walk on a treadmill or in circles around a track. That is not what Paul has in mind when he says "walk." Christians should be walking toward a definite destination: complete conformity to Christ's character. The little choices of each day, guided by the truths you are studying, should be aiming at that destination—Christlikeness. But why? Not for self-improvement, but for the pleasure and honor of our God.

With these in mind, go back and review this week's lessons. Below, write how you can apply these truths about God's holy zeal and jealousy in everyday, apparently insignificant, ways that lead to the destination of Christlikeness.

_____

_____

_____

_____

_____

Take my life and let it be
Consecrated, Lord, to Thee.
Take my moments and
my days;
Let them flow in ceaseless
praise.

Take my love; my Lord,
I pour
At Thy feet its treasure
store:
Take myself, and I will be
Ever, only, all for Thee.

— Frances Ridley Havergal

2. Sink Your Roots in Him

Paul says that God has rooted every believer in Christ. Following Christ means daily sinking the roots of your life into the truths of God. Roots gain nutrients from the soil. Your soul may find temporary satisfaction in the junk food of our culture, or it will find lasting satisfaction in the feast of the immutable realities of God.

Go back and review this week's lessons. Below, write some of the truths that you feel are the most significant food for your soul. What things did you learn this week about God's zeal and jealousy that you realize you must feed upon if you are to live out the Christian life?

_____

_____

_____

_____

_____

3. Building a Life on These Truths

Each truth you learn in this study can be seen as a brick. Combined with other truths, each brick will be an essential part of building a life with Christ as the foundation. Coming to Jesus in repentance and faith is the only place to begin, but good beginnings are not all there is to Christianity. Paul knew that the Colossian Christians needed more than a foundation built on Christ; they also needed a life built by His grace with His biblical truths. To leave the truths you are studying piled like bricks in a corner of your life would be a grave mistake. You don't want to look back after twelve weeks and see a pile of bricks! You need a life that is a true dwelling place for God Himself.

Review this week's lessons and ask yourself, "In what ways can I build my life, marriage, family, or friendships at work on the realities of the zeal and jealousy of God?"

_____

_____

_____

_____

4.   **Become Established in Your Faith**

Paul used a word, translated in the NASB as "established," which conveys the idea of firming something up, making something stable, solid. In spiritual life, we might use the word *maturity*. You must grow to maturity in your faith (your grasp of the great realities of God), in part, so that you will not be easily shifted by false teaching or half-truths.

CONSIDER HEBREWS 5:12-14.

> *For though by this time you ought to be teachers, you have need again for someone to teach you the elementary principles of the oracles of God, and you have come to need milk and not solid food. For everyone who partakes only of milk is not accustomed to the word of righteousness, for he is an infant. But solid food is for the mature, who because of practice have their senses trained to discern good and evil.*

There is only one safeguard against error, and that is to be established in the faith; and for that, there has to be prayerful and diligent study, and a receiving with meekness the engrafted Word of God.

— A. W. Pink

Here the writer is speaking to people who have heard the truth many times but have remained immature in their faith. He tells us that maturity comes from a life that applies and practices what it is learning. Through application, you are established, or matured, in the great realities of God.

Review this week's lessons on God's zeal and jealousy. Below write some areas in which these attributes of God need to be applied to your faith so you will be established, solid, unwavering in your grasp of biblical truth.

_____

_____

_____

_____

_____

With these four pictures as guides, we never want to settle for new Bible-truths which are undigested, unapplied, unsettled, and sitting like a wasted pile of bricks.

There is one more picture we need to employ. Without this final metaphor our Christianity will not reflect God.

5.   Do All of These with an Overflow of Gratitude to God

You can attempt to apply 1-4, but without a grateful heart, how can you honor God?

*All that I am, and all
I have,
Shall be forever thine;
Whatever my duty bids
me give
My cheerful hands resign.
Yet if I might make some
reserve,
And duty did not call,
I love my God with zeal
so great
That I should give him all.*

— Isaac Watts

In the Old Testament Moses warned the people before they entered the Promised Land:

> *Because you did not serve the LORD your God with joy and a glad heart, for the abundance of all things; therefore you shall serve your enemies whom the LORD will send against you, in hunger, in thirst, in nakedness, and in the lack of all things; and He will put an iron yoke on your neck until He has destroyed you.* (Deuteronomy 28:47-48)

Surely that is a shocking message for us as well. If we go about our Christian lives trying to walk in truth, sink roots in truth, build upon truth, and be established in truth, but we do so with ungrateful hearts, we can expect divine discipline.

Review the lessons on God's zeal and jealousy. What reasons for gratitude toward God arise from the study of these?

_____

_____

_____

_____

May the God whose love moves Him with an unquenchable and holy zeal grant you such a sight of these perfections that you can:

* walk (go about the normal things of life) in its atmosphere . . .

* sink roots for nourishment in it . . .

* build a life with it . . .

* grow firm and be established in your grasp of God's truth because of it . . .

* do all of this with an overflowing sense of gratitude to Him.

DAY 5: PRESS ON TO KNOW THE LORD

You have come to the end of this twelve-week study. There is some sense of accomplishment in completing a study like this, but that was never the intended destination. There is so much more of God that is yet to be explored! For some of you this study has been a fresh reminder of things you already knew; for others it has been a starting place. But whether you are a babe in Christ or a mature follower, you are faced with an infinite God. As we come to the end of this workbook you will be taking a few moments to consider what God has taught you about Himself.

In the 6th chapter of Hosea the prophet calls a drifting Israel back to their God:

> *Come, let us return to the LORD . . . . So let us know, let us press on to know the LORD.* (Hosea 6:1, 3)

The call to repentance is interwoven with promises of mercy, and it includes a continuing growth in the knowledge of their God. Pressing on in the knowledge of God is not just for Old Testament Israelites who have backslidden. Paul's prayer for the Colossian church includes these requests:

> *. . . that you will walk in a manner worthy of the Lord, to please Him in all respects, bearing fruit in every good work and increasing in the knowledge of God.* (Colossians 1:10)

The phrases, "press on to know the LORD" and "increasing in the knowledge of God," demonstrate that knowing God is not a thing once done and forever accomplished. Every believer is called to embrace a lifelong pursuit of an ever-sweeter and deeper knowledge of God's perfection. Knowing the living God is an adventure that will not end with the grave.

A REVIEW OF GOD'S ATTRIBUTES

Let's review the attributes of God that you have studied, the perfections that make up the weight of His majesty.

HE IS INFINITE AND INCOMPREHENSIBLE

God's perfections possess no essential limitation and cannot be measured. His greatness cannot increase or decrease. He is beyond being fully understood. His person and His actions are wonderful (full of wonder), unfathomable, and unsearchable.

HE IS SELF-EXISTENT AND INDEPENDENT

God alone owes His existence to no one. He is the "I AM." He is independent of all others for both his origin and the sustaining of His person. In fact, He has never nor will He ever experience need. He is complete in Himself.

HE IS SUPREME

He is the Most High, transcending every other. He rises above every effort to define Him. He is, in fact, solitary, beyond compare and standing forever apart from all else in the perfection of His character and actions.

HE IS IMMUTABLE

As Timothy Dwight wrote, God is subject to no change in His manner of being, His perfections, His thoughts, His desires, His purposes, or His determinations. He is now what He always has been and always will be.

HE IS ETERNAL

God alone exists above the influence of time. He is without beginning or end. He is the Ancient of Days, yet He does not suffer the effects of old age. He is from everlasting to everlasting, filling each moment. He is in the beginning and at the end simultaneously.

HE IS ALL-PRESENT

We learned that God dwells throughout the known universe and the uninhabited regions of immensity. He is in all places at once, essentially and without effort. God never travels. He is never absent. Desired or not, God is ever-present and active.

HE IS ALL-POWERFUL

Blessed be God, He has revealed Himself! Again and again His attributes are set before us. Let them be our constant study and our constant trust.

— Henry Law

God possess all power. He has the ability to do all He pleases, all His perfect wisdom devises, and all His pure will resolves. He cannot be restrained, and His purposes cannot be frustrated.

HE IS ALL-KNOWING AND ALL-WISE

He knows instantly every item of knowledge without possibility of error or incompleteness. He knows all that is past, present, and future. He knows effortlessly, without reasoning. He cannot forget. He cannot be mistaken. He has never asked advice. He has never been corrected. His wisdom makes use of this knowledge, choosing the best goal and accomplishing it in the best manner.

HE IS SOVEREIGN

God is by His very nature a monarch. He is the highest king, the King of all kings and the Lord of all lords. He has the right to do all His pleasure with all His creation. His authority is essential to His person. He was King before creation, and no one aided Him in establishing His throne. His kingdom has no borders and will never end.

HE IS HOLY

God is separate. He is essentially distinct from all His creation and morally uncontaminated by sin's pollution. He cannot be tempted with sin, nor does He tempt anyone.

HE IS RIGHTEOUS AND JUST

God is perfect; all His ways are just. He is morally straight. It is impossible for His thoughts or actions to have any crookedness in them. When He deals with issues of right and wrong, He is always straightforward, just, and equitable.

HE IS WRATHFUL

He is filled with a fiery displeasure and an enduring opposition to sin. He hates sin in all of its forms—culturally accepted sins and shocking sins. He hates sin when He finds it in His enemies. He hates it when He finds it in His children.

HE IS GOOD

God is the origin and source of all that is truly wholesome and virtuous. His goodness includes His moral perfection and beauty as well as His benevolence, generosity, and kindness.

HE IS HUMBLE

Though God transcends all else as the Most High, He delights to stoop low to express His pity for His enemies. His humility is seen in His daily awareness of and dealings with creation. Yet nothing so perfectly unveils this trait as the sending of His Son to take upon Himself our humanity and to become the sin-bearer on the cross.

HE IS FAITHFUL

He is steady. He is firm in His determinations. He is honest, unwavering, and immovable. He is therefore trustworthy. He cannot fail to be what He says He will be and do what He says He will do.

HE IS LOVE

He is the one person who possesses mercy, grace, and pity in an infinite degree, and He exercises these without error or indulgence.

HE IS ZEALOUS

There is in God a keenness, an intensity of earnestness which goes beyond that which any created being possesses. When this zeal is turned toward the objects of His love, it is expressed in an unstained jealousy.

HE IS PATIENT

God bears with the offenses and provocations of His creatures who deny His rights and rebel against His rule. He is slow to anger, long-suffering, and not easily provoked. His patience never results from any confusion in Himself regarding how to deal with a situation, nor any inability in Himself to respond appropriately.

SELF-EXAMINATION

Having reviewed the attributes you studied these past weeks, here are two exercises for personal consideration.

CONSIDER again the list of God's attributes above.

- In light of each of these attributes, consider how perilous it is to face God outside of the mediating work of Jesus.

- In light of each of these attributes, consider the indescribable privileges that are ours through Christ's mediation.

FOR YOUR CONSIDERATION

1. To which attributes had you given very little thought before this study?

_____

_____

_____

_____

2. To which attributes had you given most thought prior to this study?

_____

_____

_____

_____

3. Which attributes in this study have had the most significant impact on your life, and how has this changed you?

_____

_____

_____

_____

4. Considering again the attributes of God, write a prayer of praise, gratitude, and consecration to the one God who is infinitely worthy.

_____

_____

_____

_____

_____

_____

_____

Pursuing an increasing knowledge of God is not merely for your own benefit. On the contrary, knowing God must never stop with you. Though not all are called to pastor or preach, it is every Christian's privilege to speak and live so as to spread the truth about God throughout the world. The words of a nineteenth-century preacher and author, Henry Law, are fitting to conclude our study. He writes:

> *It is good to call others to the knowledge of the Lord. This is a wondrous theme, and well demands our utmost powers . . . . But who can tell His essence as God! His name is opened out to us in His blessed attributes . . . . With joyful lips let us speak of all His goodness. It is unsearchable, unmerited, infinite, everlasting. Let us here begin the testimony which can never end. From age to age His truth shall live; from age to age let joyful lips proclaim it!* [48]

Notes

1. Herman Bavinck, *The Doctrine of God* (Edinburgh: The Banner of Truth Trust, 1997), 33.

2. Stephen Charnock, *The Existence and Attributes of God* (Grand Rapids, MI: Baker Books, 1996), 200.

3. A.W. Tozer, *The Knowledge of the Holy* (New York: HarperCollins Publisher, 1961), 8.

4. John Owen, *The Mortification of Sin*, New Edition (London, 1831), 299.

5. Selected from the hymn, "O Lord Enlarge Our Scanty Thought," by Nicolaus Ludwig von Zinzendorf, translated from German by John Wesley.

6. A.W. Tozer, *The Knowledge of the Holy* (New York: HarperCollins Publisher, 1961), 11.

7. George Swinnock, The Works of George Swinnock, M.A. (Edinburgh: James Nichol, 1868), vol. 4, 389.

8. A.W. Tozer, *The Knowledge of the Holy* (New York: HarperCollins Publisher, 1961), 32.

9. Greg Nichols, *Doctrine of God*, n.d. TS.

10. The grace of God is "the unmerited love of God toward those who have forfeited it, and are by nature under a judgment of condemnation." Louis Berkhof, *Manual of Christian Doctrine* (Wm. B. Eerdman's Publishing Co., Grand Rapids, Michigan, 1995), p. 67.

11. A.W. Tozer, *The Knowledge of the Holy* (New York: HarperCollins Publisher, 1961), 34.

12. Herman Bavinck, *The Doctrine of God* (Edinburgh: The Banner of Truth Trust, 1997), 144.

13. Martin Luther, *The Bondage of the Will* (London: Printed by T. Bensley for W. Simpkin and R. Marshall, Stationers-Hall Court, 1823), 37.

14. A.W. Tozer, *The Knowledge of the Holy* (New York: HarperCollins Publisher, 1961), 69.

15. *Ibid.*, 76.

16. Herman Bavinck, *The Doctrine of God* (Edinburgh: The Banner of Truth Trust, 1997), 14.

17. Rev. Andrew A. Bonar, D.D, *Letters of Samuel Rutherford: With a Sketch of His Life and Biographical Notices of His Correspondents* (Edinburgh and London: Oliphant Anderson & Ferrier, Letter CCXXVI), 446.

18. https://www.merriam-webster.com/dictionary/immutable.

19. Timothy Dwight, *Dr. Dwight's System of Theology*, (London: William Baynes, 1819), vol. 1, 81.

20. Herman Bavinck, *The Doctrine of God* (Edinburgh: The Banner of Truth Trust, 1997), 154-157.

21. A.W. Tozer, *The Knowledge of the Holy* (New York: HarperCollins Publisher, 1961), 39.

22. https://hymnary.org/hymn/PsH/46

23. Timothy Dwight, *Dr. Dwight's System of Theology* (London: William Baynes,1819), vol. 1, 142.

24. Hildebert of Lavardin, as quoted in A.W. Tozer, *The Knowledge of the Holy* (New York: HarperCollins Publisher, 1961), 74.

25. A.W. Tozer, *The Pursuit of God* (Camp Hill, PA: Wing Spread Publishers, 2006), 65.

26. *Ibid.*, 115.

27. Stephen Charnock, *The Complete Works of Stephen Charnock, B. D., Volume 2*, (Indiana: Sovereign Grace Publishers, Inc., 2001), 106.

28. A. W. Pink, *Attributes of God* (Grand Rapids, Michigan: Baker Book House, 1978), 46.

29. Matthew Henry, *An Exposition of the Old Testament, Volume IV*, (Edinburgh: J. Wood, 1763), 721

30. A.W. Tozer, *The Knowledge of the Holy* (San Francisco: Harper & Row, 1978), 56.

31. J.I. Packer, *Knowing God* (Downers Grove, IL: InterVarsity Press, 1993), 90.

32. A.W. Pink, *Attributes of God* (Grand Rapids, Michigan: Baker Book House, 1978), 32.

33. *Propitiation* is the turning away of anger by the offering of a gift. This was a common theme among pagans in antiquity as they attempted to appease their gods and to avert disaster. In the Bible the term refers to the turning away of God's righteous anger, caused by our law-breaking, through the substitutionary death of Jesus Christ. As the sin-bearer, His death satisfied the wrath of God by removing the offense. Hence, God's justice is upheld and His mercy is exercised in the same great event.

34. Paul Washer, *Knowing the Living God* (New Albany, MS: Media Gratiae, 2016), 80.

35. *Ibid.*, 80.

36. Stephen Charnock, *The Works of the Late Rev. Stephen Charnock, B.D.*, (London: Baynes, Paternoster Row 1815), vol. 2, 495.

37. I am indebted to Mr. Richard Owen Roberts for the constant reminder of this fact.

38. A.W. Tozer, *The Knowledge of the Holy* (New York: HarperCollins Publisher, 1961), 87.

39. John Newton, "Let Us Love and Sing and Wonder."

40. Stephen Charnock, as quoted in J.I. Packer, *A Quest for Godliness: The Puritan Vision of the Christian Life* (Wheaton: Crossway Books, 1994), 251.

41. A. W. Pink, *Attributes of God* (Grand Rapids, Michigan: Baker Book House, 1978), 82.

42. Andrew Murray, *Humility*, the Beauty of Holiness (Fleming H Revell Co., London, 1969), 5-6.

43. A.W. Tozer, *The Attributes of God*, Volume 2, (Camp Hill, PA: WingSpread Publishers), 165.

44. Robert Murray McCheyne, *The Works of the Late Rev. Robert Murray McCheyne: vol. 2, Sermons, Sermon 30: The Love of Christ* (New York: Robert Carter, 1847), 181.

45. J.C. Philpot, *Meditations on Matters of Christian Faith & Experience, On the First and Second Chapters of Ephesians*, Grace e-books, http://www.grace-ebooks.com/library/J.%20C.%20Philpot/-JCP%20On%20Ephesians%201%20and%202.pdf (Sept. 20, 2017).

46. Isaac Watts, "From Heaven the Sinning Angels Fell."

47. D. Edmond Hiebert, *James* (Chicago: Moody Press, 1988), 255.

48. Henry Law, Psalms, 1878, Grace e-books, http://grace-ebooks.com/library/Henry%20Law/HL_Psalms.pdf, Ps. 100.

_____

_____

_____

_____

_____

_____

_____

_____

_____

_____

_____

_____

_____

_____

BIBLICAL FOUNDATIONS FOR THE CHRISTIAN FAITH

A SERIES OF BIBLE STUDY WORKBOOKS BY

PAUL DAVID WASHER

KNOWING THE LIVING **GOD** · DISCOVERING THE GLORIOUS **GOSPEL** · DISCERNING THE PLIGHT OF **MAN** · UNDERSTANDING THE DISCIPLINE OF **FASTING** · STUDYING THE HOLY **SCRIPTURES**

Biblical Foundations for the Christian Faith by Paul David Washer

Only the truths of Scripture, understood with the mind and communicated through doctrine, can provide that sure foundation upon which we should establish our beliefs and our behavior and determine the validity of our emotions and experiences. The study of doctrine is both an intellectual and devotional discipline. It is a passionate search for God that should always lead the student to greater personal transformation, obedience, and heartfelt worship.

- **Knowing the Living God**
- **Discovering the Glorious Gospel**
- **Discerning the Plight of Man**
- **Understanding the Discipline of Fasting**
- **Studying the Holy Scriptures**

The workbooks in the series are primarily biblical studies and do not contain much in the way of colorful illustrations, quaint stories, or even theological expositions. It was the desire of the author to provide a series of works that simply point the way to the Scriptures and allow the Word of God to speak for itself.

The great goal of these studies is for the student to have an encounter with God through His Word. Founded upon the conviction that Scripture is the inspired and infallible Word of God, these books have been designed in such a way that it is literally impossible for the student to advance without an open Bible before him or her.

Download the first chapter of each workbook free at **http://shop.mediagratiae.org**.

Behold Your God: Rethinking God Biblically

Behold Your God: Rethinking God Biblically, led by Dr. John Snyder, is a 12-week multimedia Bible study that seeks to help the believer apply the attributes of God to all of life. There are two components to the study: a daily devotional workbook, and a set of 13 DVD. Each week the student will work through the workbook (five days per week) in preparation for watching the DVD lesson. Behold Your God can be used as an individual, family, group, or church-wide study.

Each week's DVD is made up of three segments. The historical introduction is a short biographical sketch of the life of a significant figure from Christian history whose ministry illustrates the truths that you have been studying that week. These were all filmed on location in Wales, England, Scotland, and North America at sites associated with Charles Spurgeon, George Whitefield, Martyn Lloyd-Jones, Jonathan Edwards, Robert Murray M'Cheyne, Amy Carmichael, Samuel Rutherford, A. W. Tozer, George Müller, et al. After these introductions, a half-hour sermon from Dr. Snyder reinforces what we have been studying in the Bible that week. Finally, we hear a collection of interviews footage from contemporary ministers whose lives and labors reflect these same truths. These men include Paul Washer, Richard Owen Roberts, Jordan Thomas, Anthony Mathenia, Eifion Evans, Andrew Davies, and Conrad Mbewe.

For more information, visit us online at **www.beholdyourgod.org**.
The entire study is also available as an online interactive course at **http://online.beholdyourgod.org**.

Logic on Fire: the Life and Legacy of Dr. Martyn Lloyd-Jones

When Dr. Martyn Lloyd-Jones (1899—1981) gave a series of lectures on the subject of preaching in 1969, he coined a phrase that became an emblematic description of his own ministry: "What is preaching?" he asked. "Logic on fire!" But what exactly does it mean, and how does it manifest? *Logic on Fire: The Life and Legacy of Dr. Martyn Lloyd-Jones* is a deluxe documentary package which charts the story of this most remarkable man, widely considered to be one of the most influential preachers of the 20th century.

Shot in historic locations across Wales, England, Scotland, and the United States, Logic On Fire features interviews with Jeremy Bailey, Ben Bailie, Keith Batstone, Ann Beatt, Christopher Catherwood, Elizabeth Catherwood, Jonathan Catherwood, Andrew Christofides, John Cheeseman, George Curry, Andrew Davies, D. Eryl Davies, Ian M. Densham, Adam Desmond, Liz Desmond, Kevin DeYoung, Ligon Duncan, Eifion Evans, Philip H. Eveson, Sinclair B. Ferguson, Ian Hamilton, W. Vernon Higham, Basil Howlett, John MacArthur, Bethan Marshall, Anthony Mathenia, Conrad Mbewe, Jason Meyer, Iain H. Murray, Robert Oliver, Bruce Powell, Richard Owen Roberts, John Snyder, R.C. Sproul, Ceinwen Swann, Justin Taylor, Geoff Thomas, David A. Tucker, Rhiannon Tunnicliffe, Jeremy Walker, Paul Washer, and Donald S. Whitney.

This deluxe documentary package contains the 140-minute feature film, over 3.5 hours of extended interviews, deleted sequences, and additional material on 3 DVDs, 5 postcard prints, and a 128-page clothbound book full of never before published photographs, sermons, and more.

For more information, including the opportunity to view several cinematic trailers, web-only extended interviews, or to steam the entire film online, visit our website at **www.logiconfire.org**.